WIZARD 6

Joseph G. Dawson III, General Editor

Wizard 6

A COMBAT PSYCHIATRIST IN VIETNAM

Douglas Bey

Texas A&M University Press   College Station

The paper used in this book
meets the minimum requirements
of the American National Standard for Permanence
of Paper for Printed Library Materials, Z39.48–1984.
Binding materials have been chosen for durability.

LIBRARY OF CONGRESS CATALOGING-IN-PUBLICATION DATA

Bey, Douglas, 1938-
    Wizard 6 : a combat psychiatrist in Vietnam / Douglas Bey.— 1st ed.
        p. cm.— (Texas A&M University military history series ; 104)
    Includes index.
    ISBN 1-58544-482-0 (cloth : alk. paper) —
    ISBN 1-58544-519-3 (pbk. : alk. paper)
    1. Vietnamese Conflict, 1961–1975—Psychological aspects
2. Vietnamese Conflict, 1961–1975—Personal narratives, American.
3. Bey, Douglas, 1938–   I. Title: Wizard six.   II. Title.   III. Texas A&M
University military history series ; 104.
DS559.8.P7B49   2006
959.704'37—dc22   2005025899

To my wonderful
wife & cheerleader,
Debbie

Contents

Acknowledgments

I would like to acknowledge my grandchildren, Keslie Ward, Audrey White, Kyle Ward, Andy White, and Rachel White. I hope they will pass on some of the stories to their children someday.

I am glad to have an opportunity to acknowledge and thank the many people who helped and encouraged me, but as I was writing this, the image of the Hollywood Oscar acceptance speeches came to mind and I felt a brief wave of narcissistically induced nausea! "I'd like to thank all of the little people who helped to make me into the awesome person I turned out to be." I used to become impatient with the long list of people thanked by the Oscar recipients but, given a similar opportunity, find that I'm just as verbose.

As a kid, I loved to hear my grandfather Rudy tell about his childhood in the old country. He was a storyteller, and people would gather around him when we were fishing to hear his tales. I think I either got his storytelling genes or identified with him, or both, because I tend to see each day as a story.

My dad was a professor who saw, as his primary mission, giving his students confidence that they could be good mathematicians. He made a big deal over their successes and minimized their errors as his shortcoming for not teaching them better. He raved over my lousy play on the golf course and, throughout my life, kept telling me that I should write a book. I finally did it, but he is no longer here to read it and tell me how great it is.

My mom passed away last year at age eighty-nine. She had a difficult life with two open-heart valve replacements and bypass surgeries and several serious depressive episodes. She would be pleased to know that I wrote a book but probably wouldn't have read it because of the profanity. My mother-in-law, Mildred Yockey, probably won't like the profanity either, but I think she will enjoy reading the book.

My brother, Dick, calls several times a week to keep in touch and exchange jokes. We make a special effort to keep our relationship close. He's more intellectual than I, but he read the manuscript and said he liked it. His genius daughter Alex liked it.

I have been blessed by having some outstanding teachers over the years. University High School, Cornell College, and the University of Illinois College of Medicine in Chicago all provided great instruction. Harry Levinson shared his work with organizational diagnosis and intervention. He supervised my third-year psychiatric residency research paper on this topic and allowed me to participate on the faculty of some of his industrial psychiatry seminars at Menninger's. I can still recite Karl Menninger's lectures verbatim. In addition to being my "ego-ideal" during training, Karl Menninger took the time and made the effort to write to me and to send me books and articles while I was in Vietnam. His grandson, Karl Menninger II, was very helpful in obtaining permission to print excerpts of those letters in this book.

I arrived at writing this particular book through the coaching of my literary agent, Bert Krages. Bert held my hand throughout the process and patiently put up with my insecurities. Harry Harlow reared baby monkeys with substitute wire or terry cloth–covered substitute mothers. When frightened, the baby monkeys would press a lever to get a look at their substitute maternal figures and acquire some security. I compulsively e-mailed Bert, my wire-monkey mama, for the security of knowing that he was there. This has been my first serious effort to put together a book. I had no idea how much work it was going to be or how much time it would take when I began. Bert said that I should not expect the immediate results I was accustomed to seeing in the practice of psychiatry and offered to send me a tranquilizer! I felt as though I had been working on this book for years and was surprised to discover that Bert made his suggestion about a book on Vietnam in February 2002 (of course, I had spent a couple of years in the 1970s putting together the original book on division psychiatry).

I want to thank Mary Lenn Dixon, editor-in-chief; Cynthia Lindlof, copy editor; Wendy Lawrence, Janet Mathewson, Diana Vance, Gayla Christiansen, and all the rest of the Texas A&M University Press publishing team who have been very kind to an old novice writer.

Mary Lenn put me in touch with Dale Wilson, who is a wounded Vietnam vet, retired military history professor at West Point, and retired editor for TAMU. His input and feedback were very help-ful. Thanks to Bill Wills, editor of our local newspaper, *The Pan-tagraph,* for his helpful tips and advice. Three friends read some of the manuscript and offered excellent criticism in a supportive manner.

Garold "Bud" Cole is a retired librarian at Illinois State Univer-sity who is *the* authority on Civil War literature. He has written three Civil War reference books over the years. He looked over my preliminary efforts and offered excellent suggestions to improve the continuity and flow of the work. Karen Zangerle is the head of one of our local social service agencies. I call her "Our Lady of PATH." She is a kindhearted genius who generously spent time she didn't have to spare helping me make the book readable. Jerry Parsons was willing to read the manuscript and give me the benefit of his wisdom and experience.

Walt Smith was one of my social work/psychology technicians in Vietnam. He is a brilliant, courageous person of great integrity. He helped me in Vietnam and more recently when we discussed our memories of Vietnam by e-mail. I know he disagrees passionately with my political views, but we have remained friends despite our political differences. I appreciate his sharing his views on Vietnam, our work there, and our current political situation.

During the writing I located and started corresponding with my good friend and mentor in Vietnam, John Hamilton. We hadn't been in contact since Vietnam. Since returning home in 1970, we both have been divorced, both have had open-heart surgery, and both have returned to our churches and have been trying to live Christ-centered lives. I also heard from Ross Guarino recently, and we were able to share memories. Ed Colbach ran into Bert, my agent, at a Northwestern University alumni picnic and learned of the book. He got in touch, and we were able to compare notes on our experiences as psychiatrists in Vietnam and have remained in contact ever since.

I would like to acknowledge and thank a couple of locals who made it in Hollywood—the late McLean Stevenson (star of *M*A*S*H*) and Mike Laughlin (movie producer)—for taking the time and making the effort to visit me in the hospital after my heart surgery in 1992. The nurses gave me much better service after their visit.

Thanks to Greg, Chuck, Joe, Mary Joe, Eddie, Candice, Mike, Mandy, Cindy, Trish, Curley, Frosty, Winnie, Tony, nurse Tracy, Jerry, Heather, John, and all of the gang at Jim's Steakhouse, which has become our pub.

Of course, I have to thank the love of my life—my wife, Debbie, who put up with my hours of isolation in the study over the past two years and still cheered me on when I became discouraged or impatient. She didn't hesitate to give me much-needed verbal kicks when I was twitching about not hearing from a publisher.

My kids, Cathy, Barb, Sarah, Matt, and Alvis, were encouraging, as were our good friends Gabriel Telot, Dave and Ruth Anne Klumb, and Ron and Carol Naae.

My good friend Bill Taylor died of a heart attack shortly after my first go-around with heart disease. I miss him; my brother Donn; my cousin John (who did two tours in 'Nam as a marine pilot); my uncle Wayne; my parents; my father-in-law, Wayne Yockey; and my grandparents. I'm sure they would have enjoyed the book. I hope Bill's widow, Sharon, will like it.

My friend John Donovan and his son Matt are real American warrior heroes but might enjoy hearing a few REMF stories. They have been of great help to my son Matt, who, I'm proud to say, wants to follow in their footsteps and enlist in the army this year.

When you get older, the maintenance goes up. I am thankful that I have had good doctors who have kept me alive and bolstered my morale through and after two heart attacks and two open-heart surgeries: Gabriel Telot, Andy Patel, Tom Ocheltree, Kelley Kennedy, Rual Wright, James Seehafer, Tony Dustman, Jerry Bratburg, John Esch, Dan Scott, Frank Mikell (my main man), Eric Thompson, Mark Hansen, John Zander, David Roszhart, Thomas Shanahan, Don Stacy and staff, and Lawrence Dunkleberger at the VA, and my nurse practitioner, Joanne O'Brien. Thanks also to my extremely intelligent "tooth fairy," John Keller, who has kept me from having to gum my food.

Thanks to the VFW for sticking up for Vietnam vets even when it was unpopular to do so.

Finally, best wishes to my old buddies from the 1st Infantry Division and all the Vietnam veterans who sacrificed at the request of their country but missed the welcome home that they deserved.

WIZARD 6

Introduction

The Vietnam equivalent of Klinger from *M*A*S*H*. A killer dentist. Soldiers addicted to alcohol, drugs, and killing. Black pride, Vietnamese prejudice, and racial conflict. Soldiers who didn't want to go home! The Viet Cong's fear of mental illness. Doughnut dollies, sautéed feces, car washes, steam baths, and sex. Passive aggression, counterphobia, and homophobia. Vietnam was *Apocalypse Now, Catch-22,* and a little of *M*A*S*H* rolled into one! *Wizard 6* describes my tour of duty as a psychiatrist assigned to the 1st Infantry Division in Vietnam during 1969 and 1970. It was another existence. We referred to home as "the world." *Wizard 6* is also about who I am, how I became a psychiatrist in Vietnam, how I coped with the experience, and how I think it affected me.

As with any combat environment, there was the irony of military psychiatrists helping men adjust to a crazy place. To make it through the year, you had to initially forget about "the world" back home and focus on the day-to-day life in the hot, noisy, smelly, sometimes dangerous, often boring, world of Vietnam. You were stepping through the looking glass, entering a parallel existence, trying to be normal in an abnormal situation.

There were few psychiatrists in Vietnam. In 1965 there was only one, whose psychiatric training consisted of fourteen weeks of working on the job under a trained psychiatrist. At the height of the buildup in 1969, there were 543,000 troops in Vietnam. That same year there were twenty-five army psychiatrists, four navy psychiatrists (two in country and two on ships), and two air force psychiatrists in Vietnam. Six of the army psychiatrists were in the field assigned to combat divisions. I was one of the six and was assigned to the 1st Infantry Division. The idea to put psychiatrists in combat divisions arose during World War II. It was based on the concept of seeing soldiers near where their symptoms arose, treating them right away, and getting them back to duty. Basically it is like chemical-dependency counselors being former addicts themselves, pediatricians and child psychiatrists having kids of their own—you are better able to evaluate and treat individuals if you understand where they are coming from and have been there (or are there) yourself. The backup for divisional services was the 935th KO team (mobile psychiatric detachment) in Long Binh, which had four psychiatrists, one psychologist, one neurologist, and two neuropsychiatric nurses. Nha Trang's 8th Field Hospital had a similar KO team. The mission of these teams was to serve as evacuation centers for army psychiatric and neurology casualties in Vietnam. They also served as a twenty-four-hour mental hygiene consultation service for soldiers in their areas. There was a psychiatrist at the 3rd Field Hospital in Saigon, one at the 67th Evacuation Hospital in Qui Nhon, one at the 91st Evacuation Hospital in Chu Lai, and one at the 95th Evacuation Hospital in Da Nang. Five more were assigned to other divisions: 1st Cavalry, 4th Infantry, Americal, 25th Infantry, and the 101st Airborne. The 9th Infantry Division and its psychiatrist were being withdrawn from Vietnam when I arrived. Serving as one of the six division psychiatrists was a unique experience. I published and presented a number of papers on my return and wrote a book on military psychiatry in Vietnam that was primarily directed to military psychiatrists. I gave a rough copy to the army psychiatrists at Walter Reed who were putting together a history of psychiatry in Vietnam. I then put the book aside, as I tried to do with my memories of the entire experience. More than thirty years later my literary agent, Bert Krages, asked me if I had anything on Vietnam and, after reading the rough book, suggested I modify it for a lay audience. This was the conception of *Wizard 6*.

Thirty-plus years ago things looked different in this country. In 1969 John Wayne received an Oscar for best actor in *True Grit*. An average new car cost a little over three thousand dollars, the average new home cost less than sixteen thousand dollars, and a gallon of gas cost thirty-five cents. The antiwar movement had been steadily growing. On campus there was a saying, "Girls only say yes to men who say no." Marchers were chanting slogans such as "Hell no, we won't go" and "Hey, hey, LBJ. How many babies did you kill today?" On the other side the hard hats and Nixon's silent majority still supported the military and the war in Vietnam. The peace sign was known as the chicken foot by this group. Blacks were rioting and burning cities after Martin Luther King and Robert Kennedy were assassinated in 1968. The Tet offensive by the North Vietnamese Army (NVA) shocked the nation, who had been told by Gen. William C. Westmoreland and the government that we were close to winning the war. Walter Cronkite changed his opinion about the outcome following Tet. This caused the public to doubt any positive news from the government or the military about the war. The My Lai massacre of five hundred Vietnamese civilians by Lt. William Calley and his butchers turned more Americans against the war.

Soldiers who were advisers in the early sixties, soldiers who served in the mid-sixties, and soldiers who were in Vietnam after 1970 all had different experiences than I did during 1969 and 1970. Even those who were in Vietnam when I was there but served in other units or in a different capacity probably experienced the tour differently than I did. It was a pivotal era in our country. The antiwar movement was gaining momentum, the hippie drug movement was in full force, and racial tensions were high. The silent majority was rapidly becoming the silent minority.

I have changed the names of a few of the people whose names I've forgotten and a couple who I thought would be embarrassed or get in trouble if they were recognized, but most are real names. Due to glitches in my memory, I may have mixed up some people and attributed stories to some that belong to others. I did have extensive notes, tapes, pictures, and records to help me, but I am sure that what I recall now is not perfectly accurate. In some instances I have the actual words that were spoken written down or recorded, but in many instances I have reconstructed what we probably said based on the particular case involved. The rendition of the experience is accurate, and this is what I hope to share with the reader. Wizard 6 was my radio call name in the 1st Infantry

Division. I was the division psychiatrist (aka Wizard); and since I was the chief, I was "6," or the one in charge.

When I tell people who never served in Vietnam that I was there, they tend to form a mental picture of me slogging through rice paddies doing battle with the Viet Cong (VC). For most of us this wasn't the situation at all. Eighty-five percent of the soldiers in Vietnam were support troops. Only 15 percent passed the "ass-in-the-grass" test, meaning they were out in the jungles and rice paddies shooting and being shot at. Assigned to a combat division, I was as close to the action as a psychiatrist could be in Vietnam, but I was an REMF (Rear Echelon Motherfucker) to the combatants in the field. There was an informal pecking order, and anyone among the support troops with a safer, more comfortable assignment was an REMF to us. There was a constant, real presence of danger. We had no control over the intermittent rocket or mortar attacks. But as REMFs, our main struggle was with boredom. We always said that if we were to make a movie that accurately portrayed our experience in Vietnam, we would heat the theater up to 120 degrees, blow in the smell of feces burning in kerosene, and then have someone talk about a lizard for thirty-six hours. If the audience tried to leave, they would find the doors locked! I was tempted to start each chapter with a description of our morning routine in Vietnam to attempt to convey how tedious our existence was much of the time. I dropped this idea because boring the reader is generally not considered to be good form when writing. I was more fortunate than most guys in 'Nam because I had interesting work, good guys to work with, and the ability to travel in, and to some extent, out of the country.

There is, I believe, an unconscious desire on the part of Vietnam veterans to shock those who haven't shared this experience. An example of this provocative tendency was demonstrated by Maj. Gen. George S. Patton III, who did three tours of duty in Vietnam between 1962 and 1969 in command of the 11th Armored Cavalry Regiment. He referred to his men as "a splendid bunch of killers." Once, when his armored unit received fire from a village, the proper protocol would have been to contact the village chief and his own superior officer and obtain clearance before returning fire. Instead, the then Colonel Patton turned his vehicles and leveled the village. He received considerable negative press and criticism for this act.

One of the reporters who was attempting to interview him after the incident asked, "Do you love war, Colonel Patton?" He looked at the reporter and answered calmly, "No, I hate war—but I do love the sight of arms and legs flying through the air!"

I was not immune to this provocative tendency. P. K. Worley, who was then in charge of public relations for the Menninger Foundation (where I did my psychiatric residency prior to entering the service), wrote to me early in my tour to ask if I would send him some informal observations of my experiences in Vietnam to share with the alumni and foundation friends in the Menninger *Alumni News*. I wrote back a description of American aircraft dropping candy outside villages and then napalming the children when they came to get it and of the joys of having sex with the toothless, Vietnamese women who burned GI feces (known as "shit burners"). The candy story was just that, and we basically left these particular Vietnamese women alone. Civilians back home thought we were "baby killers," and instead of denying it, we shoved it in their faces. In reality, the doctors and technicians I knew in Vietnam were very kind to the Vietnamese. When we treated Vietnamese patients, we gave them the same level of care that we provided to American patients. We were especially kind to the children we saw on MEDCAPS (Medical Civic Action Programs) and at the orphanage we adopted. In the same way, no one that I ever knew actually had sex with one of these Vietnamese women, but it was a common statement that evoked a very ugly mental image. I'm sure that P. K. was taken aback by my response, and he sent me a proof of the proposed newsletter article that I have preserved over the years that detailed exactly what I had reported to him.

Looking back, I think that even though I was a psychiatrist, my coping style in Vietnam was typical pre–Alan Alda male. Women share and express their feelings. They talk at length about their traumatic experiences. They openly cry and hold each other. Men tend to hold things in and kid one another to bolster their counterphobic defenses. By "counterphobic," I mean we deny our feelings and our fears and act as though we aren't upset. For example, when I went through a divorce years ago, my ex spent a good deal of time crying, sharing, and emoting with a therapist and with her friends and family, who held her hand and offered opinions about my mental health (I had to be nuts to leave her—even though she kicked me out). My friends offered me the following support on the golf course at about the fifth tee:

"You okay?" asked Andy.

"Yeah," I muttered.

"You look okay," commented Tom.

"Nice shot!" added Jack.

"Wanna beer?" asked Andy.

I once thought it likely that a group of women helping each other adjust to a combat division in Vietnam would have had different and probably healthier ways of dealing with their stress than my buddies and I did. After reading *War Torn,* written by several female journalists who covered the war, I decided they just had different ways of coping—but not necessarily healthier.

We used profanity in Vietnam. The "f" word was used so frequently in Vietnam that we inserted it between syllables. When I started writing *Wizard 6,* I used genuine "'Nam speak"; but it seemed offensive and, what was worse, boring. So I dropped a good deal of it—but that was the way we communicated. This wasn't a big adjustment for me, as part of my rebellion against my academic family was to hang out with jocks and speak in "locker-room language." I once had a bumper sticker made that said "Eschew sesquipedalian verbiage."

When I began to write *Wizard 6,* I reported the stories I thought were interesting and funny from my year in Vietnam. As I thought a little more deeply about the experience, I realized that my year in Vietnam was not just a collection of humorous anecdotes. Many of the feelings I had isolated and experiences I had suppressed at the time I was there were unpleasant. I realized that my own feelings and reactions to the experience were an important part of the story. Therefore, in order to convey the experience, it is necessary to provide some information about who I was thirty years ago and how I came to be that way. My responses and actions in Vietnam were influenced by a number of factors: growing up in an academic, midwestern, conservative, German American family right after World War II; the early trauma of visiting a state hospital "snake pit"; my conflict between my role as the family hero and wanting to be true to myself; the trauma of my brother's mental illness and suicide. These were all factors that led to my developing a compulsive, type-A, workaholic, guilt-ridden lifestyle.

I adapted to Vietnam by taking on the counterphobic defenses most people in the military developed: forgetting about home and distancing myself from negative feelings by becoming an observer and a photographer of events rather than a participant. At times, my defenses failed and I was hit with unpleasant feelings or lost control of my own aggression. Keeping busy, focusing on work, reading the military psychiatric literature, and traveling (in the division, in country, and out of the country) all helped reduce stress and made the time go faster. Self-medication with alcohol was a less healthy coping device I employed as well.

I describe my work as a division psychiatrist in the areas of direct service, identifying high-risk individuals and high-stress periods in units. I present a variety of disguised case examples of the types of patients we saw and the treatment we provided. There is a tendency to forget the routine cases and remember those that were difficult or unusual. I have tried to overcome this tendency and to describe some of the everyday work that we did. My initial optimism in our work was based on the low rates of gross stress reactions (aka combat exhaustion) we saw. Even in the division, a large percentage of our patients were support troops. We were always aware that there was danger, and periodically we would experience a frightening event (mortar attack, rockets), but our main struggle was to survive the deadly routine and boredom and make it through the year. Later, I noted that stress associated with racism, drug and alcohol abuse, and background differences between command and enlisted men was unique to Vietnam. It appeared that stress in Vietnam was manifested in ways other than the classic symptoms of combat exhaustion described in the prior military psychiatry literature. I describe our efforts to help with these problems and the results of our work. I have attempted to share with the reader some of the unique individuals, situations, behaviors, and places I encountered. I also try to state what I think I learned from the experience.

CHAPTER 1

Prelude to Vietnam

In order to convey my year in Vietnam in 1969 and 1970, I need to back up and tell you who I am, where I came from, and how I got there. My first year in the army in 1968 is also an important prelude to my year in the division in Vietnam.

My mother's father died after gall bladder surgery when she was nine years old. She was interested in medicine and wanted to be a doctor but majored in home economics, which was a more conventional vocation for women of her era. She transmitted her interest in medicine to my younger brother and me.

My grandfather came from Alsace-Lorraine, and a good many of my relatives were both German and French. I inherited the German work ethic (*Arbeit macht das Leben süss und Faulheit stirbt sich*—"Work makes living sweet and laziness kills you"). I started working in eighth grade and have always had at least one job since that time.

When I was four years old, I made rounds with a navy physician while my father was stationed in Cape May, New Jersey, during World War II. I knew at that point that I wanted to be a doctor. I was bored in grade school and clocked a lot of time in the nurse's office. Miss Shea, RN, read poems to me and caused me to develop a lifelong respect and admiration for nurses (and poetry).

During high school I visited a "snake pit" ward at Peoria State Hospital. It was before the first antipsychotic tranquilizer Thorazine was introduced. I was interested in psychology and hypnotism but wasn't in the psychology class. I just went along on their field trip out of curiosity and was unprepared for what we were to see. Fifty screaming, naked women smearing themselves with feces and menstrual secretions, urine and feces on the floor, no furniture or curtains on the ward, some catatonic patients having sat in the same position for so long their muscles had atrophied—and the attendants showed off the patients as if they were freaks in a carnival. (This is reminiscent of a form of entertainment at Bedlam Hospital in London, where patrons would tip the attendants for the opportunity of watching the mentally ill patients.) I was deeply traumatized by this experience. I could not believe that these were human beings and that they lived in these terrible circumstances. As an idealistic teenager, I decided I wanted to help these people. My father encouraged my compassion by observing that the mentally ill were the "lepers" of modern society. I now knew that I wanted to be a doctor who helped mentally ill patients.

I was the oldest child and the family "hero" to whom the family turned in time of crisis. I was called home from medical school to break down the bathroom door to prevent my younger brother Donn from killing himself and to make arrangements for his psychiatric hospitalization. He suffered from "manic depression." This was six years before lithium was approved in the United States to treat bipolar disorder. Donn felt that he had failed as a patient, and his last words to me were "Three strikes and you're out." Donn barricaded his hospital room during his third hospital stay and hanged himself while his psychiatrist was talking to him through the door. I tortured myself with guilt thinking of the times I had been mean to him or "one-upped" him. I've never been able to read his suicide note, although I knew that it was kept in my parents' top dresser drawer. Our family was so guilt ridden when he died that we had a closed-casket funeral. We rationalized that we wanted to remember him the way he was—in actual fact, we couldn't stand to look him in the face. Our family felt alienated from others who hadn't shared our traumatic experience and who, we thought, couldn't understand our feelings. We felt we had failed Donn as a family. As a result, my parents; my youngest brother, Dick; and I felt overwhelmed with frustration, sadness, shame, and guilt that we could not save him. Both Dick and I had a strong desire to try to do something in life to keep people from killing themselves and to keep families from going through the agony of losing a loved one in this tragic way. We were both driven when it came to learning and applying our specialties. We felt we could not expect any help from God (since he had not saved Donn) and we would have to do it ourselves. Dick graduated summa cum laude from Yale medical school and did his residency in neurology at the Mayo Clinic. He is currently in private practice in Winston Salem, North Carolina.

I attended my father's alma mater, Cornell College, in Mount Vernon, Iowa. I had a scholarship because of my high school grades and my ability as a wrestler. In college I hung out with the "animals" rather than the premed students. I was accepted and attended, on a general assembly scholarship, the University of Illinois medical school in Chicago. As the family hero, I tried to protect and please my folks. I married a girl who had a genius IQ, which was important to my academically oriented parents (my father would check on the IQs of the girls I dated in high school). We married for very irrational reasons, and I made the bizarre rationalization that this would enable me to study and work harder if I wasn't distracted by a happy, loving relationship at home. I worked every fourth night and one weekend a month at the Inland Steel medical department in East Chicago, Indiana, to support my wife and two baby girls while I attended medical school.

Although I strove to please my progenitors and those in authority, there was some rebelliousness on my part as I sought to have my own, independent identity. In an effort to help me understand this tendency in myself, a therapist once told me the story of Rabbi Horowitz. The rabbi was dying and one of his students came to him and said, "How are you?" "I'm depressed," answered the rabbi. "How can that be possible?" asked the student. "You are a great religious teacher and leader. You've published many books and taught many students." "I'm not Rabbi Horowitz," answered the dying man. The point being that you can live your life according to what you think others want you to be and not be true to yourself. Looking back, I can see that my hanging around with "animals," my use of profanity, my sometimes crude behavior, and later my divorce and remarriage have been, in part, efforts to rebel and to be my own person in life. My choice of psychiatry fits this paradigm as well. Most parents would be pleased to see their son become a physician, but few are eager to see him specialize in psychiatry. My experience in Vietnam tended to reinforce this rebellion against the conventional and the expectations of others.

My first contact with the U.S. Army was the induction physical that took place during my internship in 1965. I was twenty-seven and found myself in a huge barnlike structure on the south side of Chicago, going from station to station "spreading my cheeks" with several hundred seventeen- and eighteen-year-olds. One of the seventeen-year-olds came up to me and asked, "May we smoke, sir?" I asked him if he had missed the fact that I was also in my underwear and told him I didn't care what he did! This is the first time that I remember feeling old.

I received my specialty education in psychiatry at the Menninger Foundation in Topeka, Kansas. I felt fortunate to have been accepted for my residency training by what was probably the best psychiatric training program in the world at the time. Both Karl and Will Menninger were part of the teaching staff. Dr. Will had been a general and the head of army psychiatry in World War II. Dr. Karl and his wife, Jean, walked over to our house with a bouquet of flowers from their garden to join us for dinner one special evening (we were living in Dr. Helen Sargent's old home, which was down the street from the Menningers' house on Westwood Drive). The top psychiatrists and psychologists in the world came to Topeka to lecture and to participate in our instruction as visiting lecturers and instructors. I was a member of Dr. Harry Levinson's industrial psychiatry faculty and wrote my third-year paper on organizational diagnosis and intervention under his supervision. In order to take care of my patients, attend the required classes, read the assigned literature, and take advantage of the many elective classes, lectures, and seminars available in Topeka, I had to work from early morning until 10 or 11 P.M. nearly every day. I registered for every course available and attended all the elective seminars I possibly could. Karl Menninger said that to be successful in any field, you had to be neurotic, because truly happy, balanced people did not put all their energy and efforts in any one direction. By that definition I was definitely neurotic.

The number-one song the year of my internship (1965–66) was "The Ballad of the Green Berets" by S. Sgt. Barry Sadler and Robin Moore. The movie *Green Berets* with John Wayne was popular as well. During the Vietnam era it was impossible to be deferred from military service if you were a medical doctor. However, there was a "Barry Plan" that permitted deferment until your specialty training was completed if your specialty was needed by the military. There was a shortage of psychiatrists, and I was allowed to complete my specialty training. I was not opposed to serving in the military, and from a practical standpoint, it was much better for me financially than what I had been receiving during residency. Looking back, had I not been required to go into the military, I would have probably gone into analysis and ended up on the Menninger Clinic staff, now located in Houston, Texas.

My official introduction to the military came soon after the end of my residency training when I reported to the army's basic medical training class at Fort Sam Houston. I arrived in San Antonio, Texas, in July in a brand-new, army green, V-8, four-barrel, dual-exhaust GTO convertible. I drove from Illinois with the top down and nearly fried my brains going through Oklahoma. I lived in a local motel in San Antonio, compliments of the army, and went to the post, where I purchased uniforms, brass, shoes, boots, and so on with my uniform allowance. After the poverty of college, medical school, internship, and residency, it was exciting to have a nice paycheck, stay in a motel at government expense, and go to the plush officers' club for drinks and dinner. Rank was determined by the number of years out of medical school. Most of us went in as captains, but some went in as majors and even lieutenant colonels.

We were assigned to a sharp Mexican American drill sergeant. Sergeant Rodriguez (pseudonym) had a mirrorlike helmet, spit-shined boots, knife-edge creases in his spotless shirt and trousers, and brass that sparkled in the sun. He spotted one of our group wearing a bird colonel's insignia (named for the eagle on the insignia) on one shoulder and a lieutenant's bar on the other. "What are you supposed to be, sir?" asked the sergeant. "I'm a lieutenant colonel," answered the doctor proudly. "Oh, we have something JUST for that," replied Sergeant Rodriguez, shaking his head in amazement. He showed the new lieutenant colonel the silver oak-leaf cluster that signified his rank.

We learned to march a little. Sergeant Rodriguez thought it would be nice if we could execute "To the rear, march," even though it was not among our requirements. He demonstrated it and had a couple of our group do it; then we all tried it. After half of us collided with the other half twice, he said he guessed that was why it wasn't on our list and he'd just stop us and have us do "about face" instead. The corpsmen and nurses came to the parade ground to watch and laugh as our class of five hundred male and female doctors in army and air force uniforms, some in khakis, some in fatigues (there were always a few who forgot the proper uniform), all carrying briefcases and books, tried to march. It was impressive to me that all these drafted doctors, half of whom were heading directly for Vietnam and most of the rest expected to go later, were trying to do their best to learn to march and be "good little soldiers." I think it demonstrates that most of us doctors, at least at that time, wanted to please our parents, teachers, and anyone in authority.

Despite our efforts to learn to march and to score on the tests, we were a little ornery. The Fort Sam faculty were used to teaching doctors, and our smart aleck stuff didn't seem to faze them in the least. They repeated basic information several times and beat on the stage with a pole if a particular statement was going to be on the test. We'd laugh when they repeated several times something like "Last name first, first name last, then your social security number." The faculty would point out that we could laugh, but about a third of us would get it wrong! On the rifle range we were cautioned not to touch our weapons without permission and to fire only when ordered. Just then some ducks flew over the range, and most of the class started taking pot shots at them. We had a night-compass course, crawled under machine-gun fire (most of us liked this because it was just like in the movies), and learned how many holes were supposed to be in a privy for a squad versus a platoon versus a company (this was in case we had to do unit health inspections). At the end of the course we had a graduation ceremony at 8 A.M., complete with an army band. Our class sang "Mickey Mouse," and the band, being good sports, joined in and then played inspirational numbers. The finale was the band blaring "Up, Up and Away" by the Fifth Dimension.

The only choice given to me by the army had been the location of my assignment. I put down in order of preference the East Coast, the West Coast, and Europe. I was assigned to the South at Fort Knox, Kentucky, and later to Vietnam.

At Fort Knox I was assigned to serve as chief of the inpatient psychiatric service at Ireland Army Hospital. Sergeant DeLeon was my ward master. He was a stocky, well-built, neatly groomed Puerto Rican with heavy, dark-rimmed glasses and a full head of black hair. He always presented himself in a very humble manner. He had more than twenty years of experience in army psychiatry. As a hospital doctor at Menninger's, I had been assigned to a team of seasoned social workers, psychologists, nurses, occupational therapists, art therapists, music therapists, recreational therapists, and aides. These people had years of experience working with hospitalized psychiatric patients. I learned quickly that although I was the team leader on paper and signed the orders, I had better listen to what the people who knew what was going on had to say. Although I was the new chief, I candidly told Sergeant DeLeon that I knew nothing about military psychiatry and was open to his suggestions as to how we could best accomplish our mission. He responded by sharing his experiences in the military, coming up with many innovative and successful approaches to problems and generally keeping me out of trouble.

The first morning I reported to the hospital commander and then to the chief of psychiatry. There were several psychiatrists assigned to Fort Knox, but most served in the Mental Hygiene Unit. That morning the Regular Army psychiatrist chief, Maj. Noel Goodman, greeted me by saying, "The bathroom is over there." I later mentioned this to Capt. Gus Cretekos, a child psychoanalyst assigned to outpatient evaluation and treatment, and commented that this was a strange welcome. Gus explained that the major was so preoccupied with himself that since he had to go to the bathroom, he assumed everyone else did also!

Serving as a psychiatrist in a stateside military post was the easiest job I have ever had. I was thrilled to have a nice paycheck. In addition to receiving army pay, I was able to moonlight at the Elizabethtown mental health clinic and earn some additional money. Even with two jobs I had plenty of time to fish, bowl, eat out, and see an occasional play in Louisville. Compared to my life as a resident in Topeka, my job was soft. I would put on my uniform in the morning and drive to the hospital. I would then go to the psychiatric unit where my social work/psychology technicians were waiting. One would help me off with my uniform coat, another would hold up my starched laboratory coat, and a third plunged his arms down the sleeves to open them up (so I would not have to strain pushing my arms through the starched sleeves). Next they would help me on with the lab coat, give me a cup of coffee, and leave me alone in my office to "collect my thoughts." After this "break" I would make rounds on the unit accompanied by the head nurse, Sergeant DeLeon, and some of the technicians and medics. Following this, I would take another coffee break and then do some paperwork (which meant signing the forms the technicians had completed). The military insisted that every blank on a form be completed, and there were lots of forms. It didn't seem to matter what was actually in the blanks, just that they were completely filled. The technicians had fun putting silly, off-color names in the blanks, but as long as the blanks were filled, the paperwork did not come back—but miss one space and it would be returned for completion.

When I returned from lunch, there would be several soldiers lined up on chairs in the hall memorizing their excuses, waiting to be seen. These were men who had gone AWOL (absent without leave) and had been picked up by the military police or local law enforcement and sent to the nearest military facility. They had to be seen by a psychiatrist before they could be returned to their units or sent to the stockade. Typically, the interview would go like this:

"Why did you go AWOL?"

"My sergeant yelled at me, my girl friend is pregnant, and my best friend got killed on a motorcycle."

"The army only allows one excuse; which one do you want?"

"I'll take my girl friend is pregnant."

"Okay, now get back to your unit."

Usually the soldiers were able to make it back on their own. Chronic offenders were either incarcerated in the stockade or escorted by the military police back to their units. The county sheriffs near Fort Knox would keep an eye on AWOL soldiers until right before the holidays and then would round them up and collect a fifty-dollar bounty for returning them. There may have been some sadism involved in seeing that the AWOL soldiers spent Christmas in the stockade, but primarily it seemed to be a sort of Christmas savings plan among the local law officers. During the Vietnam War the desertion rates increased 400 percent between 1966 and 1971, when they reached 73.5 per 1,000 soldiers. By comparison, only 25 per 1,000 deserted during the Korean War. Of the 500,000 deserters in Vietnam, only 93,250 remained away longer than thirty days.

Regular Army officers preferred Regular Army doctors and thought that the higher the rank, the better the doctor. In my experience, this wasn't true because, in general, the best physicians returned to civilian life and Regular Army officers were often promoted into administrative positions, such as hospital commanders, where they had little clinical activity. In our department, for example, Capt. Barry Gault was a Harvard-trained psychiatrist who had better training and more clinical experience than Major Goodman, who was army trained and whose activities as chief of the department were largely administrative. Despite these differences, Regular Army officers would ask to see Major Goodman.

You cannot order doctors to do much, even in the military, because they need to exercise their own judgment and skill to help patients. You can make them serve in a particular place, give them the hours they must work, and have them see certain patients, but you cannot make them listen, care, or think appropriate thoughts. Once in a while a Regular Army medical officer would try to assert rank over the doctors who were in for two years. The chief of the medical staff for Ireland Army Hospital was a young, freshly army-trained, lieutenant colonel urologist who was a "lifer" (career soldier). Shortly after I arrived and had taken over the job as chief of the inpatient service, the young, trim, somewhat hyperactive Lieutenant Colonel Plumber (pseudonym) marched onto my unit and asked about one of my patients.

"I'm Lieutenant Colonel Plumber, chief of the medical staff."

"Hello," I replied instead of snapping to and saying, "Yes, sir."

Plumber frowned. "I understand that you saw a patient in the emergency room last night and ordered one hundred milligrams of Thorazine four times a day."

"Yes."

Plumber flushed and appeared a little flustered at my lack of defensiveness. "Isn't that a lot?"

"No."

"Your coat is unbuttoned," Plumber stammered.

"Yes, sir!" I saluted and responded in military fashion, buttoning the offending button. He stormed out of the unit, and I did not see him for the remainder of my service at the hospital.

The social work/psychology technicians were enlisted men, but they also had some slack because of their jobs. Lieutenant Bixby, a tank commander, called the unit about one of his men, Private First Class Jones, who was undergoing psychiatric evaluation, and spoke to Specialist Kelly. Bixby informed Kelly that Jones was nothing but a goldbrick who ought to have his butt kicked. Kelly pointed out that Bixby's specialty was tanks and he would get a report as soon as Jones's evaluation was completed.

Shortly after my arrival I was asked by one of the judge advocate general (JAG) officers to evaluate a soldier facing court-martial charges because of his failure to follow orders, multiple AWOLs, and disrespect to officers. I had taken two elective forensic courses at Menninger's and was anxious to show my legal skills. I interviewed the soldier at length and then did the typical lengthy, detailed, Menninger forensic workup. I stated in about twenty-three different ways that the soldier had a personality disorder and did not have a psychiatric illness that would explain his behavior. I turned in the report and waited for days without hearing any feedback. By chance I ran into the referring attorney and asked him about the soldier.

"Oh, they let him off," he replied.

"Let him off!" I exclaimed. "Didn't you read my report?"

"Well, to tell you the truth, Doc, we didn't—but it was so long we figured the guy must have been pretty sick!"

I explained the contents of my report and that reports of that length were the norm where I trained. The attorney shook his head and smiled. "The worst of it is, the board was so frustrated at having to let that schlep off, they nailed the next guy."

I learned a lesson in communication that day. My extensive report had accomplished the opposite of what I had intended. As a result of my compulsive workup, the individual who should have been punished was free and the next unfortunate person to be heard received unduly harsh treatment. Following this experience I attached a cover letter in which I summarized my conclusions to the court (and called the referring JAG officer before trial to clarify the content).

The patients on the psychiatric unit wore blue coveralls. Patients on other hospital units wore white hospital pajamas. Patients from my unit who were ambulatory and in control of themselves would go in a group on the elevator to the basement hospital cafeteria for meals (those who were too ill were served on the unit). Patients and staff from other floors would appear startled and uncomfortable when they found themselves alone on the elevator with "psych" patients. In the dining room the psychiatric patients sat together, feeling ostracized. My patients developed their own ways of coping with their alienation. When a new person from another hospital floor got on the elevator with a group from the psychiatric unit, someone in the group would say, "You're stepping on our dog." The person would look, and one of the patients would be holding an invisible leash. The person would dutifully step back and apologize. Another patient would say, "Pet the dog." The person would pretend to pet an invisible dog. In the cafeteria they had the kitchen staff get scraps and water for their "dog." They got a big kick out of turning the tables and having people do silly things for their invisible pet because they were frightened by what they viewed as "the crazy" patients from the psych unit.

I had an on-the-job training (OJT) psychiatrist named Captain Raneri who was a doctor of osteopathy (which is the equivalent of an MD as far as the army and medical licensing bureaus are concerned). He had already served a year in Vietnam as a general medical officer. I called him Count Raneri because he was from a wealthy family in Philadelphia and had a very cosmopolitan air about him. He was thin, with black hair and a neatly trimmed mustache. Raneri's aristocratic background and his year in Vietnam resulted in his not taking any guff from anyone. When I had a patient I was trying to transfer to Walter Reed, I would ask Raneri to make the call. (Typically, the admissions officer at Reed was reluctant to accept any transfers.) Captain Raneri was not above a little fabrication in order to accomplish his mission. And usually he intimidated the admitting officer into doing what he wanted. On one occasion, however, he was making his case with the admitting resident at Reed, who said he would have to check with his supervisor. Raneri said to "put him on." Soon a voice introducing himself as Captain Black (pseudonym), U.S. Navy, came on the phone. Raneri introduced himself in a condescending way as a lieutenant colonel. Captain Black asked Raneri if he knew that a navy captain is the same rank as a bird colonel in the army. Raneri stammered, laughed, and said that Captain Black had gotten him with that remark. Needless to say, that patient didn't get transferred.

Sergeant DeLeon recruited a young medic, Sergeant Medina, to work on our unit. He was the all-weight judo champion of Puerto Rico, and his calm presence on the unit kept everything quiet and under control. For example, Medina would go to the emergency room to escort a violent, psychotic soldier to our unit. The medics would be trying to restrain the soldier, who was trying to hit anyone near him. Medina would put his hand on the man's wrist and say softly that he would like it on the psychiatric unit, would receive good care, and would be safe there. The agitated soldier would jerk his arm to take a swing at Medina, but the arm wouldn't move! He would look questioningly at Medina (who was like a piece of steel) and at his wrist still in Medina's grasp. Medina would smile, and the soldier would walk meekly with him to the unit.

Sergeant DeLeon, who had been a drill instructor before becoming a psychiatric ward master, wanted to drill the inpatients each morning. I went along with his idea, which turned out to be an excellent diagnostic tool. The schizophrenic patients awaiting medical discharge loved it. They felt they were part of the army. They put on their blue hospital uniforms and marched to Sergeant DeLeon's cadence. The men with personality disorders who were trying to get out of the army hated it and complained that they should not be made to drill because they were "sick."

Sergeant DeLeon knew how the army worked. Whenever we had a Regular Army noncommissioned officer (NCO) or officer on the unit, he would call the man's sergeant major or first sergeant and speak about the patient, explaining that "we are taking real good care of him." He would be thanked and asked if there was anything he needed. Sergeant DeLeon would reply, for example, that the boys like coffee (or steaks, or whatever Sergeant DeLeon felt we needed). And it would be sent right over.

I learned that this is how the military worked. If you did not want something to happen, you went through channels—if you did, you bartered. It was a good system once you got used to it. When I needed some dental care, I asked around to find out which dentist on the post had the best reputation. I then asked his medic what he liked to drink—"scotch" was the response. At my first dental appointment I presented the "tooth fairy" with a bottle of Chivas Regal. He was very appreciative and replaced all of my worn-out fillings with gold, compliments of Uncle Sugar.

I was glad that I had an opportunity to repay, in a small way, some of Sergeant DeLeon's kindnesses. We had a psychotic Puerto Rican patient who was diagnosed as having acute paranoid schizophrenia. He was being medically discharged from the army and transferred by air to a Veterans Administration hospital in Puerto Rico for long-term treatment. I wrote a note stating that he needed to be accompanied by a staff member and that Sergeant DeLeon was the person on the unit who knew the patient best and who was trusted by the patient. I strongly recommended that for the patient's safety and the safety of the staff in the plane that Sergeant DeLeon accompany the patient. As a result, Sergeant DeLeon was able to spend two weeks back home in Puerto Rico on temporary duty with all expenses paid by the government.

One day a huge black soldier arrived by medical evacuation from Vietnam with no medical records. He was wearing a tag that said "Private Brown (pseudonym)—Paranoid Schizophrenia—Thorazine 300mg/day." It was just before Christmas, and he seemed to be doing well, so I let him go on leave as part of "Operation Snowman," in which we emptied the ward of patients so that the staff could take it easy over the holidays. Shortly after he left, I received his medical records and orders to conduct a sanity hearing on him because he was charged with premeditated murder in a riot at the U.S. Army Installation Stockade in Long Binh, South Vietnam (popularly known as the Long Binh Jail, or LBJ). According to the records we received, Private Brown had hit a white prisoner in the head with a metal rod and beat him again after he fell to the ground. I immediately went to the hospital commander, who asked me if I thought Brown would come back. When I said I did, he replied, "Don't worry about it." Brown did come back but was stuck in the psychiatric unit because no one wanted to hold a trial. Walter Reed wouldn't take him, Vietnam didn't want to try him, and the lawyers at our post didn't want to get involved because it would mean having to call in witnesses from all over the world.

His mother was a psychiatric nurse and seemed to be an intelligent, caring person. She came over from St. Louis to visit her son several times. I told her that she should contact her congressman and the NAACP and put some pressure on the situation or he would be sitting on that ward indefinitely. When I left for Vietnam, he was still there.

The head nurse on the unit, Lieutenant Mantha, was a young, attractive woman who had been sent to work on the psychiatric ward as punishment by the chief of nursing of Ireland Army Hospital. The chief of nursing was an old, crabby colonel who barked out orders and enjoyed the privileges of her rank. Sergeant DeLeon made a point of waiting on her hand and foot whenever she appeared on the unit. He invited her to the psychiatric department Christmas party and stayed with her as long as she remained to make sure that she had plenty of spiked punch. Lieutenant Mantha hated to see Sergeant DeLeon fawning over the colonel, but our unit enjoyed the goodwill of the chief nurse even though Mantha did not.

Lieutenant Mantha was an excellent surgical nurse who had gotten in trouble with the chief of nursing by criticizing some of the outmoded procedures she observed on the surgical unit. Even worse, she had tried to institute change without going through the proper channels or getting the colonel's approval. She was young and idealistic, but short on tact. When she arrived on our unit, she told me that she didn't know anything about psychiatry, didn't particularly want to learn anything about psychiatry, and had hated her psychiatric rotation during her nursing training. One thing I learned from my training in group psychotherapy was that if a person was passionate about a topic, it didn't make too much difference if the person was positive or negative—there was some emotional investment in the subject. I took her on morning rounds and had her sit in during initial interviews with patients; the psychologists had her sit in as a cotherapist with some of the groups on the unit. Dr. Richard Doiron was an excellent clinical psychologist from Maine. He briefed her on psychological testing and supervised her group work. Lieutenant Mantha was very bright, compassionate, and energetic and soon came up with several ideas to improve the care on the unit. In contrast to her chief's response, we listened to her suggestions and nearly always implemented them. By the time I left for Vietnam, she was leading groups herself and had become an excellent psychiatric nurse. I received a letter from her while I was in Vietnam in which she said she had left the army and was pursuing a career in psychiatric nursing.

Gus Cretekos was a pudgy, Greek American, "teddy bear" sort of a guy with dark crew-cut hair, prominent eyebrows, dark-rimmed glasses, a good sense of humor, and a very sensitive, kindly disposition. Children loved him. Like many child psychiatrists I have met, he loved children, but at the time he and his wife, Elaine, did not have any of their own. He caused considerable stress to the Regular Army officers at Fort Knox by refusing to buy (because of the additional expense) a new field-grade cap with gold leaf on the bill after being promoted directly from captain to lieutenant colonel. Most Regular Army officers couldn't wait to buy the new field-grade cap with "scrambled eggs on the bill" to visually demonstrate their promotion from company grade. Second lieutenants, lieutenants, and captains are "company-grade" officers. Majors, lieutenant colonels and colonels are "field-grade" officers. There is a saying in the military that "honor among company grades is like virtue among whores." It is a big jump to go from the plain-billed company-grade officer's cap to the gold-braided bill of a field-grade officer's lid. Gus was a unique person, with no interest in military trappings.

One problem we had on the unit was that soldiers would be evacuated to the hospital from other army posts for a psychiatric evaluation, which included psychological testing. It typically would take several days to schedule the testing and write up the report that included my consultation with the patient. Then, when we tried to send the soldiers back to the referring facility, we had to wait weeks to get them scheduled on a return flight. As a result, these patients would "silt up" the unit and take up beds that could be used for patients who were ill. Those who had personality disorders were griping every morning about Sergeant DeLeon making them march and drill. In addition, the plane (which was under air force control) did not always take them to their point of origin, so they would then be evacuated again until, sometimes after several plane rides, they would arrive back at their posts. It took so long for this process that the patients with psychiatric illnesses such as depression or anxiety disorders were often well by the time they returned to their original posts. The phenomenon was referred to as "air therapy."

Sergeant DeLeon, several of the key technicians, and I met to see what could be done about this situation. Specialist Kelly was an "operator" whose talents included playing golf with the commanding general. I told him when I first met him that he was too slick for me and I didn't want to try to keep track of him—I wanted two hours of productive time every day and after that he could play golf, hunt, fish, or whatever. This was satisfactory with him, and he accomplished a great deal during the two hours he actually worked. Kelly, DeLeon, and I decided that if we could get a referred soldier evaluated within a few hours, we could put him back on the same plane and return him immediately to the referring unit. I told Sergeant DeLeon that I could do the psychiatric evaluation and the report, but how could we possibly get psychological testing that quickly? Sergeant DeLeon said to leave this to him. He went to the psychologists and asked them if they liked coffee. They all said yes. He replied that if they wanted to keep having coffee, they would do the psychological testing on air-evacuated patients as soon as they arrived. He also explained why we wanted to accomplish this speedy workup. From that time on every evacuee who came up to our unit was tested immediately. I saw the patient for the psychiatric consultation and wrote up the report, and Specialist Kelly put the patient's travel orders into a typewriter and added "and return." We put the soldiers back on the same planes in which they arrived, along with a sealed envelope containing their psychiatric and psychological evaluations. I'm sure the referring doctors who were expecting an "air-therapy cure" were surprised to get their patients back the same day!

I evaluated a number of interesting cases at Fort Knox. One of them was the most frightening person I have met in thirty-seven years of psychiatric practice. He came to the psychiatric unit after he tried to break into the post armory to steal a weapon to use to kill his sergeant. The MPs thought he was strange and brought him to us for evaluation. He was tall, thin, fish-belly pale, with unkempt black hair and intense Charles Manson–like eyes. From my years of wrestling, I have a habit of sizing up guys to anticipate their strength. What I learned over the years was that you did not have to worry about the guys who look like Charles Atlas. They usually have been pumping so much iron that they are muscle bound, slow, and generally not that strong. The guys to look out for are those that are thin and pale (because they are indoors working out all the time) with piano-wire sinews. This man looked very strong. He grew up in eastern Kentucky. His father worked in a coal mine, drank heavily, and was physically abusive to the patient, his siblings, and his mother. The patient got into fights as a youngster, wet his bed, and tortured animals (he denied setting fire to things). I mention these because the triad of bed wetting, abusing animals, and setting fires used to be considered symptoms of sociopathic or psychopathic personality disorder. He ran away as a teenager to get away from his father's abuse and joined a carnival at first as a laborer and later ran the shooting gallery. He married a woman who was six years older but didn't consummate the marriage. Instead, he enlisted in the army, requested duty in Vietnam, and was sent to a combat unit. The men in the unit thought he was odd and made him a point man (the lead man on patrol who cuts through the brush and is exposed to dangers such as booby trips and first contact with the enemy), hoping that he would get killed.

After a few months in country he was asked to guard some Vietnamese prisoners. When he was alone with them, he shot them in the knees, tortured them, and finally killed them. He cut off their ears while they were still alive and made a necklace of them. The men in his unit said that he was crazy. He heard about this and said that he would kill the next person who called him crazy. They stopped calling him crazy. He started sneaking into Vietnamese villages and killing people at random. He decided to kill his wife when he returned home, because he thought she was a whore, and wrote his cousin in Hazzard, Kentucky, about his plan. Instead of his cousin trying to talk him out of this notion, the cousin replied that they were building a road and if he wanted to put the body under the road, no one would ever find it. The man returned to the States and was assigned to Fort Knox. He picked up a prostitute, planning to kill her, but the woman sensed danger and ran away. He returned to the post where he attempted to steal a weapon to kill his sergeant.

He described in detail the way he tortured and killed Vietnamese. He said that he would shoot them in the knees and that it
excited him to hear them screaming and begging for their lives. He
mutilated their bodies while they were alive. He reported that he
experienced an orgasm the first time he tortured and killed prisoners and that following this experience, he had a sexual tension that
would build up over time until it reached a point where he either
had to kill someone or cut himself to relieve the tension. I presented
him to the team on the psychiatric unit. He repeated the detailed
descriptions of his torture and murder of Vietnamese prisoners and
villagers. It was chilling to see him do this in a calm monotone
with the same emotion you would use to describe washing your
car. I've since seen patients who have fabricated stories of killing
and torture in Vietnam, but none of them came across as being
truly frightening—this guy was. One of the psychologists asked,
"You told us that you were very religious—how do you reconcile
torturing and killing these people and the Bible's commandment
'Thou shalt not kill'?" The patient responded to the question as
if he were answering the question of a small child: "That commandment does not pertain to sinful abominations," he patiently
explained. "I am doing the Lord's work by ridding the world of
homosexuals, prostitutes, and heathen [Vietnamese] sinners." He
said that he had no guilt or remorse about these acts. He believed
he was carrying out God's will. When he was escorted from the
conference room, we all sat silently and thought how terrifying
this killer was.

A few days later on the evening shift one of the medics happened to hear a muffled noise. When he checked a linen closet,
he found the patient quietly strangling one of the orderlies. The
medic called for help, and the staff were able to save the orderly,
who required hospitalization and would have been killed if the
medic hadn't discovered him when he did.

I immediately made arrangements to transfer the patient to St.
Elizabeth's Hospital in Washington, D.C. I gave the admitting doctor
a detailed report over the phone and sent along a lengthy written
report that included a description of what the patient had told us,
our observations, and his attempt to kill the orderly. They were
aware that the man was extremely dangerous, and hopefully, he
is still under their care.

WHEN I RECEIVED ORDERS to go to Vietnam, I told Sergeant DeLeon that I was very grateful to him for sharing his experience with me and appreciative of the year-long military psychiatry experience at the Ireland Army Hospital. I became familiar with the job of an army psychiatrist and some of the differences between military and civilian psychiatry before being put "on my own" in a combat unit. It would have been much more difficult for me had I gone directly from Fort Sam Houston to Vietnam.

I wrote to my old mentor Dr. Karl Menninger to tell him of my military experiences at Fort Knox and of my orders for Vietnam. I expected a show of sympathy. Instead, he wrote:

Dear Dr. Bey:

I was very happy to hear from you. Much of what you are doing sounds interesting, but I sympathize with the boring aspects of it. I think it will be more exciting when you get out. Wasn't it Thucydides that said, "War is the father of all things" meaning that if you don't get killed you learn a lot. Many great discoveries have come out of military activity.

I read the other day that the student unrest over the country can best be described as incomprehensible because it is irrational and it is irrational because the whole Vietnam business is so irrational. Some people have the right to act crazy I guess, others don't. Meanwhile, you and I have to see some people who don't just act crazy, they are crazy and the contrast is very incongruous in our minds, but probably the Lord understands it.

Sincerely yours,
Karl Menninger M.D.

I was surprised at Dr. Karl's words at the time but later felt it was the best thing he could have written to me. He was inspiring me to make the best of the situation and try to learn something and perhaps discover something new. It was flattering to hear him say that he and I were in the same business. He also acknowledged that we were not running the show. This was a typical response from him.

I was sad at the idea of leaving home and being away from my daughters, Cathy (age six) and Barby (age five), for a year. I remember getting choked up when I heard Andy Williams singing "Love Is Blue," because my world was definitely going to be blue without my daughters. Cathy was direct and asked me how long I'd be gone, if I'd get killed, and if people would shoot at me. Her innocence penetrated my facade of control and adequacy. She knew that I couldn't say for sure that I'd be all right. Barby believed in magic and made a "spell" to bring me home. At Fort Knox the girls had friends whose fathers were in or had been in Vietnam. Once the active-duty soldier left for a hardship assignment, the family was required to leave post housing. When they moved back home to Normal, Illinois, they were the only children their ages whose father was in Vietnam because there were not that many thirty-year-old draftees in the country.

I was downcast at the thought of being separated from the girls for a year, but there were other feelings that I didn't express. I was excited about the adventure of going to a foreign country and probably felt a little macho about going off to war. There was some anxiety about the unknown and the possibility of being killed. My brother, Dick, remembers shaking hands with me, saying "See you later." My response was "I hope so." There was also the interest and curiosity, largely inspired by Dr. Karl, of being in a unique situation, learning new information, and trying new things in a combat zone.

I went to Chicago where my old wrestling buddy Bill Taylor and his wife, Sharon, hosted a farewell cocktail party for me at their home in the Carl Sandburg Apartments. Bill was absolutely honest, hardworking, patriotic, and a loyal friend. He was later appointed head of the Federal Deposit Insurance Corporation by Pres. George H. W. Bush. The Sandburg Apartments were near the Cabrini Green public-housing project in Chicago. As we looked down from the window of the Taylors' apartment, we could see a mob of angry black people coming down the street overturning and setting fire to cars and to some of the buildings. We were all a little anxious, wondering what might happen if the mob came into our building. The group was anxious about my safety in Vietnam, but I was thinking that things weren't that safe at home.

I went through the paperwork to process out of Fort Knox and the arrangements to move my family off the military post and back home with my relatives. It took a long time to do anything on post because most of it was handled by civil service workers who worked at their own pace, insisting that every "i" was dotted, every "t" crossed, and every blank completed on all the "proper" forms. I took the two days' worth of inoculations in preparation for Vietnam (yellow fever, dengue, hepatitis, tetanus, smallpox, typhoid, and plague) and experienced the usual low-grade fever and arthralgia accompanying the process. I fired an M16 and a .45-caliber pistol on the range and performed the other require-ments necessary before my departure. It seemed ironic that I had to meet all sorts of mandatory requirements to qualify to go to a place where I didn't want to be sent.

On a rainy morning in May I boarded a plane in Louisville and took off for San Francisco. My old college roommate and fellow wrestler, Jim Lynn, and his wife, Linda, were at SFO to meet me. I greeted him by saying, "Howdy, Turd," and Jim laughed, remem-bering the note "Good luck, Terd" he left me before taking off for the summer and my subsequent criticism of his spelling and his academic skills in general. "Glad to see that medical school and all that shrinking hasn't altered your basic asshole personality," Jim said while taking my carry-on bag. "We've got to hurry—we only have until tomorrow morning to get you ready to protect the free world from communist aggression." Jim and Linda then took me out drinking and partying most of the night. We went from bar to topless bar and strip club to strip club all night in San Francisco. "This poor SOB is leaving for 'Nam in the morning," was the stan-dard introduction that would lead to many free drinks and offers to "change your luck."

When the Lynns dropped me off at Travis Air Force Base to await my flight to Vietnam, I was very tired, drunk, and hungover. I flopped down on a bench in the crowded terminal and tried to sleep. I watched a short, stocky army captain a few feet from my bench say good-bye to his wife and children. After they left, he sat by himself crying. I noted that he was a medical officer. I had a headache and was too hungover to be depressed. I remember thinking, "What a wimp!" Then, as I reflected, "Hell, I'm the one who's messed up—he probably has a good relationship with his wife and is in touch with his feelings—I'm the one who was out all night drinking trying to control mine." As they say in Alcoholics Anonymous, "Denial is not a river in Egypt." The situation brought to mind the song "Leaving on a Jet Plane" by Peter, Paul, and Mary—we were both lonely and hated to leave, not knowing if and when we would return.

CHAPTER 2

Stepping through
the Looking Glass

It was a huge jump from life at home to life in an infantry division in Vietnam. Looking back, it was like going through the looking glass in *Alice in Wonderland* and entering a parallel existence. To make the transition, one had to forget "the world" and focus on the day-to-day events in Vietnam.

At Travis Air Force Base we showed our orders for Vietnam and boarded a chartered Boeing 707. "Check out those stewardesses, man," my left-hand seatmate nudged me. I looked at the ones I could see, and they appeared to be somewhat matronly. "Yeah, so?" I asked. "The airline is willing to risk these," he said. I was too hungover to reflect on his paranoid theory, but it did make a little sense to me at the time. Later, I heard similar theories from other Vietnam veterans, and perhaps this was just a rumor that my neighbor had heard in the past. The aircraft had extra seats installed, making for a cramped nineteen-hour flight. The cabin started to smell like an armpit after a few hours.

My talkative seatmate was a Special Forces enlisted man who was returning from a hardship leave in the States. He wore tiger-striped (camouflage) fatigues and a beret and looked pretty fit compared to my other pudgy seatmate and me. He showed me pictures he had taken in Vietnam, including some of pigs eating dead NVA soldiers. I was hungover and irritable and didn't respond to his efforts to gross me out. My right-hand seatmate was Capt. Herbert Goldman, a psychiatrist, the medical officer I had observed saying good-bye to his family in the military airport prior to boarding. He was tearful and quiet. We stopped briefly in Hawaii and Wake to change flight crews. Our last pilot was a Vietnam veteran who couldn't resist getting on the intercom and telling stories about drawing fire when he landed at Bien Hoa during his tour of duty. We stared out the windows to get a look at the place where we'd be living for the next year.

We saw red soil, bright sunlight, a cloudless sky, and a dusty airstrip filled with military aircraft and vehicles. For a midwesterner used to rich black soil and lush green scenery, the dusty red dirt appeared foreign and unattractive. Several military and civilian aircraft were taking off and landing. Some were parked on the barren, dusty tarmac near the prefabricated hangar at the Bien Hoa Airfield. A few sick-looking palm trees stood along the edge of the runway. When the plane stopped, the temperature in the cabin rose rapidly, we started to perspire, and our breathing became labored. After a lengthy wait, we deplaned by a stair ramp and were greeted by ovenlike heat, dusty air, and a peculiar odor that was a combination of burning fuel and an unidentifiable scent. My veteran seatmate told me it was burning feces, explaining that the Vietnamese "shit burners" would take the pans out from under the privies twice a day, pour fuel oil on the contents, and set them on fire. Two lines of happy soldiers in fatigues and floppy boondock hats (aka "boonie hats") stood at the bottom of the stairway with their duffel bags, waiting to board the freedom bird and get home after their year in Vietnam.

They laughed and hooted as they saw us leaving the plane to begin our year in country. "Here come the FNGs (fucking new guys)!" "Hey, kill yourself now!" "You're going home in a body bag." "What a bunch of sorry mothers." "Grow a tree and hang yourself." "Hey turtle—you ain't going to make it." "The montagnards are shorter than you." We didn't understand this one at the time: it referred to the indigenous, dark-skinned Vietnamese and implied that they would be leaving Vietnam before we would. We trudged, heads down, through the gauntlet in our sweat-soaked fatigues.

We were entering another existence. The men who were there were helping us enter their world by flooding us with anxiety;

shocking us with stories of killing, danger, depravity, and sadism; and, all told, using the most profane language imaginable. We soon would learn to imitate the veterans, forgetting about the world and learning a new way of speaking and how to survive a year in Vietnam. I was too preoccupied to hear the constant sound of aircraft overhead. Later, I noticed that no matter where I was in Vietnam, I heard the constant "woomp woomp" of helicopter blades in the sky.

After being issued gear that included tropical fatigues, tropical boots, a poncho liner (a nylon insert into a military rain poncho, used as blanket; with an insulation rating of a four-pound wool blanket), a poncho, .45-caliber pistol, and M16 rifle, we were bused from Bien Hoa to the 90th Replacement Station, which appeared to be purposely designed to be a more miserable environment than any other in Vietnam so that we would be elated wherever we ended up. The tents were infested with mosquitoes, dusty, crowded, hot, and permeated with body odor.

The next morning, my former seatmate and fellow psychiatrist Captain Goldman and I were taken to the United States Army Republic of Vietnam (USARV) headquarters in Long Binh to meet with Lt. Col. George L. Mitchell, the psychiatric consultant, to receive our assignments. The USARV headquarters was in a large, white, modern building that was air conditioned, had modern office furniture, and seemed out of place in Vietnam. I was glad that I had contacted my buddy Ed Colbach in Vietnam ahead of time to assure myself a good assignment in Qui Nhon living in a villa on Red Beach. Lieutenant Colonel Mitchell informed us that several psychiatrists with orders to Vietnam before us had managed to avoid coming to Vietnam one way or another, leaving two combat divisions without psychiatrists. These two combat-division slots had priority; therefore, we would be filling them. This news ended my fantasies of living in a villa on the ocean. I remember asking myself at the time, "What is wrong with you that you didn't get out of coming?" Years later when I read in the paper that Donna Shalala said that the best and the brightest didn't go to Vietnam, I thought back to that moment in Vietnam and how stupid I felt to have shown up. We flipped for assignments. I won the toss and took the 1st Infantry Division. I didn't know anything about either division but assumed that *airborne* meant jumping out of aircraft. I later learned that the 1st Infantry Division was the first combat division to have a trained psychiatrist assigned to it—Dr. Herbert Spiegel, assigned as a battalion surgeon in June 1942. My sad companion got assigned to the 101st Airborne Division.

An air-conditioned car came to take Captain Goldman to a C-130 so he could fly north to airborne country. My driver and escort arrived in a dusty jeep wearing flak jackets (heavy, fiberglass-filled vests for protection from shrapnel) and steel pots (helmets) and carrying M16 rifles. As we drove to the 1st Division support command headquarters, they pointed out ambush sites and told stories of rocket attacks, firefights (minor engagements with the enemy), and mortar fire in the division. We passed large groves of rubber trees and rice paddies. Vietnamese farmers were using water buffalo to till the ground. We saw one who had a motor-driven tiller. We drove through villages made up of huts with thatched roofs. Pigs and children romped between and throughout the dusty huts. Some of the children along the road held up their fingers in a "V" for victory salute that looked like a scene from World War II. Everything appeared new to me. When there is an expectation that things are different, you tend to see ordinary things in a new light. We approached an area ahead that looked like a prison, with earth mounded up into a berm and several rows of coiled concertina wire surrounding the base camp (the semipermanent field headquarters) at Di An. An elevated guard tower with two soldiers stood next to the gate. The soldiers in the tower could set off the claymore mines (one-pound plastic explosives, often molded into an arch with six hundred steel ball bearings that would blow outward when detonated), gasoline, and TNT (fou gas, a type of "homemade napalm" consisting mainly of jet fuel and explosives) located in the perimeter defenses, sound the alert, and call in artillery fire.

My escorts pulled through the gate; drove by a number of hootches (slang for the low-lying buildings made of wooden slats separated by screen to let air through), Quonset huts, sand-bagged mortar and artillery emplacements; and dropped me off with my duffel bag in front of a semicircle of eight or nine men in lawn chairs who were drinking beer. "Here's the new Wizard," my driver shouted as he drove off, leaving me in the dust. I looked up to inspect my new medical colleagues. A thin, black man in a bright red Hawaiian shirt, shorts, and flip-flops was dancing around on the periphery of the seated assemblage. The guys in the lawn chairs (which they referred to as their "cars") were wearing green boxers; some were shirtless and others had on green T-shirts, and all were wearing flip-flops. As I looked around the semicircle of docs (as the infantry affectionately called their medics), they seemed remarkably cool. I don't mean emotionally or that they were great looking. I mean temperature-wise—I was the only one sweating. Well, actually one heavy-set guy in a green T-shirt had dark stains under his arms, but he looked absolutely frigid compared to me. In my flak jacket and fatigues I was making up for everyone else's lack of perspiration—it was dripping off me. The sound of Motown music coming from a hootch drowned out the noise of the helicopters overhead.

I felt out of it and obviously new, standing in my sweat-soaked fatigues facing the group. "Welcome to the 1st Division, Wizard," said a smiling, shirtless, well-built black man with a neatly trimmed mustache. As I was to learn, this was John Hamilton (Big John)—a former captain of the Florida A&M football team that won three national championships. He started for three years and played both offense and defense. He was the executive officer of Alpha Medical Company.

The markedly heavy-set fellow with a Fu Manchu mustache and wearing a floppy boonie hat, an army T-shirt with pit stains, and green boxers toasted me with his beer. Instantly likable, he had twinkling eyes that were kind, intelligent, and full of fun. He reminded me of a cross between Charlie Chan and Nigel Bruce (who played Basil Rathbone's sidekick Watson in the original Sherlock Holmes movies). He was Capt. Malcolm Galen, a general medical officer and an intelligent superspecialist (renologist/kidney doctor).

"If you've got to be one—be a Big Red One," Alpha Company commander Capt. Lenny Dunford smiled and waved. He was a thin, topless doc with a heavy mustache. I didn't know it then, but he was "short," with only a few weeks to go on his tour of duty.

Maj. Szaboles Szentpetery was a 6-foot, 6-inch muscular surgeon and former Hungarian freedom fighter. He had a short military haircut; a green T-shirt; and a loud, booming voice with a strong Hungarian accent. "You look a leetle hot," he laughed at the sweat pouring off me. "Vanta beer?" "Sure," I said and gratefully accepted the cold beer he tossed to me. I promptly inhaled it.

Captain Zappia was a short, dark-haired, Italian American, shirtless, general medical officer from the East Coast. He was loud, extroverted, and pushy, with a Napoleon (little-guy) complex. His haircut was Napoleonic as well. Ray Troop, the commander of Bravo Company, was tall, shirtless, blond, wholesome, and good-looking—a sort of "Jack Armstrong, the all-American boy." He was built like a rodeo cowboy. Ray was a West Point graduate who had a year of psychiatric training at Letterman Army Hospital. He decided he didn't care for psychiatric training and came to Vietnam as a general medical officer. He was made company commander because of his previous military service. He was hyperactive and found it difficult to sit still; even when he was sitting and relaxing, he fidgeted constantly.

Capt. Beau Lee (pseudonym), the division optometrist, was a blond, shirtless, younger man of medium build, with a Southern accent. He was similar in appearance to Troop and could have been his kid brother, but he was shorter and softer looking. He was a Regular Army Medical Service Corps (MSC) type and had the distinction of having the only air-conditioned workplace in the medical battalion. His handsome features and soft Alabama accent made me think of a slick riverboat gambler in the old South. As I think back, he was a sort of "poor-man's" Matthew McConaughey. You could see that he enjoyed being the center of attention and performing the initiation ceremony.

Beau sat back in his "car" and said, "Wizard, we just have one question we ask FNGs, but it is an important question, so think carefully before you answer and when you answer, answer truthfully with no hesitation or mental reservation what—so—ever." His tone and speech reminded me of a Masonic initiation where he was the Worshipful Master and I was the candidate. I said, "Okay." I was still wearing my flak jacket, and the sweat was dripping off my nose. He then slowly and pompously asked me a question about my sexual habits. He enunciated it clearly as if I'd just gotten off the short bus. By this time I was extremely hot, exhausted, tired of war stories, irritated, half sick to my stomach from the smell of the place, and I thought to myself, "This cherry wimp is trying to gross me out." I responded with a lengthy, extremely vulgar answer that concluded with my referring to myself as "Colonel Lingus." The other docs laughed, and I think I grossed Beau out, but he quickly recovered and said, "Wizard—you are okay; we've found there are two kinds of guys: those who admit what they do and those who lie about it. John spoke up and said that was "bull—real men don't do that stuff." Beau said, "See what I mean—John is one of the liars." "Bull," snorted John, "my stuff works."

Every unit had their way of initiating the FNGs. The pilots were located near our area in the base camp. Their method was to have a party, and after the FNG had a few drinks, they'd stand him up on a table and sing to him (to the tune of "Camptown Ladies"):

You're going home in a body bag
Doo dah, doo dah
You're going home in a body bag
Oh dah doo dah day

Shot between the eyes
Shot between the legs
You're going home in a body bag
Oh dah doo dah day

The FNG would stand in front of the group giving off an SEG (shit-eating grin) but also developing the counterphobic defenses needed to adjust to and survive in 'Nam.

As I was being initiated into the medical group, a man walked out of a nearby hootch wearing only a towel and carrying a bar of soap. He was a pale, average-built, hairy, somewhat dark-skinned Italian American doctor named Capt. Anthony Columbo (pseudonym). One of the doctors in the semicircle looked up and asked with great interest and curiosity:

"Where are you going?"

"Going to take my shower now," responded Columbo.

"Going to take a shower?" asked another doctor.

"Yep, I thought I'd shower."

"Let me know how the water is."

Tony then walked over a few paces to a makeshift shower consisting of a barrel mounted on a wooden frame and a string from the barrel that controlled the flow of water. He showered in sight of all of us. He then dried off and walked back by the group of doctors on his way to his hootch.

"Done showering?"

"Yep," responded Columbo, "had a nice shower."

"How was it?"

"Well, it started out sort of warm but not as warm as yesterday—then it got colder near the end."

"How cold was it?" asked another doctor.

"Well, it wasn't really that cold—it felt pretty good actually."

"Was it like yesterday?"

"Well, it wasn't as warm at first—but it ended up pretty much like yesterday."

I watched and thought to myself, "What sort of place is this?" and "Who are these people?" "What caliber of docs ask such dumb questions?" It seemed perfectly obvious to me that Tony was going to take a shower and then that he did take a shower—why all of the interest and detailed questioning about the obvious? As we used to write on our charts in medical school, it seemed "innately obvious to the most casual observer" (IOTTMCO).

After passing my initiation by Captain Lee, I walked to the medical battalion headquarters to meet the division surgeon and medical battalion commander, Lt. Col. Klaus Koberle. Galen accompanied me on the short walk along the white gravel path to his office. It was in a hootch with a sign in front: "1st Medical Battalion" along with the battalion emblem—a white background with a red Maltese cross on top; and a red background with a golden bear ("Fremont") at the bottom and the motto "Ready for Anything." A sergeant sat at the desk in the waiting area. When I identified myself, I heard a loud voice with a heavy German accent yelling, "Send da Vizard back." The NCO nodded toward the door from where the shout had come. I walked into the office and saluted the lieutenant colonel seated behind his neat, spotless desk. He was a husky, clean-shaven man with short, dark blond hair who looked as if he could have been a German panzer or a U-boat commander in a B movie. He stood up quickly and greeted me.

"Velcome Captain. You are the new Vizard—ya?"

"Ya. I mean, yes sir."

"Vell, I must tell you dat I don't know if I believe in psychiatry."

"That's okay, sir; I'm not sure I believe in colonels."

Lieutenant Colonel Koberle stood silently looking at me and then laughed loudly. "Maybe you are okay, Vizard!"

"Thank you, sir."

Columbo had given me some background information about the lieutenant colonel prior to our meeting. Tony said that he was born in Germany, was Regular Army, and was getting short. The division surgeon, Weinburg (pseudonym), in Lai Khe was even shorter, and Lieutenant Colonel Koberle was going to take over as both division surgeon and commander of the 1st Medical Battalion when Weinburg left. Lieutenant Colonel Koberle had completed his residency training in internal medicine. Lt. Col. James Hefner, who was soon to replace him as both division surgeon and battalion commander, completed his residency in obstetrics and gynecology. I was the only other doctor in the division who had completed specialty training.

I went to finance to process into the division, exchange my American dollars for military payment certificates (MPCs), and make sure I got paid. I was impressed that military personnel in Vietnam actually worked. What typically took days with civil service workers in the States was accomplished in less than one hour in Vietnam. This wasn't a fluke. One of the Regular Army guys told me that if you want to see how the army works, you have to go to a combat area. In the States much of the routine work was done by civil service personnel who could not be fired and could care less about getting things done. They were the sort of people who would tell you to stand behind the line until called when you were the only one there. In Vietnam everyone wanted to keep busy because it made the time go faster.

I was assigned to a section of the hootch occupied by the former division psychiatrist. He had built a bunker next to it, so I didn't have to run anywhere if we were rocketed or mortared. The base of the hootch, excluding the bunker, was surrounded by barrels filled with sand, which gave some protection but blocked any airflow up to a height of about three feet.

Each company-grade officer's hootch was divided into four rooms, each eight by ten feet, separated by plywood partitions. I had a cot with a camouflaged poncho liner for a bedspread, a plywood box that was used for storage, a metal locker, a steel chair, a large sealed plastic jug to use for potable water, a light bulb, a couple of electrical outlets in the wall, and a telephone. The outside walls were made up of slats with screen between them to permit some airflow. Each day a layer of dust would cover everything in the room from the red soil blowing in through the screened areas. The room had a dusty smell, and when I lay back on the cot, I felt as though I were inside a large wooden crate. You could hear what everyone was doing in their little boxes through the quarter-inch-thick plywood walls. I thought that these guys must be like the Japanese, who learned to pretend they didn't hear things through the thinly screened walls of their houses. Since my hootch had been vacant for several weeks, the dust was nearly half an inch deep! Big John was on the other side of one wall. I could hear his huge speakers booming out through the thin plywood that separated us. The bass made the wood vibrate. Stevie Wonder's voice came through the wall, singing "My Cherie Amour." Malcolm was across the street, and I could hear Zappia coughing and moving around next door.

The fourth room was empty when I arrived but was soon occupied by Capt. John Pabst, who had been a social work officer at Fort Knox. He had accepted three years in the army to come in as an officer. He was not happy about being sent to Vietnam, but there was no one for him to complain to because we were all in the same boat. He looked a little like Clark Gable with large ears and a dark mustache. He supervised the technician's clinical work and provided direct service evaluation and treatment himself. Pabst was a quiet guy, but when he spoke, people listened because he had a deep radio-announcer voice. He was given the title "Little Wizard," although he was several inches taller than I. We had worked together at Fort Knox, and I was glad to have him in the division.

The outhouse was located at the end of Broadway, our name for the "street" between our hootches. It was a standard four-hole privy that had been dug out underneath so that corrugated steel pans could be placed under each hole. These would be removed, the contents covered with a flammable liquid, and then ignited and burned by Vietnamese women. There was a screen panel in the outhouse door because ventilation was more important than privacy. On the outside of the privy door were two signs with doctor's names: one had gone home on hardship leave and failed to return, and the other had once hidden in the outhouse until another doctor in the company had to take an unwanted assignment. Both were long gone by the time I arrived, but their names remained in infamy. Inside there were a few lines of graffiti scratched in the walls. Since most of the men who utilized the facility had advanced degrees, the graffiti was a little better than most but still not memorable. The ones I remember are "We are the unwilling being ordered by the unqualified to do the unnecessary for the ungrateful"; "Fighting for peace is like screwing for virginity"; a brief biblical message, "Begat thyself"; and the pithy "There is no gravity—the world sucks."

I borrowed a broom and a rag and got rid of the top layers of dust in my hootch. Then I threw my duffel bag in the room, filled my pipe, and joined the other docs (now dressed in fatigues) for dinner in the mess hall.

The mess hall was a large Quonset hut with wooden picnic tables that featured silverware, napkins, and pitchers of pale gray Kool-Aid (the guys reported that the Kool-Aid was laced with chlorine to disinfect it). Our dinner consisted of thin slices of roast beef, potatoes, gravy, bread, butter, peas, a piece of cake, and coffee. Captain Galen explained that the army had the same menu worldwide. Even though it was 110 degrees in Vietnam and fresh fruit was readily available, this meal was shipped in so that every soldier in the army around the world would be able to sit down to the same meal—just like one big family.

The veterans were eager to fill me in and to help me obtain what I needed to get with the program. They told me I needed to go to the PX (Post Exchange) to buy a plastic wash basin, a straw mat for the floor, a fly swatter, bug spray, and my own "car" (lawn chair), which could be "parked" in the hootch when not in use. A good set of "tires" (flip-flops) was also suggested. They said I could fill my water jug with potable water at the officers' club. I also got some rubber rings to put around my dog tags so that they didn't jangle together and make noise. This wasn't necessary, of course—I wasn't planning on crawling through the jungle at night, but they looked cool and the others used them (John didn't, but he was Regular Army and knew better). I hadn't ordered my Nikon yet and did not have a camera with me, but I noted that film in the PX was $1.00 per roll, including developing. I also noted that liquor was remarkably inexpensive ($1.65 per fifth).

The docs told me that there was a guy in Bravo Company who was leaving and had a small Japanese refrigerator for sale. It would be good to have in case I woke up at night and needed a cold beer, so I bought it for fifty dollars. When I got rid of it thirty-two years later, it was still working. Later I hung up a couple of straw mats on the walls of my hootch and tacked up pictures that Cathy and Barby had drawn for me. The place looked better, and now that it was filled with my belongings, it began to feel like it was mine. Malcolm yelled that it was time for dinner, so I shut the door of my hootch and joined the guys on the gravel path to the mess hall.

Discussions at meals could be quite inane, such as whether it was better to pee on the bamboo shoots or on the wooden fence near the officers' club. There was an ongoing debate as to whether a bowel movement or sex was the most pleasurable activity. Sightings of lizards and doughnut dollies (American Red Cross volunteers) could lead to discussions that lasted several days. The temperature of the shower water, the amount of stool, the outdoor movie that night, and any variation in the day's routine were frequent topics of discussion.

At my first dinner Captain Columbo told me that they had developed two possible solutions for winning the war. The first was to put all the friendly Vietnamese on boats and kill everyone left in country—then sink the boats. The other idea was a way to win and to save the country money. Malcolm said that someone had taken the total cost of the war and divided it by the number of NVA killed. The resulting figure of seventy-five thousand dollars was what it cost the U.S. taxpayer per NVA killed. This plan involved taking bags containing fifty thousand dollars in quarters up in helicopters and dropping the bag whenever you saw a Vietnamese. If you hit the person, you killed him or her and saved twenty-five thousand dollars. If you missed, the Vietnamese would take the money and retire—either way, you got rid of a Vietnamese with a savings of twenty-five thousand dollars.

Captain Troop felt that the main problem with Vietnam was that there were no professional sports. He felt having professional teams distinguished civilized from uncivilized countries. The guys, with the exception of John, referred to Vietnamese as "slopes," "dinks," and "gooks." Looking back, I find that this was inconsistent with what I knew was a kind and sympathetic attitude toward the Vietnamese on the part of the medical staff. I think it may have been part of our counterphobic attempts to imitate the seasoned veterans through the use of profanity and tough, albeit racist, language. There may have also been an effort to dehumanize the Vietnamese through labels to avoid being confronted with what we were doing to them and their country. The men in the field did not always share this positive attitude toward the Vietnamese. I saw men from field units who had to be restrained from attacking Vietnamese patients in the clearing station. These soldiers had just come from situations in which their buddies had been killed and wounded, and they were ready to attack any Vietnamese they saw—including the wounded prisoners being treated in the base camp.

The docs didn't talk much about politics. In general, they were down on Jane Fonda and the antiwar people who they felt were working for the other side, but we just didn't discuss things like that. We tried to lose ourselves in our work, and when we weren't working, we focused on silly details in the day-to-day existence of our own world—at times very intensely. I made an early faux pas by advancing a theory at dinner, based on what I had heard from my marine pilot cousin, about why we were having military problems in Vietnam. The docs quickly let me know that they weren't interested in talking about this topic and that I was just an FNG fresh from the world who didn't know what I was talking about.

"If they would have let the military do what they could do, we would have creamed the NVA and VC and been out of here by now," I said, advancing what I thought was great insight into the war.

"What are you talking about?" asked Galen.

"The NVA and VC go to free-fire zones, and we can't shoot them."

John jumped in to correct me. "No man, free-fire zones are areas where they move out the civilians and shoot anything that moves."

"Okay, but I heard that there were places we weren't allowed to shoot and that this is where they hang out until they get ready to strike."

"Hey Wizard—do you know why rabbit shit comes in little pellets?" Zappia asked.

"What?" I replied.

"Just answer his question," Galen directed.

"No."

Zappia then proceeded to ask me other questions in a similar vein. After I answered, he smiled and said, "Just what we thought. You want to talk about military tactics in Vietnam and you don't know shit!" Everyone laughed at my getting sucked in by Zappia, but I got the point. I was an FNG, and no one wanted to hear my theories about the war in Vietnam.

After dinner we passed on the movie and went to the medical company's officers' club, which consisted of a hootch with a bar; outside grill; and a large, roughly framed picture behind the bar of a nude, four-hundred-pound woman named Ruby Begonia. When Ruby started looking good, you knew you were getting close to going home. Mixed drinks were twenty-five cents, and beer was a dime. The bartender was an enlisted man who doubled as a barber. Typically, the bar was smoke filled (most of us smoked back then), with loud music and crowded with doctors and MSCs in their underwear and flip-flops, screaming profanities.

Still feeling the jet lag, I went to bed early to the sound of artillery shells (ours) and trying to remember what I'd been told about the difference between incoming and outgoing fire. John hollered through the plywood wall that I should NOT stand up and look if I heard an explosion. The other docs had said that it wasn't the shell that had your name on it that you needed to worry about but the one that was addressed "To whom it may concern."

As I lay on my bunk the first night, listening to the sounds of my hootch mates getting to bed and snoring, I thought that I would get a tan, lose my gut, grow a mustache, study for my boards, learn all I could about military psychiatry, and see if I could apply some of the new material I'd learned at Menninger's. I tried to keep my mind focused on constructive activities, because thinking about "the world" brought sadness and thinking about possible dangers produced anxiety.

I woke early the next morning. The bright, hot sun was shining through the slats in my hootch, and I was already perspiring. I lay on the poncho liner for a few minutes listening. I heard John stirring and the sound of helicopters overhead. I thought how I'd often lain in bed at home listening to the wrens, cardinals, and the mournful cooing of doves. "You're not in Kansas anymore," I thought. I filled my plastic bowl with water and went out on the porch to brush my teeth, shave, and get cleaned up before breakfast. I loaded one of my favorite Dunhill pipes with an aromatic tobacco I'd brought from Chicago. Just then John's stereo kicked in with Diana Ross and the Supremes singing "Someday We'll Be Together."

Breakfast was served buffet style with eggs any style, juice, bacon, sausage, toast, grits (compliments of the Southern officers, who demanded that they be included), pancakes, and coffee. The cooks would make you an omelet if you requested it. Tony was responsible for omelets being on the menu. He had them when he went on R&R (rest and recuperation) to Bangkok and taught the cooks to make them after he returned. At his suggestion, the cooks had cheese, green peppers, tomatoes, onions, ham, and bacon available so that we could have a customized omelet. We greeted each other as we went down the chow line, talking about how much more time we'd have to spend with each other, and the cooks loaded our plates. "Well, the good thing is you have only 363 days to go in country," Zappia quipped. "No, the good thing is he'll only be spending part of it with you," responded John.

After breakfast I walked over to the psychiatric headquarters next to the clearing station to meet the social work/psychology technicians. The building was a hootch with two large desks and a small one. There were cubicles divided by plywood panels (obtained by "midnight requisition," or ripping it off someone else) with "doors" made of vertical strips of blue and white plastic one and a half inches wide. A sign, "Fire evacuation plan," was posted on the wall, showing arrows leading from behind each of two desks to the exits at both ends of the building. My technicians were waiting to meet me. Most of them had completed the ten-week 91G20 (social work/psychology technician) training at Fort Sam Houston.

During World War II, enlisted personnel were trained to assist psychiatrists, psychologists, social workers, and psychiatric nurses in order to extend the influence of these scarce professionals. After the war, formal training programs were instituted to train enlisted specialists to work on hospital wards and as social work/psychology technicians in the newly formed Mental Hygiene Program. The formal training program was started in 1947 at the Medical Field Service School at Fort Sam Houston. At the time of my service in Vietnam, there were 250 persons in training for each of the five annual ten-week courses. These courses covered developmental psychology, sociocultural analysis, recognition of the types of mental disorders, interviewing techniques, and current methods of treatment. Afterward, the students received clinical training to develop practical skills, such as observing patients, interviewing, taking histories, and conducting psychological tests. The concentrated course of 360 academic hours was credited for 1,200 graduate semester hours at Baylor University. In 1970 there were eight hundred social work/psychology technicians in the army, one hundred of whom were stationed in Vietnam. Initially nine of them were assisting me (five in Di An, two in Lai Khe, and two in Dau Tieng). It was possible to receive the 91G20 specialty without taking the course if individuals could demonstrate that they had a bachelor of arts degree with graduate work or occupational experience in a related field. We were fortunate in that nearly all of our technicians had taken the course at Fort Sam. In addition, most had graduate degrees in social work, psychology, criminal justice, nursing, or anthropology.

Specialist 6 Ford was a regular army NCO who had worked in the mental health field for many years. He was a stocky, clean-shaven, older man with a crew cut, who looked more like a sergeant than a mental health technician. Clinically, he was probably the weakest tech. His strong suit was that he knew the army, how it worked, and how to get things done.

Spc.5 Walt "Dusty" Smith was a tall, thin, young man with a neatly trimmed mustache. He wore wire-rimmed glasses and looked professorial. He was also a conscientious objector. (There were more than 170,000 classifications granted during the war in Vietnam for conscientious objectors.) Being a conscientious objector did not keep you out of Vietnam—it just prevented you from carrying a gun while serving there. Regular Army personnel didn't think much of them. Some new inductees would claim to be conscientious objectors, saying, "You can make me go to Vietnam, but you can't make me shoot anyone." The sergeants would respond, "That's okay; you might stop a bullet for a good man!"

Specialist Smith had a master's degree in anthropology. He was idealistic and intellectual; he had once fled Guatemala because his research questions made him too visible to both the radical right and left and both had kill lists and terrorist tactics that Specialist Smith encountered too many times. He was drafted into the army and was assigned to the faculty at Fort Sam Houston, where he taught and trained social work/psychology technicians. A lieutenant colonel supervisor at the school had been angered by his views on race relations and then found out that he was a conscientious objector. He gave Smith the choice of becoming an officer in the army, completing his doctoral training at the army's expense, and teaching on the faculty for four years; or going to Vietnam as an enlisted man (social work/psychology technician) and getting out of the army in two years. Smith opted for the least time in the military and went to Vietnam. The colonel told him he would be training Vietnamese social work/psychology technicians in anticipation that the Vietnamese troops would be replacing the Americans. When he arrived in Vietnam, no one knew what he was talking about because the Vietnamese army did not have such technicians or psychiatrists. He was reassigned to the 1st Infantry Division. Dusty spoke English, Spanish, and "academese"; I respected his clinical judgment and listened to his suggestions.

Spc.4 Vincent A. Zecchinelli had a bachelor's degree and had been trained at Fort Sam Houston. With dark hair, average build, and a baby face, he looked like a paper boy or the good kid in the church choir. He also wore wire-rimmed glasses. He was quiet and had a wry sense of humor but also had a good heart. He was usually my jeep driver.

Spc.3 Gasper Falzone was another social worker with a bachelor's degree. He was from New Jersey and sounded tough but was very empathetic and skilled professionally. I did run across his name after Vietnam. He stayed in social work with the Veterans Administration and later worked with Vietnam veterans who were suffering from post-traumatic stress disorder (PTSD).

Private First Class Ortiz was a small, gentle, round-faced Mexican American, also from New Jersey. He was a kind, soft-spoken young man who quietly carried out his duties and never made waves. An integral part of the group, he was well liked. He had a college degree in social studies and had gone through the social work/psychology tech training course at Fort Sam. He was also bilingual.

The technicians greeted me in a friendly way and seemed glad to finally have a "boss" around the place. They wanted to learn new information, have goals, do a good job, and, above all, keep as busy as possible to make the time in country go faster. They were well trained and compassionate in their work. Within our psychiatric facility we related to one another much as any civilian mental health team might interact. The technicians took off their tropical fatigue shirts and just wore green underwear T-shirts or went shirtless. Later, when Specialist 4 Pattburg and Specialist 4 Simon joined us, they wore blue surgical scrub shirts. When Regular Army brass came in, the technicians put on their starched fatigue uniforms, saluted, and followed military protocol. As a joke they would frequently snap to attention and salute when I arrived in the morning because they knew I liked to say "As you were," which I'd learned from the movies.

Two technicians were officially assigned to each of four medical companies in the division. Two of the medical companies (Alpha and Bravo) were initially in the support command base camp in Di An. At first, I had five technicians in Di An, and we recruited three additional technicians and a clerk typist. Later in my tour, Bravo moved to the base camp near Cambodia (Dau Tieng) with two technicians. The other two medical companies (Charlie and Delta), with two technicians each, were located in the division headquarters base camp in Lai Khe. We had seventeen thousand men in the division with additional attached units of about three thousand men. Thus, the social work officer (soon to be Captain Pabst), twelve to fourteen technicians, and I provided the psychiatric support to twenty thousand soldiers in the division.

The technicians showed me the Alpha Company clearing station—a large Quonset hut containing some cots where we could treat our patients for a couple of days if necessary. My new buddy John had gotten me a jeep, and the Vietnamese sign painter had painted "Division Psychiatrist" in large letters below the windshield.

The technicians explained that since there had been a hiatus between the departure of my predecessor and my arrival, there had been a drop in referrals to psychiatry in the division. Seriously ill patients were being evacuated directly to the KO team in

Long Binh. Just then Zecchinelli ran in from the clearing station to report that there had just been a call about a psychotic patient who was being dusted off (medically evacuated) and would arrive momentarily. "I guess the word is out that we've got a new Wizard in the division," commented Falzone as he left to join the other technicians at the helipad outside the clearing station. Soon we spotted the helicopter approaching with a stretcher on the outside. Our patients were typically transported sandwiched between two stretchers. The technicians ran to the helicopter and transported the stretchers containing the patient into the clearing station. They unbelted the two stretchers and removed the top one to reveal a dull-eyed, disheveled, sweat-soaked infantryman covered with red dirt. The technicians helped him remove his clothing and escorted him to the shower and then furnished him with a hospital scrub suit. He was passive and cooperative but unresponsive. Despite his passivity, his muscles seemed tense and his palms were clammy with sweat. His heart rate was rapid and his blood pressure slightly elevated. All of this suggested that he was very anxious. The technicians explained each procedure before doing it and tried to give him as much control as possible. For example, they would ask, "Would you like a can of pop or a glass of water?" When he didn't respond, they offered him water and said, "Let's start with water." The technicians were very kind and seemed to do a good job in their approach to a frightened, uncommunicative patient. Since this was our first patient, I verbalized my thoughts so that they would begin to see how I worked.

"According to the information we have, you are an eighteen-year-old, Caucasian, eleven Bravo [infantryman] from the Second Battalion of the Second Regiment armored unit. You are unable to respond verbally at this time, but you seem to be cooperative and you do respond to direction. You don't show the waxy flexibility that we associate with catatonia. You've had a nice shower, have dry clothing and something to drink. You shut your eyes and your lips when offered food, so we assume this means you aren't hungry right now. You seem to be anxious and tense. I'd like to give you a sedative and let you get a good night's rest and see how you feel in the morning. Specialist Falzone will give you a shot of fifty milligrams of Thorazine, which is a major tranquilizer. It will sting a little, but then you will feel very relaxed and drift off to sleep. We'll be keeping an eye on you while you are sleeping, and then we can talk in the morning."

A medic approached the patient with a syringe. "Okay, I'm going to give you a shot of medicine now that will relax you and help you get some rest."

The next morning the patient awakened and was able to converse with Falzone as I listened.

"How do you feel after a good night's rest?"

"Better. Where am I anyway?"

"The clearing station in Di An. You were medically evacuated here yesterday afternoon."

"I sort of remember—you were here last night."

"Yeah, and so was Captain Bey and Specialist Zecchinelli. What happened to you anyway?"

"We were on patrol. All of a sudden we started getting hit with mortars and rifle fire from the tree line. I guess I sort of froze up." He was asked how long he had been here.

"I just arrived in country last week."

"So was this your first firefight?" asked Falzone.

"Yeah. I heard what it was like, but it scared me when they opened up on us."

I interjected. "I just got here myself. From what I understand, even the combat veterans are scared when they find themselves under fire. You had what we call a normal reaction to an abnormal situation."

"It was weird. I remember the mortars going off and the AK-47s, and I remember being scared; and then everything got black, and I think I must have passed out."

Falzone resumed the conversation. "Well, part of your problem may have been the heat; you may have been dehydrated, and it was your first firefight, which would have been scary to anyone."

"So you've seen other guys react like this?"

"Yeah, it's pretty common actually. You just get rested up, have a nice hot meal, and your buddies will be down to pick you up."

Later, two men from his squad arrived to take him back to his unit. They brought a clean uniform, socks, and underwear as Zecchinelli had requested. One of the squad members looked at the patient. "What a gold brick. How do you rate?" The other squad member added, "Hey, look at this guy. He gets a shower, hot meals, and waited on—do they have American nurses here?"

"Hey—cool it. I'm a hospital patient."

"You're a gold brick—move over; I could use some of this TLC myself."

The friendly "pimping" continued as they helped their buddy get back into a clean uniform and then accompanied him back to the unit. "Pimping" was the term we used for kidding each other. On some occasions it sounded a little sadistic, for example, when we were told we were going home in body bags by the troops waiting to depart on our plane. Psychologically, it boosted our counterphobic defenses, as they told us what we were secretly fearing. Most of us laughed and acted as though we weren't frightened at all. Sometimes pimping seemed to be a preadolescent male way of showing affection (like pulling a girl's braids). When the guys told me they were disappointed that I had returned from a pass, it was their way of saying they missed me. I took "the psychiatric care around here sucks" to be the highest compliment. In this case, the men from this soldier's unit were kidding their buddy about the wish that everyone had to stay out of the field. It was both a reinforcement of his counterphobic defenses and a show of affection.

My diagnosis at the time was gross situational stress reaction. The soldier recovered rapidly and returned to duty, as expected from what I had read in the military psychiatry textbooks from previous wars. I felt pretty good about the intervention and the soldier's response.

The next patient presented a familiar situation and not nearly as dramatic. The transportation unit sent a young man for psychiatric evaluation as part of the procedure for a general administrative discharge under Army Regulation (AR) 212. This regulation permitted the speedy discharge of undesirables who could not be rehabilitated by their commanders. A court-martial hearing was not required. A psychiatric examination helped determine if the individual suffered from a psychiatric or medical illness and, if so, should go through medical channels for treatment or medical discharge. I had done several of these evaluations at Fort Knox and was familiar with the procedure. Commanders preferred soldiers to be medically discharged because it meant less paperwork for them and because the number of 212s in the unit was one of the indicators reflecting the commander's ability to motivate and rehabilitate his troops.

This young man had a long history of difficulties in civilian life. His academic record was poor, with a history of disciplinary problems, and he had dropped out of high school. He had a few minor scrapes with the law for drunken driving, possession of alcohol, possession of a controlled substance, and selling marijuana. The latter charge resulted in the judge giving him the choice of jail or the army, so he chose the army. During basic and advanced infantry training he had received several Article 15s (a disciplinary action for less than a court-martial offense) for disobeying orders and going AWOL. His medical record showed that he had sought discharge by complaining of a bad back. He had been sent to Vietnam four months earlier and assigned to the division transportation unit. He was identified as one of the unit's "heads" (drug users) and was considered to be a shirker and troublemaker. From the psychiatric standpoint he had poor impulse control, poor judgment, difficulties with authority, and a low tolerance for stress. He flaunted his drug use by displaying at various times a marijuana leaf badge, writing "FTA" (Fuck the Army, or Free the Army) on his helmet, and wearing a peace sign. All of these were prohibited and were confiscated by his NCO. His attitude and behavior were not improved by punishment, counseling by his NCO and commanding officer (CO), nor by threats of incarceration at the LBJ. The CO decided that it would be best for the unit to get rid of him and initiated the paperwork to have him discharged. When the man came to division psychiatry accompanied by his NCO, he seemed to have a chip on his shoulder. He swaggered into the office, gave a halfhearted salute, and dropped into the chair by my desk. I had already read his medical records and been briefed by his NCO and by Zecchinelli, who spoke with the unit and the soldier before I saw him.

"How do you see the present situation?"

"The lifers have it in for me, man."

"Do you think that you did anything to cause them to single you out?"

"Nah—they're a bunch of juicers—they don't get it." ["Juicers" refers to drinkers. Hard liquor was not available to enlisted men in

Vietnam, but drugs were accessible and inexpensive. Hard liquor was available and cheap for NCOs and officers. There was also a generational factor in the drugs of choice. The drug culture was in full swing in the United States, and many of the enlisted men arriving in Vietnam had already experimented with drugs prior to their arrival. The NCOs and officers, in general, traditionally celebrated and self-medicated with alcohol. Booze was condoned and often supported by the military organization, while drug use was "bad" and illegal.]

"Looking over your record, it seems that you've had problems before coming into the army and that they've continued since you've been in."

"I've been screwed over all my life, man."

"Do you object to a 212 discharge? It will be a general discharge with no benefits."

"Fine with me. The sooner I get out of this place and the army, the better."

"What do you plan to do when you get out?"

"I don't know—maybe drive a truck. I might help my old man—he drives a truck."

"Have you learned anything from your experience in the army?"

"Yeah, that I never should have gone into the army in the first place."

Thinking back on the 212s I saw in the army, I would predict that most of them continued to have difficulties in civilian life. Many of the ones that were stationed in Vietnam probably told "war stories" on their return and used Vietnam as an excuse for their inability to function in adult life later on.

Not all of our patients did as well as our first patient or were as cut and dried as the second one. One of the early psychotic patients who was medically evacuated did not respond to brief treatment in our clearing station. When he arrived, his arms and legs flailed out between the belted stretchers, and he had to be restrained to prevent him from attacking the medics and technicians when they placed him on the clearing station cot. He shouted at Falzone and Zecchinelli to leave him alone. When Falzone told him he was safe and asked if he wanted something to drink, the patient screamed that he didn't want any help.

Eventually the patient did swallow some fluids, and the medic gave him an injection of Thorazine. The technicians and medics observed him throughout the night. In the morning we attempted to interview him.

Falzone started by asking, "How do you feel after a night's rest?"

"Don't answer, don't answer, don't answer," the patient whispered to himself.

"Don't answer what?"

"I know what you want."

"We want to help you. You seem scared," said Zecchinelli.

"You've been messing with me for a long time now."

"We just met you yesterday."

"You've got a radio in here."

"Yes, that's the clearing station radio where the dust-off helicopters call in."

"You've been using it to mess with me."

Falzone asked the patient, "You think we've been sending radio signals to you?"

"Somebody has and you've got the radio."

As we continued to interview the patient, it became clear that he felt that he was being controlled by radio beams that were broadcasting voices into his head. He admitted hearing voices that told him what to do. His medical record gave no information about previous psychiatric contacts in civilian life or in the army. He was described as quiet, a little odd, and a loner by his NCO. He had been in country for less than a month and had not had any real contact with the enemy. Other men in his unit observed him talking to himself. When the medic attempted to question him, he became agitated and attacked the medic because he believed the medic had something to do with the voices in his head. The medic had him evacuated to us for further evaluation and treatment. We kept him in the clearing station for another day with no change in his delusional thinking. He was calmer and said that the voices were less distinct but still present. We sent him to the 93rd Evacuation Hospital in Long Binh for further evaluation and treatment. They attempted to treat him in their facility, but he was eventually sent back to the States with a diagnosis of schizophrenia-paranoid type.

Early on, I decided that I needed to have face-to-face contact with my technicians in Lai Khe and Dau Tieng. We decided to drive up "Thunder Road" (Highway 13, called "Thunder" because it had been mined). Smith called it "Lady Bird Johnson Freeway" because it was rumored that she was a major stockholder in the civilian firm Pacific Architects and Engineers, who, at great expense, built our base camps and installations in Vietnam. So we put on our flak jackets and steel-pot helmets, the techs got their M16s, I strapped on my .45, and we headed north for division headquarters in Lai Khe, about twenty-five miles from Saigon on Highway 13. Bob Hope said he knew why they called it Lai Khe—"because I no likeee."

On the way we passed small villages and rubber plantations where the Rome plows had knocked down the trees to clear an area on each side of the highway to reduce the risk of ambush. (Rome plows, made by the Rome Company in Georgia and also called "hogjaws," had a special blade and protective cab on a D73 bulldozer. They were also used in combat as point elements for mechanized units on reconnaissance-in-force operations in thick trees.) Much of the jungle in our area had been defoliated using the herbicide Agent Orange. We turned in through the gate, passing the guard tower and rows of concertina wire with claymore mines. Lai Khe was known as "Rocket City" because it received more rocket attacks than any of the other base camps and was rocketed during the 1968 Tet offensive. The rumor was that the army threatened to close the "plaza," consisting of Vietnamese whorehouses, nightclubs, and shops, in the nearby village if the base camp continued to be attacked and that this threat caused the rocketing to stop. Looking back, I think it was more likely that rocketing decreased because the division implemented Gen. Creighton Abram's strategy to shut down the VC infrastructure and to intercept NVA coming down the Ho Chi Minh trail. Lai Khe did unfortunately receive rockets during my tour, including the night I invited our psychiatric consultant to visit.

At the clearing station I met Specialist 4 Matthews and Specialist 4 Foley. They showed us the area where they saw patients, introduced us to the medical company mascot (a mongrel dog named Snoopy who rode in the front seat of the ambulance), and gave us a tour of their clearing station. The "meat wagons" were a holdover from the Korean War. The ambulances were supposed to ferry patients from the battalion aid stations to the clearing station, but in Vietnam they were used primarily in base camps for local transportation. Everything else was handled by helicopters. I was glad to see that our Lai Khe technicians were large, husky men who could physically handle agitated patients when necessary.

During the visit the clearing station was hit with a mass casualty. Helicopters landed with wounded soldiers strapped to the sides. The medics and technicians ran to the helicopters to grab the stretchers and carry the wounded into the clearing station. They crouched low, running through the rotor wash and the large clouds of dust that rose beneath the rotating blades. They carried the stretchers into the clearing station and gently moved the wounded men onto the waiting examination tables. They then piled the stretchers in a rack next to the clearing station and ran to get more. The medics inside the station cut open the soldiers' fatigues, which were soaked with blood, urine, and feces, and applied fresh compresses to the wounds. Other medics started intravenous fluids to keep the wounded from going into shock and to facilitate blood transfusions. The clearing station became crowded and hot, and the stench of sweat, blood, excrement, and medications permeated the air. The odors seemed to be magnified by the temperature and humidity inside the Quonset hut. As more wounded arrived, the noise level increased. Patients were screaming and moaning, doctors were shouting orders, and the medics were yelling for materials and equipment. The doctors quickly assessed which of the American patients needed the most immediate attention. The Vietnamese prisoners were treated with the same care and skill as the American soldiers, but it was understood that the Americans would be tended to first.

The doctors from the medical company crowded into the clearing station and together with the corpsmen began working on the wounded. Although I had had plenty of emergency experience (from Cook County Hospital ER, covering the emergencies at Inland Steel, during my internship at Illinois Masonic Hospital, and on call at Ireland Army Hospital), I was told that the Wizard's assignment was to report to the morgue to examine the dead and fill out death certificates.

Matthews, Foley, Zecchinelli, Smith, and I went from the clearing station to the Doctor Delta Morgue next door. Although it was hot outside, there was a breeze, so the morgue was more comfortable than the crowded clearing station. The air had the ubiquitous scent of burning feces and exhaust fumes from the helicopters that were taking off and landing with a seemingly endless supply of wounded. After the wounded were carried in, the technicians started bringing the body bags to the morgue. As the body bags were brought to this area, the technicians and I would unzip them and confirm that the men inside were dead. Some were hardly recognizable as humans, and some looked like sleeping teenagers. Once opened, the bags smelled of blood, rubber, and excrement. We did our assessment, but it was shocking and very sad. During college I had opened bodies, weighed organs, and done the drudge work for a local pathologist in exchange for lessons on pathology and anatomy—working with dead bodies wasn't something that was new to me. The shocking aspect was seeing one dead teen after another and thinking about their families, girlfriends, my dead brother, and how little of life they had experienced. As the body bags were unzipped, I was shocked at seeing the faces of young men who looked like Donn. Their faces and Donn's showed up in my dreams at the time and still do on occasion.

I later told Specialists Matthews and Foley that they should feel free to refer any soldier to me if he made them uncomfortable. It didn't matter if the diagnosis was schizophrenia or anxiety reaction. If they weren't sure or if they were concerned about the person's welfare, send that soldier to me or keep him in the clearing station until I could come over to see him. Matthews and Foley had been essentially on their own since my predecessor left, with only the general medical officers for backup. I knew they could function on their own but felt that it would help them relax and do an even better job if they knew they could have me see anyone, regardless of diagnosis. It took pressure off them to know they had psychiatric backup.

THE TYPICAL ROUTINE for the officers of the medical battalion was the morning constitutional and hygiene, breakfast, brief return to hootch, off to work, and lunch at noon. After lunch each day we would head back to our hootches, strip down to our underwear, and take a break. The Vietnamese soldiers and civilians took a siesta after the noon meal and would rest in the shade on the ground or in a hammock. American soldiers also took a break but couldn't seem to just relax. Szentpetery and Troop lifted weights; Columbo, Zappia, and Galen played volleyball. My preference was to read a book while getting a tan. Big John wasn't into tanning and would relax inside his hootch while listening to music or occasionally play volleyball. After the midday hiatus, we would return to our work and then go to dinner at 4:30 P.M. After dinner, we would shower, change into underwear, and either go to the officers' club or the outdoor movie or play volleyball. The "drive-in theater" consisted of a rectangular, white billboard-sized sign outside the clearing station. Movies were projected on the board. The officers would "drive" their "cars" to the gravel area, "park" in front of the billboard, drink beer, and add their own lines to the movie.

LIEUTENANT COLONEL HEFNER replaced Lieutenant Colonel Koberle a couple of months into my tour. He had held every rank in the army up to lieutenant colonel, starting as a private in a tank unit in World War II. He served in Korea before medical school and did his residency in the military, specializing in obstetrics and gynecology. He had been in the army "since Christ was a corporal." He was a skinny, clean-cut, high-energy guy with a graying flattop haircut. As a good friend of the commanding general of the division, he had considerable clout. The day he arrived in the unit Lieutenant Colonel Koberle took him to the officers' club during an altercation in which I threw the division optometrist through the door. Following this unbecoming event, he entered the club to find the medical officers drunk and screaming profanities. This was also the night that Major Szentpetery came in drunk, waving a loaded .45 and screaming that he was going to kill Ross Guarino for ruining his Nikon. Lieutenant Colonel Hefner said he was shocked at what he was seeing.

After the lieutenant colonel arrived, another common evening activity was to drive our cars to his hootch, sit around in a circle with the battalion brass, discuss the day's activities, tell jokes, and drink beer. Lieutenant Colonel Hefner encouraged these gatherings, as it kept him up to date about what was happening in the battalion. They also kept us from going to the club and getting wasted.

One characteristic that set the brass apart from the rest of us (besides rank) was that they were clean shaven, whereas the rest of us all sported 'staches of varying length, thickness, and grooming. I believe the absence of mustaches among the battalion brass and Regular Army officers reflected the fact that there wasn't a facial hair on the general or any of his staff. If the general grew a big mustache, you can bet most of the regulars in the division would sport one as well. The general and his staff had crew cuts right out of World War II, and the Regular Army officers also opted for this style.

I'm not sure why most of us grew mustaches. I don't think it had anything to do with the peace movement or rebellion on our part; probably it was just something we could do. We would do the same thing on a fishing trip to Canada or on a motorcycle trip just because we were away from home and in the boonies. Hair, mustaches, and such were "in" during this era. I thought I looked pretty cool, for an old guy, with my aviator glasses and mustache. John was the exception—he sported a neatly trimmed mustache, but he was the only Regular Army officer in our unit who did.

We all liked the lieutenant colonel because he knew the army and he tried to accomplish positive changes in the division medical service. He appreciated the things we were trying to accomplish in psychiatry. He was very supportive and, in general, good to those who served under him.

One evening as we were seated in our cars shooting the breeze with the colonel, he asked, "How are things going, Wizard?" I told him about an incident that day in which a major, who was the new executive officer (XO) of an infantry battalion, had reamed out one of my technicians because I had refused to medically discharge a soldier from the XO's unit. The soldier had some Article 15s and was probably messed up but was not, in my opinion, mentally ill and didn't qualify to be medically discharged. The lieutenant colonel immediately picked up the phone, which he kept next to him at all times, and called the battalion commander.

"Hi, George, this is Jim at First Med."

"Hi, Jim—what can we do for you?"

"You have a new executive officer, and I'd like you to give him a message for me."

"Sure thing Jim—shoot."

"Tell him that if he ever sets foot in my medical area again and behaves in the disrespectful way he did to my men today, I'll arrange to have him transferred to a unit where it will take him six months to get his mail."

"Will do, Jim."

The next day the major appeared at our psychiatric facility with his hat in his hands to apologize for being completely out of line, complimenting us on the wonderful work we were doing, and stating that he had been absolutely wrong in criticizing us. I didn't have a chance to look, but I imagined the seat of his pants had bite marks on it. The technicians thought it was great and felt reassured that there was some justice in the world—even in the army.

Typically, we'd talk about the day's events and then start telling jokes. One of my own strong suits has been being able to remember jokes, so we would get started on categories and then tell one after the other. Lieutenant Colonel Hefner had been an emcee and knew lots of them. He also had some good stories about his experiences in the army. He told us that Vietnam was nothing like World War II, when they had to re-form their tank outfit every week because of the number of casualties. Also, in Vietnam we had absolute air superiority and didn't have to worry about being bombed or strafed by enemy aircraft.

He once related his experience as surgeon for Mamie Eisenhower. Mrs. Eisenhower came to Walter Reed several weeks before a scheduled surgery and had the entire floor she was to occupy completely redecorated. Following her surgery, Lieutenant Colonel Hefner was making rounds, and she asked, "What's the matter, Jim?—you seem a little down." The lieutenant colonel explained that he had been trying to get housing for himself and his wife in Washington, D.C., but nothing seemed to be available. "I'll tell Ike," responded Mrs. Eisenhower. Lieutenant Colonel Hefner said that the next day the head of housing for Washington, D.C., ran up to him and in a breathless voice said, "I don't know who you know—but you can have any house you want in Washington."

In contrast to Lieutenant Colonel Hefner, Maj. Martinet (pseudonym), our new battalion executive officer, was a certified public accountant. Major Martinet had never held a command position in the military nor had he served in a combat area. He had worked most of his army career as a bookkeeper in the finance department at a major army hospital. He was thin, bald, and chicken-necked. He dealt with his anxiety about his new assignment by carrying a swagger stick, smoking a cigar, and bullying the enlisted men under his command. The latter is a "no-no" in the military. Experienced commanders such as Lieutenant Colonel Hefner took care of their men's comfort before attending to their own. Field commanders in Vietnam who mistreated their men were often killed by their own troops. Major Martinet had not learned this and eventually paid a price for his abuse. He was obsequious, and it was rumored that when Lieutenant Colonel Hefner turned over in bed, Major Martinet's nose twitched.

ONE EVENING AT SUPPER Zappia and Galen were involved in an intense conversation about a lizard Zappia had seen in the area. I left the table, having already heard about several of these sightings. I dug a cold beer out of the refrigerator in my hootch and slipped into my skivvies, which were the after-dinner uniform of the day. John joined me, and we took our "cars" and headed to Lieutenant Colonel Hefner's hootch. The lieutenant colonel, Major Martinet, and Sergeant Major Brown (pseudonym) were already there sitting in their lawn chairs.

As John and I pulled up, Zappia and Galen arrived, still talking about the lizard. Lieutenant Colonel Hefner noticed that John's flip-flop strap was loose and commented on it.

"Did you have a blowout, John?"

"Yes, sir," John answered, "looks like I may have to get a new set of tires—too many miles on these." The rest of us, prompted by Major Martinet's nodding and guffawing, chuckled.

"Are you up for a steak fry Friday night?" Lieutenant Colonel Hefner inquired.

"Yes, sir!" we all chorused.

Lieutenant Colonel Hefner then turned to Sergeant Major Brown and asked, "Sergeant Major, why don't we have any skin flicks?"

"Skin flicks, sir? I didn't know you wanted any, sir."

"Well, Transportation has them, Maintenance has them, Supply has them, the Engineers have them—I just thought it would be nice to have them Friday with the steak fry for a little entertainment."

"No problem, sir," responded the sergeant major.

Then the lieutenant colonel turned to the group and said, "Let's get serious for a moment, gentlemen." He got out a sheaf of papers and said he wanted to talk about an incident that had happened the previous evening. An enlisted man had come to the clearing station staggering around. The medic assumed he was drunk and had called Major Sanchez (pseudonym), who was the doctor on call, and described the situation. Sanchez was from Argentina, where his father was a senior military officer. Sanchez told the medic to send the man back to his unit and have him report to sick call in the morning. When the soldier returned in the morning accompanied by a couple of his unit members, he had a dilated pupil with an elevated optic disk, suggesting increased pressure inside his skull. He was also disoriented and uncoordinated. He was sent to the evacuation hospital at Long Binh where X-ray images revealed that he had a fractured skull and a blood clot on the brain. Lieutenant Colonel Hefner turned red, obviously angry. "This is incompetent, negligent, half-ass medical care, and I won't have it in my battalion or in the First Division!" the lieutenant colonel nearly shouted. He said he wanted to present the situation to the rest of us for our opinion about what should be done to Sanchez. He said his own inclination was to court-martial him, but another alternative would be to write him up and transfer him to another unit in Long Binh. We all looked at one another.

Lieutenant Colonel Hefner was right. This wasn't good medicine, and Sanchez should have checked the soldier. On the other hand, most soldiers who stagger into the clearing station at night are drunk—it is rare to have a skull fracture or a blood clot. Most doctors didn't get up to examine every drunk or stoned soldier who showed up at night. We felt sorry for Sanchez. He was Regular Army, and his career would suffer if he was written up. It would be embarrassing to get kicked out of your unit, but a court-martial would have been worse. We all said that reassignment would be preferable to a court-martial and that writing him up and being reassigned would be pretty severe discipline to a career medical officer. Lieutenant Colonel Hefner said, "Okay, that's what it will be," and told Major Martinet to "get him out of my sight ASAP."

"Yes, sir!" responded the major, who elevated his eyebrows and chomped down on his cigar with a self-righteous expression as though he wouldn't tolerate any medical incompetence either.

I'm pretty sure that Lieutenant Colonel Hefner had already planned to write up Sanchez and transfer him but got us involved to give rest of the doctors a "kick in the butt" about seeing patients when they were on call. It was sort of shocking to see this normally supportive, relaxed, fun commander come down hard on Sanchez. He wasn't too keen on "foreigners," and the only Regular Army doctors we had around, besides him, were all foreign-born (Lieutenant Colonel Koberle, Major Szentpetery, Major Reinosa, and Major Sanchez). I don't know if this caused the lieutenant colonel to come down hard on Sanchez or if he would have done it anyway. In any event, Sanchez got nailed for failing to go to the clearing station and see the soldier. Later, Lieutenant Colonel Hefner, who was a pretty active juicer himself, came down hard on a Regular Army sergeant who got in trouble for alcoholism, but he didn't let us in on the decision that time.

Brown, the ranking sergeant major in the division, was a miracle worker. When Ross Guarino and I wanted to travel on a specific day to Thailand for R&R and return on an exact date, we were told by headquarters, "The commanding general of the division himself can't name specific dates for his R&R." Sergeant Major Brown said he'd see what he could do, and the next morning we had orders for the exact dates we requested! This sort of accomplishment was typical for the sergeant major.

Although I continually tried to find out from him how he accomplished these magical feats, only once during the year of duty did he let me in on his modus operandus. When Lieutenant Colonel Hefner asked him to get some skin flicks for a Friday steak fry and party, the sergeant major had responded with the customary, "Yes, sir." He told me that immediately afterward, he put out the word among the NCOs throughout the division that his lieutenant colonel wanted skin flicks. The word came back that there was a soldier from the engineering battalion who was leaving country with a duffel bag full of movies. Sergeant Major Brown drove to the airport and found the enlisted man and his bag.

"Corporal, I understand that you have pornographic material in that bag—give it to me."

"Yes, Sergeant Major!" The startled corporal immediately handed over the bag.

"You realize that transporting pornographic material out of

country is a court-martial offense punishable by jail time in LBJ, don't you?"

"Yes, Sergeant Major." The enlisted man was sweating and about to cry.

"Well, since you served in Vietnam in our division, I'm not going to mention this. You can go home as scheduled, but don't let anything like this happen again."

"No, I sure won't, Sergeant Major." The enlisted man took the sergeant major's hand in both of his as his eyes welled up with tears. "I'll never forget this, Sergeant Major. If I can ever do anything for you, don't hesitate to ask."

I've often thought of this as an example of the pinnacle of manipulation. The sergeant major got all of the enlisted man's films, pleased his superior officer, and made the victim of the theft feel grateful for the experience. I've since heard this referred to as "Irish diplomacy." It's a situation in which you tell someone to go to hell in a way that the person thanks you for giving directions.

The following Friday we had so many skin flicks that the guys were getting bored and betting on such things as whether there would be a dog in the next film or whether the actor's feet would be dirty. We used to get pornographic films at our medical fraternity, but I've never seen so many or such a variety. Every nationality, sexual preference, fetish, perversion, and combination that you could dream up was represented. Some guys rated the skin films on a scale of 1 to 3, with 3 showing the most skin. There was also a "fuzz" rating of 1 to 3 on the basis of the amount of pubic hair that was visible. These were nearly all skin 3 and fuzz 3 films.

A few weeks into my tour in Vietnam, the medical company gained a new first sergeant. Sgt. Ivan Ivanoff was a Russian-born, tan, wrinkled, gray, crew-cut, tough-looking lifer. He parachuted into Normandy during World War II. He had no family that anyone knew of, and the rumor was that his only mail came from Sears Roebuck. When he took over the company, he immediately made the enlisted men shine their boots, wear their "covers" (caps) except indoors, and generally follow all of the military rules and regulations to the letter. Since we were a combat unit located in the boonies, where laxity was considered one of the benefits, there was considerable griping about this unfair turn of events. Complaints, covert threats, feelings of injustice—none of these changed Ivanoff's behavior in the slightest. He seemed to thrive on the negative feelings he engendered. As strict as he was, he was also very consistent in his discipline and showed no favoritism. Eventually, the unit adjusted to his style and went along with it. One night, a few months after Sergeant Ivanoff had taken over, three enlisted men from the company approached him at the NCO bar where he was drinking with some other sergeants. Several other enlisted men were watching the interaction from afar. The group of men told the sergeant that they hadn't liked him at first. They didn't like the way he tightened up discipline, but they could see that he was fair and consistent, so now they thought he was a good sergeant. Ivanoff looked at them with fury in his eye as he paused trying to think of an appropriate response and threatened to take them outside and "kick the crap out of them."

The three enlisted men were stunned and backed quickly out of the NCO club as the onlookers laughed. Ivanoff remained consistent throughout his tour. It didn't matter if you griped, it didn't matter if you toadied up—Ivanoff was the same! Some of the men did get to him a little during the year when they poisoned the stray dog he had adopted. As far as we knew, the dog was his closest relationship. John told me recently that Ivanoff went on to become a command sergeant major later in his military career.

I DIDN'T HAVE MUCH TO DO with the really big brass in the division. Maj. Gen. Orwin Talbott was the commanding general. Lieutenant Colonel Hefner communicated regularly with the big brass, including General Talbott, and I filled him in on whatever he wanted or needed to know about matters pertaining to mental health in the division. My medical school experience had trained me to keep a low profile. And since I had no ambitions in the military, I did not see any particular benefit to increasing my name recognition among the division leadership.

The new USARV psychiatric consultant, Col. Thomas Murray, invited me to visit him in Long Binh. He had a full-sized, air-conditioned trailer. He proudly showed me his kitchen, refrigerator, flush toilet, television, stereo, and comfortable furnishings. I was reminded of the military tradition of RHIP (rank has its privileges). I don't believe it was a negative reaction to his quarters, but I invited him to come and tour our division. Colonel Murray asked me specifically if there was any risk involved in his coming to the division for the visit. I assured him that he would be completely safe. Unlike many who were invited to visit Di An, Colonel Murray followed through and did actually visit. We toured the psychiatric facilities in Di An and then drove to headquarters in Lai Khe. He was invited for cocktails and dinner with General Talbott, who presented him with souvenirs of the division. Colonel Murray and Lieutenant Colonel Hefner were enjoying predinner cocktails with the general and his staff when we were suddenly hit by one of the largest rocket attacks of the year. Colonel Murray distinguished himself by running to the bunker with his martini and was complimented by the brass for not spilling a drop en route. Lieutenant Colonel Hefner praised our work during his discussions with Colonel Murray, and Colonel Murray said nice things about us to the general. So, for the most part, our points went up—Colonel Murray did look at me a little differently after his experience with the rocket attack, however.

I occasionally attended the command daily briefings with all the big brass, including the commanding general, in Lai Khe but more frequently attended the support command briefings in Di An because they were closer. These were similar to the daily hospital reports we had at Menninger's (which Dr. Peter Fleming, a World War II veteran of the 101st Airborne Division, probably copied from the military). The brass would be seated in front of the room, coffee cups in hand, facing a lieutenant or captain in starched fatigues and spit-shined boots who stood by a map of the division area of operations with a pointer. He would rattle off the news of the day to the lower-ranking officers sitting behind the brass, and mildly interested types like me either stood or sat at the back of the room. The report would be given in objective language: "Second of the Second received fire near the Iron Trapezoid at seventeen hundred. Fire was returned. Blood trails were located. Will search at dawn." The report always ended with the "score": friendly forces, 1 KIA (killed in action) and 10 WIAs (wounded in action); aggressors, 200 KIAs and 50 WIAs. It always seemed that the friendly forces did more damage than the aggressors.

The division had a bird colonel assigned to the commanding general's staff at headquarters in Lai Khe who was a higher ranking version of Major Martinet. He was known as the "super squad leader" among the division's company commanders because of his penchant for hovering over firefights in a helicopter and radioing down orders to the company commanders on where to position their men. On one of these occasions the colonel landed his helicopter and jumped out with his aides. They threw themselves onto the road with their arms extended and pointed their .45s toward the jungle. One of the company commanders walked over to the prone officers, leaned down to the colonel, and pointed in the opposite direction. "They're over there, sir."

IN A RELATIVELY SHORT TIME I made the transition to the new existence in Vietnam. I met the men I'd be living and working with for a year, and they helped me adjust and settle into the work and daily routine. My approach to work was to read the military literature, make use of the practical tips I'd gotten from Sergeant DeLeon at Fort Knox, and try to apply what I'd learned from my training at Menninger's. I followed Dr. Karl Menninger's suggestion and kept notes of my observations. By studying what we were doing in Vietnam, I was able to chronicle events in a neutral fashion and distance myself from some of the emotional trauma of the experience. In the same way, when I photographed the day-to-day events in Vietnam, I had the camera between me and the life experience. I walled off my feelings about "the world" and tried to fill up my day with as much work and activity as I possibly could. Downtime led to reverie, thoughts of home, and unpleasant emotions.

"Killer psychiatrist" outside hootch and homemade bunker.

*Capt. John Pabst, social work officer, and social work/psychology techs
Louis Straka and Vincent Zecchinelli.*

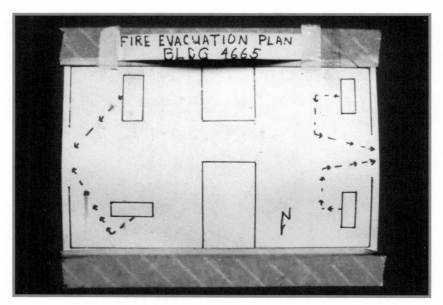

Required fire-evacuation plan. Our building had a door at each end and four desks. The arrows indicate that you walk from behind your desk out the nearest door.

Our "four-holer" outhouse. Names of the notorious docs are posted above the door.

Interior of psych "headquarters." Plywood partitions to separate interviewing areas were obtained by midnight requisition.

*Doctor Delta Morgue, where we opened the body bags and
verified that the contents were dead.*

*1st Division mental health team. Back row: Specialist 4 Simon, Specialist
4 Foley, Maj. Doug Bey, Private First Class Ortiz, Specialist 4 Vincent
Zecchinelli, Specialist 6 Ford, Capt. John Pabst, Specialist 4 Mike
Weissman, Specialist 4 Pattburg. Front row: Specialist 4 Walt Smith,
Specialist 4 Tony Grella, Specialist 4 Wech, Specialist 4 Gasper Falzone.*

Psychiatric conference in Nha Trang. U.S. psychiatrists, psychologists, and social workers in attendance with Maj. Michael Downey, Australian army psychiatrist (center).

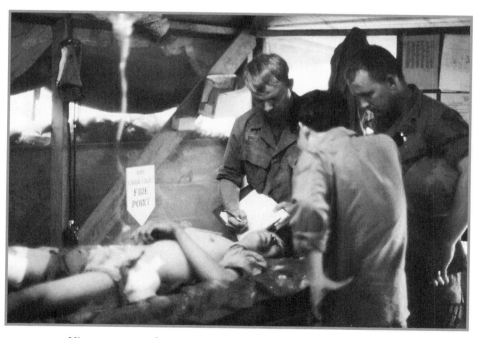

Vietnamese and American intelligence officers interrogating a wounded NVA soldier.

Capt. John Hamilton, A Company executive officer, and Maj. Doug Bey enjoying after-hours brews in informal uniforms.

Spc.4 Vincent Zecchinelli, Maj. Doug Bey, Capt. Ray Troop, Spc.4 Louis Straka, with the division psychiatry jeep.

Black and White in Vietnam

One problem not addressed in the earlier military psychiatric literature was that of race. We began by following our individual psychotherapy model in which we tried to help individuals who had difficulties to look at themselves to see what they might be doing to contribute to their own problems. It soon became apparent that the problem was not one of individual psychopathology but one of ignorance, prejudice, lack of communication, and lack of understanding between racial groups. Despite our lack of training and experience in the area of race relations, we found that we were being forced to educate ourselves and attempt to address the racial problems that were causing difficulty within units in our division.

"Hey, Wizard," Big John yelled from behind me as I left the mess hall. "Come with me tonight, there's something I want you to see." I agreed, not knowing what I was agreeing to but always looking for something that varied from the daily routine. We sat for a while on the steps of the hootch and drank a couple of beers with John's stereo playing in the background. Instead of changing into underwear and flip-flops as usual, we stayed in our tropical fatigues and boots. I followed John over to the enlisted men's area of the base camp.

It was still light, and I could see a group of black enlisted men standing in front of a hootch. They were laughing and greeting each other with ritualized handshakes, called "dap," and statements such as "Wassup blood" and "Hey, Bro." They glared at me as John and I approached. They continued to stare with hostility as we entered the hootch and sat on the cot next to the door. John walked over to the group and explained why I was there. "He's okay, man—he's with me—I asked him to come."

"So what if you axed him? Chuck ("Whitey") always gets ta look at our hole card but he don't show us shit."

"Nah, man, he isn't looking at your hole card; I'm just showing him what is happening."

I didn't make out the rest of the conversation, but apparently there was reluctant agreement that I could stay. John returned and nodded that it was straight. I didn't feel welcome and it was hot and difficult to breathe in the building, so I was glad to sit near the open portal, which provided some ventilation and a quick means of escape if needed. The hootch itself was dark and filled with forty to fifty black enlisted men. Some were wearing bracelets made from shoelaces, presumably from the boots of buddies who had been killed in action, and some had combs sticking out of their hair. Others had Afro hairstyles, and a few had berets. The army had limitations on the length of a soldier's hair but had not anticipated soldiers whose hair stuck straight out of their heads. The air was hot, musky, and saturated with the scent of marijuana. Although the hootch was of the same slat-board construction used in the officers' quarters, the enlisted men's cots were set in a common area instead of being separated by plywood partitions. The hootch was surrounded by a three-foot-high wall of sandbags and barrels, which significantly reduced the circulation of air through the building.

The young men in the room continued to stare at me with anger and suspicion. A thin man wearing a black beret and dark glasses stood up before the group and began an angry diatribe about the oppression of blacks in America. He started with slavery, segregation, and economic oppression. He said that the blacks had not fought back but had put up with the mistreatment they received. Black churches had been bombed and set on fire. The civil rights activist Medgar Evers had been assassinated in 1963 by a white man. He noted that Martin Luther King had preached nonviolence and had been killed by a white man. The Kennedys had tried to do what was just, and they had been killed by white men, too. He went on to say that blacks were not going to be pushed around any longer and that they were ready to do whatever was necessary to protect themselves. He stated that their fight was more with the white man than the people of color in Asia. "No Viet Cong ever called me nigger. The Viet Cong don't burn crosses or hang black men." He went on to describe Vietnam as a "white man's war" and said that blacks were fighting and dying in Vietnam for Vietnamese freedom while in America blacks were fighting for the basic civil rights and self-respect that had been denied them by the white power structure. He said that blacks should be home fighting for their own rights and dignity and not fighting to keep the Vietnamese free from communism.

Although the talk expressed anger and rebellion, the atmosphere in the hootch was almost churchlike with the congregation of young blacks interjecting shouts of "Right on," "You said it, blood," "Uh-huh, that's right; you got that right, " and "Black is beautiful, man." Both the speaker and audience spoke in the mixture of English and profanity typical of Vietnam with the words "whitey, honky, or chuck" usually being preceded by "motherfucking." John sensed that I was about to speak up and put his hand on my arm. "Don't say anything," he told me.

After the talk, John did the dap with several of the brothers in the room, including the speaker. I stood back and received a few nods of acknowledgment accompanied by suspicious stares as John again told them that I was okay.

When we returned to the officers' area, John asked me what I thought of the talk. I expressed some anger about what I thought were untrue and provocative statements made by the speaker. John told me that as an officer and an older white man, it would have been wrong to challenge the young enlisted man because it would put him in a corner and force him to prove himself in some way.

Apparently the black soldiers in this unit got together on a fairly regular basis to reaffirm their solidarity. John had asked to bring me to this particular meeting as part of my education. He did not attend these meetings regularly because he did not feel it was appropriate for an officer to do so. I don't know if other units in the division had meetings of this type, but I assume that they did.

John was in an awkward position in the military. As a captain he was a role model for young blacks, but he really could not do much to give them a boost or to protect them. He was married, the father of a daughter, and college educated—all of which further set him apart from the enlisted blacks, who were primarily uneducated, single, inner-city youths. On the other hand, he had to put up with the prejudice and whims of the overwhelmingly white command. In 1969, 13.3 percent of those in the army and marines were African Americans, but only 3 percent of the officer corps of the army and 1 percent of the Marine Corps officers were black.

John followed the rules to the letter but, in subtle ways, maintained his own identity within the military. He was one of the few Regular Army officers who had a mustache, and he never used derogatory racial terms when referring to the Vietnamese.

Big John was my neighbor and friend in Vietnam. He had been the first officer to welcome me on my arrival. People tend to be goosey around psychiatrists. Many think either that we are totally useless or that we can read their minds. Many white Americans, even today, would be reluctant to invite a psychiatrist to a social gathering. Like many older siblings of mentally ill individuals, I strove to be superadequate and supernormal. I felt I had to compensate for my brother's problems, protect my parents from further stress, and try to maintain the strained fabric of our family structure. I often had difficulty knowing what my true feelings were and, therefore, inwardly felt isolated and alone. My family felt ostracized by my brother's suicide. Some of it was caused by our own withdrawal, but some was attributable to the stigma society attached not only to the victim but to the family in those days.

John had his own family traumas and had been raised in large part by his extended family. I learned long after Vietnam that his mother died of uterine cancer and his dad became an alcoholic when John was twelve. He was the only boy and took on a role of responsibility in his family. Whether it was our both being victims of prejudice, our both being family "heroes," our similar Christian backgrounds, or that we mutually had to deal with loss and family dysfunction, John and I seemed to take a liking to one another from the beginning. Possibly another reason underlying our friendship was that I was always one of the poorer kids among my peers growing up. John and I were both used to working without a safety net.

John took the initiative in showing me how the army worked and tried to give me a glimpse of how the world looked through a black person's eyes. He realized that as an athlete and as an officer, he was a role model for the black enlisted men. He felt an obligation to look after and to encourage young black soldiers under his command. I know that John often had to make a conscious effort to ignore the racial slurs and jokes that he could not help hearing in the mostly white officers' clubs.

Another reason John and I got along was, to some extent, that we were both jocks who had attended college on athletic scholarships. He was a big-time athlete who was co-captain on the three-time national champion Florida A&M football team. A running back who played behind him in college went on to become a star player in the National Football League. I wrestled in high school and college but was hardly on his level athletically. He never made a point of it, and there was an athletic camaraderie between us. I once tried to take John on in a wrestling match, but even though he knew nothing about wrestling, he was too strong for me to handle. He let me off the hook by telling the other guys he was surprised by how strong I was.

Early on, I noticed that John and I would read the same articles in the *Stars and Stripes* (the newspaper for overseas military personnel) but interpret them differently. I eventually learned that he felt that there was a white conspiracy in the United States to oppress blacks and that the goal of the whites was to put the blacks into concentration camps or send them back to Africa. He would find evidence in the news to support these beliefs.

Over time I began to understand where he was coming from and to see how he arrived at his conclusions. The blacks had been brought as slaves to the United States, and there was considerable resistance to integration and equal rights in parts of the country. Gov. George Wallace had stood on the steps of a school to resist integration of schools in Alabama in the 1960s. Blacks were, at least initially, disproportionately represented in Vietnam among the enlisted men, and there were few black Regular Army officers and NCOs. The assassinations of leaders espousing racial equality in the United States had caused major riots and unrest among the black communities. Blacks grew up and lived with prejudice throughout their lives. They were sensitive to unconscious and conscious prejudice on the part of whites. John, who was handsome, athletic, and educated, was sometimes snubbed and often overheard racial jokes told by physically unfit rednecks at the officers' club. What at first seemed to be paranoia on John's part made more sense to me when I considered the world from his perspective. John grew up in the South and went to a black college. He probably didn't have exposure to many whites, and perhaps he learned something about a white man's perception of the world from his contacts with me.

Ironically, racism in the United States may have been a small factor in the origins of the conflict in Vietnam. Ho Chi Minh, the Communist leader of North Vietnam, had left Vietnam in 1911 to work as a cook's assistant aboard a French ship. He jumped ship in New York, worked in Boston for a while, and traveled throughout the South. It was in the southern United States that he observed that there was a difference between the stated principles of democracy and the reality of life in the United States. He later wrote about the hypocrisy of a society that espoused democracy yet did not allow African Americans to share its benefits.

The Student Nonviolent Coordinating Committee (SNCC) opposed the U.S. policy in Vietnam as racist oppression of nonwhite peoples. One of their chants was "Ho ho, what ya know, white folks gotta go." John had come to Vietnam with the expectation that he would be welcomed by the Vietnamese as a fellow person of color. He was surprised and somewhat hurt to discover that the Vietnamese were more prejudiced than most whites in the United States. The Vietnamese ostracized the montagnards because of their darker skin color, and many Vietnamese refused to provide service to black soldiers. When John and I were on leave, we only went where he was welcome, making me more keenly aware of the prejudice that was present among the Vietnamese.

As the executive officer of the medical company and as a career Medical Service officer, John had considerable knowledge of the army and army medicine and essentially ran the company. When Capt. Lenny Dunford left country, Capt. Ross Guarino replaced him as the Alpha Company commander. Ross was essentially a figurehead because doctors usually spent only two years in the military and had limited training and experience as commanders. Even though Ross had been through ROTC in college, he did not

CHAPTER 3

have the military or administrative experience that John had. As executive officer, John was the hard guy, the one who kicked butt in the company.

John took it upon himself to inspect my uniform as well as my quarters. Usually he had something favorable to say about the way I dressed. He didn't care for my housekeeping, however.

"Hey Wiz—what's up with your quarters?—this place is awful."

"I'm going for that 'lived-in' look."

"This place is nasty, man! I thought you said you were compulsive."

"Yeah, but Karl Abraham in his book on the anal personality said, 'Oben beglänzend und unten beschissen,' which means compulsive guys look neat on the outside but have dirty underwear."

"Well your place is beschissen all right! You gotta get it together man—you're gonna get sick livin' like that—I'm gettin' sick just looking at it."

"You're used to the soft civilian life—we real army men can rough it."

"That hasn't got anything to do with roughing it—that's just personal hygiene, and you need to get your stuff together."

John also tried to educate me about command and administration in the military. He invited me to his office to watch him discipline his men. John's office was spacious by our standards. He had a small waiting area with an enlisted man who acted as a receptionist, typist, and gofer. John had a large desk that was bare and clean on top. He sat behind it with his back to the wall, facing the door to the waiting area. Behind him on the wall was the battalion emblem, including Fremont the Bear. On a side wall the fire-escape plan was posted as required. The walls of the office had the slats with screens between them to let the air through. There were fans running. The office furniture was the standard, beat-up, gray metal government-issue stuff we had in our office, but John's furniture was in a little better shape than ours. I imagine that administration got first pick. I was always impressed by how neat and clean John's office was compared to mine, which always seemed to have a layer of dust on everything. His part of the hootch was also much neater and cleaner than mine.

As part of my education, John would let me watch business in his office and explain why things were done the way they were. I remember one morning watching him discipline a soldier. He called in a sergeant who had fouled up in some way. He sat quietly behind his desk and said, "Well, sergeant, what is your story?" The sergeant went into a long, convoluted diatribe, the essence of which was that someone had told him to do what he did and therefore it was not his fault. At the end of his tale the sergeant fell silent. John then raised his voice and said, "Sergeant, you are like a guy in a new suit with no seat in the pants standing on the fifty-yard line of the football field and everyone in the stadium can see his bare ass but him." "Yes, sir," answered the sergeant meekly. "Don't ever let this happen again!" shouted John. "Yes, sir," answered the sergeant. After the sergeant had been dismissed, John explained that the lesson in this demonstration was to let the soldiers tell their story first. "If you start lecturing before they've told their little story, they will argue with you. Let them talk first, and then jump in their stuff."

One morning, I was sitting in John's office, looking forward to learning more about military administration, when the company optometrist Capt. Beau Lee came in. I knew Beau, of course; he was the guy who initiated me into the unit. He generously had made me and others in the unit several pairs of aviator glasses for free. This style of sunglasses was officially for pilots, but we thought they were cool, so they were popular. I remember that John did not have any aviator glasses. I don't know why; perhaps because according to the rules he could not have them (he was a stickler for the rules), because Beau refused to give him some (doubtful), because he didn't like Beau, or because he didn't like the looks of the glasses themselves (this is possible since they made you look like a state highway patrolman). Beau's Southern accent went well with his smooth, generally charming demeanor. His political views were very conservative, as were those of most of the doctors. He, like John, was Regular Army and planned to make a career of it. He tended to assume an informal leadership role among the doctors. For example, he took it upon himself to publicly interview the new arrivals to the unit.

In any event, Beau had come to request a second R&R. Most officers got a second R&R if they requested one, especially in the medical battalion where the shot cards were issued. All personnel needed to have a shot card to go on R&R, but no one wanted to go through the painful shots again just to get a new card. At the medical battalion, we would dry-lab new cards complete with stamps and signatures in exchange for steaks and similar luxuries from other units. "Dry-lab" refers to filling out the results without actually doing the laboratory tests. For example, when I processed out of the army, a WAC and the doctors at Fort Sheridan helped me make a quick exit by filling out all of my laboratory results without my actually having to take the tests. In this situation, we filled out the shot cards with the names of all the injections and the dates they were supposedly given so that the men could use the new cards to obtain a second R&R without having to go through a whole series of shots. It was obvious that Beau was feeling some resentment just at having to ask John for anything. He was openly prejudiced against blacks as well as the Vietnamese, and John had almost certainly heard some of Beau's racial jokes and slurs in the officers' club.

Although I knew John did not care for the optometrist, I was surprised when John calmly told Beau that the policy was that each person could have only one R&R. Beau flushed a little and with a slight tremor in his voice said he knew what the policy was, but he also knew that any officer in the division who wanted a second R&R got one. John shook his head and told Beau they did not in his medical company. Beau reddened and responded that this was bull and that everyone he knew got two R&Rs. John repeated the policy as if he were explaining it to a child, and Beau lost it. He screamed at John and berated John's unit. John came up from behind the desk and punched Beau square on the chin, knocking him and his chair backward onto the floor. Beau staggered to his feet and screamed "You're done! I'll see that you are court-martialed for striking a fellow officer!"

I could feel my own adrenaline working up and my heart beating rapidly. My voice was a little shaky when I explained that there would be no court-martial because what I had seen was that Beau had attacked John in a provocative manner and that Beau was responsible for what happened. I was a major by this time and outranked them both. The rank did not mean much to me except that I got more pay and some scrambled eggs on the bill of my dress uniform cover, but it did carry weight with Regular Army people. As a field-grade officer, I would have been a credible witness in a dispute between two company-grade officers. This essentially ended the matter, and Beau did not pursue legal recourse.

The situation really ended one night at the officers' club. I was drunk and semi–ticked off at the world when Captain Lee, who was also blitzed, came up to me and made a wisecrack about my unnatural affection for Big John. Whatever it was, it seemed to fire some neurons in the lizard part of my brain. I picked him up in a fireman's carry and threw him through the door. Unfortunately, this was the night that Lieutenant Colonel Koberle was introducing Lieutenant Colonel Hefner to his new command. They arrived just as Beau took the hinges off the door. Beau avoided contact with me after this event, and my access to aviator glasses ended as well.

I do not know the specific reason that made John stick to regulations and refuse a second R&R to Captain Lee. The rule was that you could have one R&R and one leave (which was essentially the same as an R&R, but the army paid fewer of the expenses). John took only one R&R during his year in Vietnam. However, Beau was correct about everyone getting an extra R&R if requested. Perhaps John did not like Beau because he was a Southerner or maybe because Beau was blatantly prejudiced. It could have been solely personal—Beau could be provocative—or maybe John was just having a bad day. This is pure speculation, but it may also have been due to John's frustration at being powerless to do much to help the black enlisted men who looked up to him while at the same time having to put up with the racism on the part of some of the white officers. John was educated, an officer, and a gentleman—but he was black. Maybe he decided, like the younger brothers, he was not going to take any more. Whatever the reason, John egged Beau into blowing up and then flattened him!

THE ENLISTED BLACKS in the base camps and support areas tended to hang out together. This is natural, since people tend to hang out with people like themselves. The sight of groups of blacks tended to raise the paranoia of the white cadre (the central leadership group), who saw their actions as provocative and rebellious. One of the important factors in prejudice is the fear of the stranger.

There is a tendency to project the feelings and characteristics you dislike in yourself onto people you do not know, especially if they look or act differently than you and your associates. Everyone in Vietnam was frustrated and angry. White officers and NCOs would see the young blacks hanging out together, wearing shoelace bracelets symbolizing black solidarity, having comb handles sticking out of their pockets (which was a violation of the dress code), and giving the clenched-fist black power salute and assume that the blacks were angry, aggressive, and threatening.

Language contributed to the misunderstanding as well. Blacks might say, "I'm going to kill yo' ass" as a way of expressing their displeasure. White commanders took that as a murder threat and would charge the individual. On the other hand, black soldiers were more than capable of doing some provoking and projecting of their own. They had their own bias and prejudice against the whites, who were in power in the military. They felt that the deaths of their leaders and the enslavement of their ancestors had been due in part to the passivity of their "step-and-fetch-it" ancestors. This generation was not going to take any guff from whites. Some groups called themselves "Mau Maus," and others called themselves "Ju Jus." These names did nothing to allay the anxiety among the white cadre.

The previous year (late summer of 1968) blacks had rioted at the Long Binh Jail and had attacked white prisoners and white guards. They put chicken bones in their hair and noses, beat on oil drums, and, according to one white witness, "went native." The prisoner I examined at Fort Knox was accused of beating a white prisoner to death with a metal rod taken from a prison bunk.

The disproportionate number of blacks in Vietnam early in the conflict was seen as another example of prejudice and the desire of the white establishment in the United States to eliminate them. Blacks made up about 10 percent of the military but about 20 percent of the combat infantry units. A little over 14 percent of the Americans killed in the Vietnam conflict were black. The majority of prisoners at LBJ were black.

There was some basis for both positions. This was a time of unrest in the United States, and many major cities had experienced riots in which buildings were burned, businesses looted, and people killed. Adding to the mix was the fact that every unit had groups of nineteen-year-old blacks armed to the teeth with weapons and explosives. Most of the black men in Vietnam were high school dropouts from ghetto neighborhoods. The officers, on the other hand, were mostly white, college-educated, newly trained lieutenants who had little or no experience at commanding troops or dealing with inner-city blacks. Commanding officers were aware that officers were shot or fragged by their men in Vietnam. ("Fragging" refers to killing someone with a fragmentation grenade.) Some company commanders and cadre tended to respond to their fears by bearing down on the black soldiers. They would issue orders prohibiting symbols of black identity, such as music, clothing, and power salutes. This led to further anger and resentment on the part of the blacks, who viewed such acts as provocations.

Combat units did not have many racial problems when in the field. There is a saying that a bullet has no prejudice. When the soldiers were faced with a common enemy who was trying to kill them all, racial differences were mostly ignored. The problems arose when units left the field for stand down at base camps. Most men who came in from the field for a stand down were irritable and ready to let off steam. They resented the REMFs, who had relatively safe and comfortable living conditions. Grunts (infantry or ground soldiers) in the field often claimed that they had more in common with Charlie (the VC) than they did with the REMFs. This phenomenon was also observed in the LBJ in 1968 when Long Binh experienced a rocket and mortar attack during the Tet offensive. The black and white prisoners came together against the common enemy who was threatening Americans in general. Later the same year, when there was no outside threat from the Vietnamese, blacks rioted and killed some of the white prisoners and guards.

REDUCING RACIAL TENSION in units was not officially part of the psychiatric unit's mission, but since many psychological issues were linked to racial problems, we did what we could to improve the situation in the division. I had no formal training in race relations, and I am white. A black psychiatrist trained to deal with race relations and capable of making policy changes would likely have been more helpful to the division than I was able to be. However, there was little time to work with the black inner-city troops and the white suburban lieutenants who led them. Had there been more time and resources, we could have done more to help them reach a better understanding and working relationship. Nonetheless, we did what we could and succeeded some of the time.

Specialist Smith counseled a black sergeant from a support unit who had been referred by his white first sergeant because of his bad attitude. In the referral request, the first sergeant asserted that the black sergeant had fraternized with lower-ranking black enlisted men and refused to enforce company policies regarding military bearing and drug surveillance. The sergeant had been a black activist before he was drafted. He felt that the military was prejudiced in general and that the first sergeant was prejudiced in particular. He also believed that the black platoon sergeant in his unit was an "Oreo" who sided with the whites against his own race.

Except for Specialist Matthews, who was black, Smith probably understood blacks better than any other member of the psychiatric team. He was also able to relate comfortably to the blacks in the division. Smith followed the model of one-to-one psychiatric treatment and met with the black sergeant. He encouraged the sergeant to vent his angry feelings and helped him see that he had a lifelong pattern of rebellion against authority figures. He also helped him see that he might have distorted and exaggerated his perception of prejudice. Specialist Smith pointed out that by wearing unauthorized clothing, the sergeant drew attention to himself in a negative way. He noted that the sergeant was a leader and could be a role model rather than a buddy to the enlisted men of the unit.

The sergeant returned to his unit, but Specialist Smith was not satisfied with the work he had done. We reviewed the case together, and I told him I thought he had done an excellent job. Smith felt that the sergeant's problems were larger than the patterns of behavior that had been addressed in the intervention. In fact, he did not think the problems were the sergeant's at all. We evaluated the unit's stress indicators and observed that they were elevated. Smith was interested in investigating the unit itself to see if the sergeant's perception of prejudice and racial tension might have some validity.

His perception of the case had merit, and we discussed how we might proceed to follow up. I discussed the situation with Lieutenant Colonel Hefner that evening as we drank our evening beer.

The colonel was very supportive of our efforts to reduce stress in the division units and thought that looking into the situation was an excellent idea. He called the battalion commander the next morning and arranged for a meeting.

On the day of the meeting, Smith, Zecchinelli, and I donned our gear and drove to the unit. The battalion commander was a tall, physically fit lieutenant colonel who wore starched tropical fatigues and spit-shined boots. The executive officer was a stocky, younger major who dressed similarly. The battalion commander stated that Lieutenant Colonel Hefner had called him and filled him in generally that we were interested in looking into some possible problems in one of his companies.

Since any organization is suspicious and defensive about outside consultants coming to analyze its problems, I quickly explained that we were trying to apply our model of organizational stress to the military environment. I also described the process of monitoring stress indices and collecting information. I talked about the Hawthorne experiment in industry that showed that just paying attention and listening to the people in an organization improved their productivity. I assured the commander that all of this information would be confidential and would only go to him and other officers in the unit. The commander seemed reassured and contacted the black sergeant's company commander to tell him that we were coming to speak with him about our consultation.

The company commander was a captain, and the executive officer, a lieutenant. They were neat in appearance but younger than the battalion commander and executive officer. The captain and lieutenant seemed uncomfortable and somewhat on the spot. Once again, I explained our interest in applying the principles of organizational diagnosis and intervention to the military setting. I assured the company commander that we planned to do this for all units in the division and that giving the men a chance to vent would in itself probably reduce tension. I also suggested that Specialist Smith could stay and work with the unit for a week to observe the problems firsthand and talk with the enlisted men. Once more, I assured the company commander that the information we obtained would not be disclosed outside the unit.

The company commander agreed to our proceeding with the consultation under those circumstances. He had to agree. I was a major, and the battalion commander had told him to cooperate. However, I wanted him to feel that he was making the decision and to elicit as much cooperation as possible. I also wanted to ease his concerns about the consultation adversely affecting his career in the military.

Specialist Smith bunked and spoke with the enlisted men, accompanying them when they did road work, cleared trees, and did other similar tasks. The black sergeant whom Smith had counseled was particularly pleased to see that we had followed up on his complaints. This was very helpful to Smith's efforts to gain the trust of the men in the unit and elicit their views. He learned that black soldiers had been ordered to take down posters featuring black women in African attire, could not give the black power salute, nor could they wear jewelry or clothes that symbolized black unity. They were forbidden to have or display an African national flag, but Confederate flags were displayed throughout the unit, including some of the officers' offices. In addition to repressing expression, the enlisted men's club for the unit played only country-and-western music during weekends. There were strong feelings among the black soldiers about command prejudice.

We prepared a report, largely based on Smith's findings, that was then given to the battalion commander and executive officer. Key individuals were briefed by us personally. The unit command reported that the consultation was helpful to them. They allowed posters to be displayed in the hootches and no longer perceived the symbols of black pride as provocative. A mixture of music was permitted in the enlisted men's club. The issue of the flags was not resolved, and the Confederate flag continued to be displayed and the African national flag continued to be banned. The issue was brought to everyone's attention, however. After the consultation, the stress indices for the unit declined.

Although we believed that the consultation was successful, we were not sure which elements had helped. Certainly the Hawthorne effect was a factor. The "Hawthorne effect" refers to an early organizational study in which investigators attempted to study the effects of lighting on employee productivity in the Western Electric Company. Office workers in each department were interviewed, and then the lighting was set at different levels. To the researchers' surprise, the productivity improved in all departments regardless of the level of lighting. The unexpected conclusion was that paying attention to the individual workers and talking to them had a positive effect on their productivity. It may have been that by focusing the unit's attention on itself, feeding back its observations, getting people to talk about the problems in the unit, and correcting some erroneous perceptions, we shook up the organization and decompressed some of the fear and anger that had been developing.

PEER PRESSURE AMONG BLACKS to prove their brotherhood was another source of problems in Vietnam. One morning two military policemen (MPs) from the LBJ arrived at our clinic escorting a black enlisted man who was thin and bookish looking, with horn-rimmed glasses. The guards presented paperwork requesting a forensic psychiatric examination on prisoner Williams (pseudonym), who had been charged with several serious criminal offenses, including attempted murder. The young man was tearful and hung his head in shame and remorse. He wasn't the typical cool, defiant offender—in fact, he seemed to be a gentle sort of kid. Specialist Smith saw him in one of the cubicles initially to take a history. Prior to doing so, he offered the prisoner a tissue and his choice of coffee or a soda. Smith also had the guards remove the prisoner's handcuffs. Zecchinelli got drinks for the guards and showed them that the only way out of the cubicle would be through the door they were guarding. The prisoner opted for soda and seemed to relax a bit.

In forensic cases we typically took a more detailed history than we did with routine medical cases. It also took more time to make the prisoners comfortable and to let them know that the information they provided would be put into a report that would likely help their attorney represent them more effectively. In Vietnam we didn't have the structured scheduling that is characteristic of civilian psychiatric practice. There was no time pressure. It was also impractical to have the prisoner returned from LBJ a number of times for a series of interviews. Smith spent approximately two hours taking a detailed history and then reviewed it with me. Then the two of us interviewed the patient together for another couple of hours.

Most criminal defendants are sullen, defiant, and worried about the extent of punishment they'll receive. They are hypervigilant and watch the interviewer closely to try to pick up clues that might help them give "the right answer." Williams relaxed as he talked and appeared to be open and cooperative. His overall emotional state was one of sadness. He showed little concern about what punishment he might receive—he seemed to feel that he deserved whatever he got.

From the history obtained we learned that Williams was an enlisted mulatto soldier who was the son of an unwed black mother and white father. His grandmother had played a significant role in his upbringing. She saw to it that he attended church regularly and emphasized the importance of education. He had grown up being teased in his neighborhood and schools because of his skin color and unwed parentage. His mixed origin resulted in others giving him the nickname "Yellow."

He was highly regarded by command of his supply unit in Vietnam because he was quiet, intelligent, and hardworking. He was relatively new in country and to his unit. He had two years of college and appeared to be a well-mannered, soft-spoken person. In the same unit a group of black soldiers had gotten into trouble for using drugs. They had been in country with the unit for several months and were generally recognized as troublemakers. These young blacks were inner-city thugs from the Detroit area who had a jailhouse mentality.

These black soldiers were convinced that a particular white soldier had ratted on them to the command. They did not trust Yellow, who was educated and came from a religious, more middle-class background. They singled him out for special treatment and insisted that he prove himself by committing a violent act against the white informer. They told him that it was time for him to pick sides. They also believed that neither the command nor the white informant would suspect Yellow. It was unlikely that his carrying out their wishes would have really won their respect and trust. Instead, they were just using Yellow to get rid of an informer and intimidate any prospective informers. If Yellow refused, they told him that they would continue to pick on him.

Yellow had always been sensitive about his color and wanted to be perceived as black. However, it was contrary to his religious upbringing and temperament to hurt another person. Nonetheless, under pressure, he agreed to cut the white soldier to intimidate him.

As he approached the white enlisted man's hootch, he debated with himself about whether to go forward with the act and had apparently decided not to harm or intimidate the white soldier. Unfortunately, the white soldier was anxious and hyperalert. He had already been threatened by the blacks in the unit and had been told that they were going to kill him for informing. When the white soldier saw Yellow enter the hootch with knife in hand, he started screaming, which excited and frightened Yellow. Yellow later described the experience as an unreal, dreamlike state seen through tunnel vision. He stabbed the white soldier to get him to shut up, causing the victim to scream louder. Yellow continued to stab the screaming soldier until the latter was quiet and motionless. He nearly killed him. It was at this point that Yellow realized what he had done and felt terrible remorse for having committed the act. He asked the soldiers outside to get the medics and turned himself in to the military police.

We reviewed what had happened with Yellow and understood that his desire to prove himself to his peers caused him to take on a mission of intimidation he would never have considered on his own. The white soldier's reaction had frightened him and caused him to react automatically in an altered mental state until his victim stopped screaming and moving. This type of reaction has been described in police work: the environment disappears while the officer focuses on the perpetrator and continues to fire until all sound and motion are stopped. We found him fit to stand trial since he did fall within the legal definition of competency at the time of the attack. We were able to present information that made his behavior more understandable to the court, to note his good Christian upbringing, and to describe his remorse when he realized what he had done.

He went back to the LBJ to await trial. We did not hear the results of his trial, but the unit commanders read our report. The unit troublemakers were already disliked by command and had been given several Article 15s prior to this incident because of their drug use. I never learned what happened to them but would assume that some, if not all, were administratively discharged or court-martialed.

ONE DAY A BLACK ENLISTED MAN came to the psychiatric unit office and asked to speak with Major Bey. Zecchinelli asked him what he wanted, and the soldier responded that his surname was Bey and he thought we might be related. Apparently someone in the division saw his name and told him that there was a Major Bey in Di An. Zecchinelli laughed and said he doubted it but brought the enlisted man into my office to meet me. The black infantryman was embarrassed when he saw that I was white, but I told him it was possible we were related in some way. Most of the Beys in the United States are black. The Bey brothers were a well-known black gang on the South Side of Chicago during the 1960s. In the eighteenth century, Napoleon Bonaparte's troops in the Middle East had captured some Beys and brought them back to France, and my relatives came from France and Germany in the Alsace-Lorraine region. My grandfather's grandfather had served as a sergeant in the French Foreign Legion. Since my ancestors came from Africa and the Middle East, perhaps we were distant relatives.

These early roots and John's influence in Vietnam may have been precursors of my informal adoption of a black teenager into our family in the 1990s. In 1992, after having two heart attacks and open-heart surgery, my confrontation with mortality and my daughter Sarah's requests brought our family back to religion. We were listening for messages carefully at that time, so when my then eighth-grade son Matt asked if a black eighth grader could come live with us, we felt perhaps this was a divine assignment. Alvis became a part of our family seven years ago and has been a gift from God and a blessing to us all. Shortly after Alvis came to our home, I took him to a speech pathology clinic because I thought he had a speech defect. A black speech pathologist sat down with me and explained that he did not have a defect. His speech was perfectly normal in his prior environment, and the defect was mine for not being able to understand him. I was a little salty when I first heard this, but I am straight with it now. It reminded me of the complaints the black soldiers had about not being able to communicate with their commanders in Vietnam.

CAPT. JOHN HAMILTON was my friend and mentor in Vietnam. Through our friendship, I began to understand and appreciate his perception of the world, which was quite different from mine. I also came to appreciate the unique stresses that he had to cope with as an officer in the military because of his race. The trend in preventive psychiatry, Walt Smith's anthropology training, and my own work in organizational diagnosis and intervention led to our looking at racial problems within the organization itself rather than trying to treat or eliminate "problem soldiers" referred by their units. The process of focusing attention on the problem and getting individuals within the unit to ventilate, offer suggestions, and discuss the problems seemed to have a positive impact. We also recognized that we weren't trained in the area of race relations and that a higher-ranking black officer with training in this area would have been much more effective than we were able to be.

Diagnosing and Treating Patients in the Division

My previous training and experience prepared me to evaluate, diagnose, and treat individuals with psychiatric problems. I was also used to working with a team of nurses, aides, psychologists, social workers, and social work/psychology technicians. My year at Fort Knox had given me some military psychiatry experience. It was interesting and familiar to provide direct psychiatric service in the division because this activity was close to the work I had done in the past. We saw two hundred new patients and about the same number of follow-ups each month in our division. Some were evaluated and treated by the technicians, who then reviewed their work with Captain Pabst or myself.

After three or four weeks in Vietnam, I received a letter from Dr. Karl Menninger:

June 11, 1969

Dear Doug:

I was extremely pleased to get a letter from you this morn-ing—dated 5 days ago, as a matter of fact. I didn't know where you were and, of course, I don't know yet but I have a little more feeling about it now than I did. And you give such a clear description of the personnel and the environment and the way of life.

I feel tempted to read your letter to many friends since I am sure there is no classified information in it. And, unless you cable me prohibition, I think I will read it to the graduating class at the dinner Friday night the 22nd.

I feel like looking up a reprint of our studies of combat exhaustion as it looked in the ETO [European Theater of Operations]. Some symptoms may sound familiar to you even though the syndrome doesn't seem to occur so often. I think your explanation of why it does not occur is exactly right.

Of course, I agree with you completely about the morale problem. Incidentally, I have been invited to speak before the Foreign Relations Committee and confer with Senator Fulbright next week in Washington, and one thing I am going to say is that continuation of the futile fighting breeds a nationwide sense of uneasiness and discouragement. Apparently many soldiers feel that they fight a very uphill war if not indeed an insoluble one. Our army tries its very best. Sometimes it sounds to me like Gulliver being pinned down by the Lilliputians. Well anyway, I think that the bad effects are not only the casualties which you see and treat, you and the other brave medical men over there, but the worried people here at home who don't know what to do about it. The President feels that some muscle-stretching exercises are in order and talks bravely about America going big and America going strong, but I'm not with him on this. I think America should go slow and go wise. It's a new role for us to play, but it's right here that I think psychiatry might be of the greatest use to the establishment.

Sincerely,

Karl Menninger M.D.

It always gave me a lift to hear from Dr. Karl. I reread his letter and then sacked out to the sound of our artillery. As usual, I was awakened in the morning by the pounding bass from John's stereo vibrating the plywood wall between us. It was Diana Ross singing

"Someday We'll Be Together." I lay on my poncho liner listening to John's music and to the helicopters flying overhead. I rolled out of bed, slipped on my flip-flops, and poured some water into my basin for shaving and brushing my teeth. Like my neighbors, I performed these hygienic tasks on my front porch. As Malcolm headed for the privy, he said, "I've been a little raggedy lately. Happiness is a solid stool."

John walked out to the porch. "As long as you take those malaria pills, your stuff is going to be raggedy and stay raggedy."

We took white dapsone pills daily and orange chloroquine/primaquine (CP) weekly to prevent malaria. A side effect was diarrhea—especially from the weekly CP pill. We completed our constitutionals, finished dressing, and headed to the mess hall for breakfast. After breakfast we went back to our hootches briefly and then headed off to work.

I trudged down the gravel path from the ghetto to our psychiatric hootch. As I entered the building, one of the technicians yelled "ATTEN-SHUN!" and Smith, Ortiz, Zecchinelli, Pattburg, and Falzone all snapped to attention. Doing my best movie British commander imitation, I said, "As you were, gentlemen." We had fun and were relaxed in our work setting, but I didn't let things get too informal nor did I joke around with the technicians the way I did with my fellow officers. It would have caused problems and would have made them uncomfortable as well. Simon came over from the clearing station, and he and Pattburg replaced their jungle fatigue tops with blue scrub-suit tops they had scrounged. Zecchinelli and Falzone wore their green underwear T-shirts. Smith, Pabst, and I remained in our fatigue uniforms.

The technicians, Captain Pabst, and I saw a lot of patients each month, but there is a tendency in our field to remember the unusual and the most difficult patients. Most of the people we saw were fairly routine cases involving adjustment reactions, with symptoms of anxiety or depression that responded quickly to short-term counseling or medication.

A young soldier named Smith (pseudonym) from the engineer battalion was referred by his CO because of symptoms of anxiety. His CO reported that he had functioned fairly well in the unit but had been showing up frequently for sick call, and the battalion surgeon felt that his symptoms were primarily due to anxiety. The patient came on his own with his medical records and was interviewed by Specialist Falzone. He filled me in on the interview.

"He's nineteen years old, Caucasian, an E-4 [enlisted man] from engineering with four months in country. He says he has always been a little anxious and hyper, but recently it has interfered with his functioning. He feels anxious when he awakens and then starts thinking he is sick. He says he is often nauseous and has thrown up. He then worries that he will become sick in public or in the mess hall. The more he thinks about it, the sicker he gets. He has had multiple checkups by the battalion surgeon, who feels the symptoms are anxiety and not organic."

Falzone said that Smith did not identify any specific stresses. Smith said he is probably more homesick than other guys in the unit and that he has always been close to his parents. He says his whole family is nervous and "worriers," and his mother takes Valium. He missed school a number of times growing up because of stomach problems.

Falzone thought that Smith seemed like a good kid. He's probably been this way all of his life, but now the symptoms are worse because he's worrying that he will become sick in the mess hall or in public and people will make fun of him. Falzone then brought Smith in and introduced me.

I asked him if had ever taken medicine for anxiety. He replied that he had once taken some of his mother's Valium. He then felt better and didn't want to see a doctor or take pills.

"Well, from what Specialist Falzone said, you are putting more pressure on yourself recently because you are afraid you are going to become anxious and sick and this in turn causes you to have more anxiety."

"Yeah, I make myself sick sometimes."

"One thing you might do is to try a little Valium, just take two milligrams—it will start working in an hour or so and last about six hours. See how it makes you feel, and try to find the dose that relieves your anxiety but doesn't make you feel sleepy. Then keep it in your pocket. Many guys don't have to take the medicine if they have something in their pocket they know they can take to control the symptoms if they have to. The idea is to give you some control so that you don't feel you have to live in fear of becoming anxious or sick to your stomach."

I asked Falzone to get him thirty Valium tablets (two milligrams each), set up an appointment for him next week, and let his battalion surgeon know what we are doing. I would call the CO to fill him in.

Smith did well and reported that, as we had anticipated, he actually took few of the tablets, but having them in his pocket and the knowledge that he could take them if needed enabled him to relax and return to his previous level of functioning.

A battalion surgeon called us to say he was referring in an enlisted man named Jones (pseudonym) from an infantry unit. He felt that the young man was clinically depressed. He arrived by jeep accompanied by a medic from his unit and was covered with red dust from the field, appeared disheveled, and showed poor personal hygiene. I could smell his body odor from the back of the psychiatric hootch when he entered. Zecchinelli spoke with the medic, took an initial history, and then presented his findings to me. He said that they were worried that Jones might commit suicide. He continued:

"He's been in country three months. He seemed to be okay until about a month ago when he began to have trouble sleeping. He lost his appetite and has lost about ten pounds. He feels worse in the morning, can't concentrate, ruminates about negative topics—mainly his girlfriend dumping him—he's tired, feels more irritable, can't make decisions, has withdrawn from other unit members, and admits he has thought of suicide but hasn't considered how he would do it. He has been depressed before but has never been treated. He says that several of his family members have been clinically depressed, and he had a grandfather who did commit suicide."

"He smells like he hasn't been taking care of himself. He's got beaucoup b.o."

"You got that right! I could hardly stand to take the history."

Falzone brought Jones in and sat in on the interview.

"Specialist Zecchinelli briefed me on the history you gave him. It seems to me that you have most of the symptoms associated with clinical depression: sleep and appetite disturbance, difficulty concentrating, loss of energy, hyperirritability, social withdrawal, negative rumination, feelings of hopelessness and helplessness, and suicidal thoughts. Was there any stress that seemed to precipitate your depression?"

"Yes sir, I got a 'Dear John letter' a few weeks ago—but I think I was already depressed when I got it."

"Depression is a very painful illness, but it is treatable and has a good prognosis. The thing you have to remember is that you are ill and can't function because of your illness—you aren't a wimp. No one can snap out of depression. What I am going to do is have Specialist Zecchinelli get you a bed in the clearing station. We are going to start you on an antidepressant—Tofranil [imipramine]—get you cleaned up, let you have some nice hot meals and rest up for a couple days. Zecchinelli will brief the medic who came with you, and I'm going to give your battalion surgeon a call as well. They were correct in their diagnosis and wise to refer you to us for treatment. It will take a couple of weeks before you see any beneficial effects from the medicine, but you definitely are going to feel better, and things are going to look better to you when that happens. We'll get you started here, and then we want you to check back with Specialist Zecchinelli on a regular basis until your symptoms are relieved. If you ever feel you are in a corner and starting to think seriously about suicide, we want you to contact someone immediately—us, your medic, your battalion surgeon. Is that understood?"

"Yes, sir."

Jones was admitted to the clearing station where he received a shower, clean clothing, warm food, and frequent visits by our technicians. Tofranil was started at 50 milligrams two hours before bedtime and increased to 150 milligrams by the time he left three days later. His battalion surgeon and medic kept an eye on him, and his duties were restricted for six weeks. He started feeling better in two weeks and had completely recovered in six weeks. We were very positive and directive in our approach to him when he first arrived, as we felt it was important to let him know that he would get better and that it was not his fault that he was ill. He also needed to know that he had people close by that he could turn to if he felt like harming himself.

I typed a modified version of the Menninger case study outline, which I gave to all of the technicians to follow when taking a history. The key to diagnosis in medicine is to obtain a good history. It takes time to get the information but is well worth it in the long run. If you take a substandard history, you are going to end up doing a substandard job. It was time consuming and considerable work for the technicians to go through this history with each client, but no one was trying to get out of doing work because work made the time go faster. There was also some pride in doing a very thorough job under primitive conditions. We had a beat-up, dusty typewriter, but we managed to turn out complete forensic and medical workups on the soldiers we evaluated. The morale of our mental health unit was always good.

COL. THOMAS W. SALMON, chief psychiatrist of the American Expeditionary Forces in World War I, developed the principles of proximity, immediacy, and expectancy. Treatment according to these principles meant that doctors saw their patients near where they got the symptoms, treated them right away, and expected them to return to duty with their units. These principles were forgotten at first in World War II but later rediscovered and used effectively. They were used immediately in Korea. Because I had read a good deal of the military psychiatry literature, I emphasized these principles to our technicians. Our initial reports and statistics seemed very optimistic in terms of seeing a low rate of combat reactions and having a high number of patients returned to their combat units.

As my experience in Vietnam grew, I recognized that there wasn't really a front as there had been in previous wars, nor were there extended periods of combat. We had air superiority, better medicines, and better screening of soldiers. (They were well screened during the initial years—by the time I arrived, most were draftees, and the screening was pretty loose.) Furthermore, the length of a tour was limited to one year. On the other hand, replacement soldiers were constantly coming in from the States, bringing with them some of the antiwar sentiment, racial tensions, and drug use that were problems at home. Because of these influences, it became apparent to me that the stresses in Vietnam were unique and were not being expressed in the same manner that had been described by previous military psychiatrists.

From our patients' histories we saw again and again that there was a huge gap in understanding and communication between the educated, suburban, white, inexperienced officers and the uneducated, urban, black, drafted enlisted men. The character and behavioral disorder cases we saw were usually associated with a Section 212 administrative discharge evaluation requested by command. Sometimes the individuals being evaluated were repeating patterns of impulsiveness, poor judgment, difficulty tolerating stress, difficulty delaying gratification, and resistance toward authority that they had exhibited prior to their entry into the military. These patterns continued in the army and led to their getting Article 15s and other disciplinary punishments until eventually they were kicked out.

We also saw soldiers who wet their beds, were sleepwalkers (a serious problem in a combat area), had phobias, were suicidal, injured themselves, had hysterical symptoms (paralysis, muteness, deafness, and blindness), were acutely psychotic and had deliriums, underlying medical problems, and stress symptoms resulting from combat. Some soldiers suffered from stress due to problems within their units. We kept track of our cases and looked for high-risk individuals and high-stress periods in units to try to prevent psychiatric casualties. The units would also refer men whom they could not tolerate. Regardless of diagnosis, we got these men out of the units to keep them from being killed.

I FLEW OR DROVE TO LAI KHE regularly to see our technicians and any patients that they wanted me talk with. We put on our gear and stooped or crouched as we entered the helicopter from the side. We fastened our seat belts and got used to flying at right angles to the ground when the helicopter banked into a steep curve. We flew to Dau Tieng, but less often. It was interesting to fly over the division area and view the checkerboard of green rice paddies. There were areas where B-52 strikes had left bomb craters the size of swimming pools. We would see huts in a grove of trees that reminded me of the farmhouses surrounded by islands of trees among the sea of corn and beans in the Midwest. The rubber trees were knocked down by huge Rome plows on each side of the highways. This produced a yellow-orange contrasting border to the forest of rubber trees. The helicopters were open on both sides and usually had a door gunner stationed on the copilot's side. It was cooler at the higher altitude, with a breeze generated by the propeller above. The pilot and copilot typically sat on their flak jackets in the belief that this would protect their genitals from taking a pot shot from below. We nearly bought it one day when our copter suddenly landed in a rice paddy. I looked forward and saw acne pimples on the neck of the youthful warrant officer piloting the helicopter. "Get the hell out of here," I yelled, and he lifted off almost directly into a Chinook that was flying above us. From then on, I checked the pilot's age and skin condition before boarding helicopters. Nearly half the deaths in helicopters in Vietnam were due to accidents.

WE SAW A NUMBER OF CLASSIC CASES of combat-induced stress. One morning I was quietly having my coffee and reading the *Stars and Stripes* when the silence was broken by Pattburg running into my office shouting that there was a dust off coming in for us.

Just then, Simon ran over from the clearing station. "Sir, we just got a call that dust off is bringing in a grunt from the First of the Twenty-eighth who is psychotic."

We soon heard the sound of the chopper descending. The technicians ran out to retrieve the patient, and I could hear muffled shouts and curses coming from within the stretchers. An arm stuck out between the strapped stretchers and waved about in an effort to grab or strike anyone within range. The technicians carried the stretchers to a cot in the clearing station and then undid the straps that held them together. The patient, fully clad in his dusty tropical fatigues and boots, was sweating, wild eyed, and agitated. The technicians held on to each extremity and placed him in the four cuff restraints that were tied to the bed. The patient seemed out of touch with reality.

"Holy Mary, pray for us now and in the hour of our death."

"Hey buddy, you're okay; this is a clearing station—you're safe," Zecchinelli told him. He was then offered something to drink and a cigarette.

The patient shouted about killing the VC and continued to thrash around on the cot, cursing and trying to get out of his restraints. He did nod yes to both the drink and the smoke, however. Simon gave him a drink of ice water, and Zecchinelli lit up a cigarette for him.

"Pretty rough out there today?" Simon asked.

"The dinks zapped my buddy Mike, man. I was talking to him, and they blew him away—they blew his head off, man."

"So how are you doing?" asked Zecchinelli.

"It should have been me—he was better than me—he was a good guy and they blew his head off."

Simon told him that he was going to get a shot to relax him and he would have a hot meal when he woke up.

One technique that I utilized in approaching potentially violent, agitated patients was to take their pulse and listen to their chest with a stethoscope. Most patients will calm down and show more control in a medical context. Most have faith that the doctor is there to help them. It also reminds patients and staff that I am a medical doctor who has specialized in psychiatry and that we need to pay attention to the medical as well as the psychological and social aspects of the case.

Simon gave the soldier a fifty-milligram injection of Thorazine, and the technicians and medics alternated keeping an eye on him while he slept through the night. He woke in the morning and had regained sufficient self-control to be let out of his restraints and eat breakfast. Zecchinelli, Simon, and I met with the patient.

"What happened yesterday?" asked Zecchinelli.

"We were on patrol and we got ambushed. My buddy Mike was right by me and caught a round in the head. I yelled for the medic, but there was nothing they could do for him. He was a good guy."

"Was this your first firefight?"

"Nah, I've been in a firefight before, and I've seen a couple other guys get hit, but Mike was my bro. I was just talking to him."

"Why don't you tell us what happened yesterday step by step," I asked.

"Well, our platoon was on patrol, and we were going down this trail single file when all of a sudden they hit us with automatic weapons. All hell broke loose. You could hear their AK-47s. We hit the dirt, and Mike caught a bullet right in the face as he started to get down. It looked like his head exploded."

"What were you doing?"

The patient began to cry. "I was on the ground. I crawled over to Mike and yelled for a medic, but I knew there was nothing they could do."

The technicians continued to listen to the patient and to offer sympathy and support. Two soldiers from his unit came to the clearing station to see him later in the day. He asked if he could return to his unit with his buddies and was allowed to do so. We told him to stop by and see us in the future if he felt the need. He didn't return.

An infantryman from B Company of the 1st of the 28th Infantry Regiment was brought to the clearing station in Lai Khe by dust-off helicopter. He was referred by his battalion surgeon for symptoms of combat exhaustion. Specialist Matthews saw the soldier and took a history.

"I can't sleep. I get nightmares of eyes coming closer and closer to me. Then I see a gun pointed at me and I wake up in a cold sweat; my heart is going a mile a minute, and I feel like I'm going to die."

"What do you do when this happens?"

"I make myself think of an ending to the dream. I get my M16 or a grenade, and I zap the eyes and the gun."

"Anything happened to you recently that might have produced these nightmares?"

"A couple weeks ago we were on patrol and got ambushed. We all hit the dirt. I was on the ground, and I heard the dinks walking by. They didn't see me but I could see the whites of their eyes, man."

"What happened?"

"I just laid there—I was scared shitless. I waited until I didn't hear anything for a long time; then I got on the radio. They must of heard me or somethin' because they fired and I caught a round in my shoulder. Our guys came in and chased them off. The medic patched me off, and I was dusted off to the clearing station where they fixed me up and gave me a shot and some medicine."

"This was a couple weeks ago?"

"Yeah. Then I started having these nightmares and couldn't sleep. I can't eat. I feel about half sick."

Specialist Matthews had one of the battalion surgeons order an initial injection of fifty milligrams of Thorazine to be followed with one hundred milligrams four times per day for a couple of days in the clearing station. Matthews continued to talk with the soldier during his stay. He let the soldier talk about his experience, his fear, and apprehension about returning to the field.

"It seems like your nightmares and fears worsened as your shoulder wound healed."

"I'm not trying to get out of going on patrol."

"No, I'm not saying that. I think the nightmares are your way of working through your feelings of anxiety about the whole experience. Probably if you'd been hit with those feelings at the time, you would have been overwhelmed and unable to radio in or do what you did."

"I'm sleeping and eating here with the medicine, but is this all going to come back when I get back there?"

"You did the right thing in the field, and you did the right thing in your dreams fighting back against the gun and the eyes—you'll do the right thing in the future, and you'll be okay."

The soldier returned to his unit. Matthews reviewed the case with me. He later checked on the soldier and reported that he not only returned to his unit but was going out on patrol and functioning well.

AMERICANS WERE NOT THE ONLY FORCES serving in Vietnam that experienced psychiatric casualties. One morning a criminal investigation officer and a Korean bird colonel named Park came to the psychiatric hootch. Falzone escorted them back to me, and Colonel Park introduced himself as the battalion executive officer. He had been sent to see me because he spoke English and had majored in philosophy in college. The Korean division brass thought philosophy was close to psychiatry and that he might be the best person to talk with me. He appeared to be in good physical shape, his tiger-striped fatigues were starched with knife-edge creases, and his boots were spit shined. Colonel Park asked if we had a tranquilizing dart or some sort of tranquilizing gas that they could borrow. I told him that we didn't.

He explained that a sergeant in one of their infantry units had been acting strangely for the past couple of weeks. The sergeant seemed to be frightened and was seen talking to himself and yelling out of the window at people who weren't there. For the past few days he had been slipping notes under his commanding officer's door, complaining that he was being persecuted. The colonel was angry with the commanding officer for not doing something earlier about the sergeant's bizarre behavior. Today, the colonel said, the sergeant began firing his rifle randomly out of his hootch—apparently to defend himself from his imagined persecutors. They had put sandbags around the hootch up to the roof so that he could only fire upward through the roof but were now asking for assistance to get him out of the hootch.

Someone had suggested that the American psychiatrist might have a tranquilizing dart, gas, or some sort of high-tech equipment to get him. We discussed the situation, and it seemed from the information we had that the sergeant didn't trust his fellow Koreans. The plan we developed was that I would go to the Korean division, stand under a light, and announce on a megaphone that I was an American psychiatrist who had come to take him to our division for care and treatment. We got into our jeeps and started driving to the Korean division. On the way I started thinking, "Wait a minute—I'm going to stand under a light and talk on a megaphone to a paranoid Korean with a loaded rifle?" The idea seemed less and less appealing as we approached the gate to the Korean division. Fortunately, just as we arrived, the sergeant walked out of the hootch and surrendered.

I was having a second cup of coffee one morning when Private First Class Pattburg led two American intelligence officers, a Vietnamese soldier, and a screaming Cambodian back to my desk. The escorts told Specialist Smith that the patient was a Cambodian scout who was "goofy." The previous day he had climbed a pole and started screaming. The fellow was obviously agitated and frightened. His eyes were rolling around in fear, and he was constantly moving. He was talking rapidly and loudly in Cambodian. The intelligence officers sat him down on a chair by my desk and told me that the Vietnamese interpreter supposedly knew some Cambodian. I spoke to the interpreter: "Ask him what he's afraid of." The interpreter asked the patient something in supposedly Cambodian, and the Cambodian babbled continuously for what seemed to about fifteen minutes in an excited agitated manner. When I asked what he had said, the interpreter responded, "Oh, he say many crazy things."

I told the intelligence officers that the fellow appeared to be psychotic, but I couldn't tell them any more than that. We really could not treat him under these circumstances because I didn't know if his condition was caused by an organic problem such as drugs, trauma, or disease or reflected a functional psychosis. I heard later that the intelligence officers took him to a Vietnamese civilian hospital and no one there knew what to do with him either. The intelligence officers then put the scout in a helicopter and flew him into Cambodia near his home village and released him.

A REPORTER FOR *STARS AND STRIPES* once asked me to evaluate and explain an interview just conducted with a sergeant who reported an out-of-body experience in Vietnam. In the interview, the sergeant described how his jeep hit a land mine, which exploded. He said that he found himself up in the air in a bright light and that he felt very comfortable and good. He could see his own body on the ground. He said that he knew he had a choice of going into the light or returning to earth. He chose to return, and as soon as he did, he found himself lying on the ground in pain. I told the reporter that in psychiatry we referred to this as depersonalization. The patient is overwhelmed with physical or emotional pain and walls it off. I gave the analogy of a surgeon doing an operation. Surgeons don't think they are sticking knives into their patients but instead wall off their emotions and think objectively about cutting through the skin, cutting though the external fascia, and so on.

The sergeant read my comments and said, "That's fine, but I know what I experienced." Interestingly, after this article was published, a number of other patients in hospitals in Vietnam revealed that they had experienced similar phenomena. When asked why they hadn't told anyone of their experiences, they explained, "We didn't want them to think we were crazy."

We saw several similar cases over the year that Specialists Zecchinelli and Falzone came to identify as a new psychiatric syndrome in Vietnam. They called it the "PR syndrome." The first case came to us in a dust-off helicopter. When it landed, Simon, Zecchinelli, and Falzone ran to the copter and carried the patient "sandwich" into the clearing station. When they unstrapped the stretchers, they found an agitated Puerto Rican soldier who appeared frightened and agitated and was mumbling in a mixture of Spanish and English. He was wide eyed and soaked in sweat. He constantly thrashed around on the cot. Smith and Ortiz spoke Spanish, but none of us could understand what he was saying well enough to take a psychiatric history. He calmed down as the technicians and corpsmen spoke softly with him and got him some food and drink. We told him that he appeared frightened, and he admitted he hadn't been sleeping or eating. After he had eaten, we offered him a sedative to help him sleep. The techs stayed with him practically one to one until he woke up the next day. Coherent, he described his experience.

"We were walking in the field on patrol, and I looked and saw *mi madre* walking through the field—it was real, man, I saw her clear. I pointed at her and started calling to her, and the medic came over and held me down and gave me a shot. I got very nervous, man. I couldn't eat or sleep or nothing."

"Did you still see your mama?" Ortiz asked.

"Yes, I saw her clearly."

"Did she talk to you?" Smith asked.

"No, I hollered at her, but she just smiled."

"Were you scared?"

"Si, I was scared."

"Do you still see her?"

"No, I know now it wasn't real—but I thought she was really there."

The patients showing these transient symptoms were all Puerto Rican. They all presented with tremulousness, excessive sweating, and vivid hallucinations of their mother appearing in the field before them. This was a transient situational type of disturbance, and recovery was quick with sedation, rehydration, food, and rest.

IN SOME INSTANCES SOLDIERS were sent because their units couldn't stand them or were afraid of them. In these situations, regardless of diagnosis, we got them out of their units one way or another, because we knew it was unlikely that they would survive if we didn't. If we decided to go through medical channels, I referred the patient to the 93rd Evacuation Hospital in Long Binh and would call the admitting doctor to advise that the soldier could not return to his unit. The soldier would then either be medically evacuated out of country or reassigned to a support unit near the 93rd Evacuation Hospital. I knew the doctors there, and they understood that I didn't send people on a whim for evacuation. It was rare that we would tell the referring unit to discharge the man by giving him an AR 212 administrative discharge. It took time to process a soldier out of the unit administratively, and leaving the man in the unit while he was being processed out put him at risk.

In one case, an enlisted man from the 2nd Battalion (Mechanized) of the 2nd Infantry Regiment was referred to us by his sergeant. The enlisted man said that his first sergeant just told him to go see a shrink. The first sergeant was angry with him because he refused to go to the field and then did poorly when given a job in the rear. The sergeant told us, "I want this coward straightened out ASAP." The technician took a history and determined that the enlisted man was very immature, lacked self-confidence, was nervous and depressed, and had a history of seldom completing work assignments. He had joined the army in an attempt to make something of himself as a mechanic. When first sent to Vietnam, he was assigned to be a tank gunner. He had been in several ambushes, subjected to friendly fire, and once was blown off a tank when it hit a mine. He was unhappy that he wasn't assigned as a mechanic and felt that he was continually pressured because he was told that he would be returned to the field if he made any mistakes. He had no friends in the platoon. Specialist Falzone thought the prognosis was guarded but felt there was a chance the soldier could stay on his job. Falzone walked two miles to the soldier's unit, where he was met with considerable hostility by the first sergeant, who told him, "These soft college kids are trying to act like shrinks and let worthless cowards off easy." The first sergeant's solution was to court-martial the soldier. The company commander seemed to favor the sergeant's view.

Falzone talked with men in the unit and learned that there were administrative problems in the unit in general. The first sergeant and commander were bearing down on the men they identified as problem soldiers in an effort to administratively discharge them and clean up the unit. Falzone discussed the case with Captain Pabst, who arranged for the enlisted man to transfer to a new company.

WE SAW SOLDIERS who were referred for nocturia (bed wetting) because the odor bothered the other members of their unit. One patient in this category was assigned to a maintenance company. He was embarrassed and said he had always had the problem and had tried avoid it by not drinking fluids at night and by setting an alarm to get up during the night. Unfortunately, these measures were insufficient to control the problem. I put him on a low dose of Tofranil, used at that time for children with nocturia, and it seemed to control the problem. The technicians saw several men from the field who had a problem with somnambulism (sleepwalking). This, of course, put both them and their units in danger. The standard treatment in the field was to tie the individual to a tree or other substantial object to prevent the soldier from getting up and walking about during the night. This solved the problem and, as far as I know, had no long-term harmful effects on the somnambulist.

SOMETIMES A PSYCHOLOGICAL CONFLICT such as the stress of choosing between the desire to flee and the moral obligation to face danger can cause a conversion disorder in which the conflict resolves itself in the form of a debilitating physical symptom. In one case, a soldier was brought in with paralysis of his lower extremities. He had been in country for one month and had engaged in his first firefight. He had dropped to the ground and was unable to get up when the fighting ceased. The medic checked him and found that he had not been wounded, had reflexes in his lower extremities, and that the patient ignored his paralysis (*la belle indifference,* characteristic of hysteria). He was air-evacuated to the clearing station in Lai Khe, where a battalion surgeon also failed to find an organic cause for his paralysis. He was then brought by ambulance to our clearing station for further evaluation and treatment. When the technicians and I opened the back of the ambulance, the soldier was sitting holding his M16 with both hands. I asked him for the weapon, and he handed it over. He said his sergeant thought it would make him feel more secure having it along. The technicians put him on a stretcher and brought him into the clearing station.

Falzone asked how he had come to be paralyzed. He replied that he was in a firefight and dropped to the ground. When he later tried to get up, he couldn't. He admitted that he had been really scared. Specialist Falzone told him that we see quite a few guys with similar symptoms, and they all say they were scared. He motioned toward two other patients in the clearing station. They confirmed how scared they had been during their first firefight and said that anyone who says he wasn't is lying or just messed up.

Falzone explained the general psychological dynamics of a conversion reaction. One part of your brain tells you to get the heck out of there and save your skin, but another part tells you that you should stay and fight. The paralysis is a way of getting you out of danger in the field and also keeps you from getting in trouble with the army or with your conscience. The soldier told him that he wasn't faking it—he couldn't move his legs. Falzone said he understood; this was an unconscious, psychological thing. He said that once he was given medicine and rested up with food and something to drink, he would start being able to move his legs.

The next morning the patient felt better and said he had "really sacked out." Falzone told him that he would be able to move his legs a little today. He should move them around, and the medics would help him walk. Later that day the soldier reported he was ready to try to walk. The medics helped him take a few steps, and then he was returned to his cot with positive feedback regarding his progress. He continued to eat and drink and was again sedated at night.

Falzone saw him the next morning and told him that he would be able to walk today. He was going to ask one of the officers to restrict him from field duty for now. The soldier protested that he wasn't trying to get out of anything. Falzone said he knew that, but guys with these symptoms aren't usually able to return to field duty right after they get out of here. He would feel better and stronger every day. When he was ready to rejoin his buddies in the field, his battalion surgeon would clear him to return to full duty.

The soldier was able to walk and return to his unit after two nights in the clearing station. Typically, patients with conversion and hysterical symptoms such as paralysis, mutism, and blindness could be quickly relieved of their symptoms through a Sodium Amytal interview (narcotherapy; discussed in greater detail in chapter 11) or by simple positive suggestion such as the kind Falzone used in this case. Few, however, actually succeeded in returning to field duty. Usually, these patients would experience a relapse of symptoms when they attempted to go back. This patient was a rare exception. His restriction was lifted, and he did return to field duty with the encouragement and support of the men in his unit.

SOME INDIVIDUALS WHO SEEMED DESTINED to fail in the military ended up making it. Psychiatrists were not good at predicting who would be successful. We had a young enlisted man from a transportation company walk in, self-referred, for evaluation of symptoms of anxiety and insomnia. He was tall, thin, and dark-haired, wearing the usual tropical fatigues, jungle boots, and floppy hat. He appeared to be mildly depressed and somewhat anxious. We learned that he had come from a broken home and that his childhood was characterized by emotional and economic deprivation. He was expelled from high school because of difficulties with teachers and truancy. He had been arrested several times for various charges, including assault, burglary, car theft, and public intoxication. When given a choice by a judge to enlist in the military or go to jail, he had chosen the former. In basic training he acquired several Article 15s for AWOL and for insubordination.

There was a note on his medical records of an evaluation by the mental hygiene unit at his post in the States, where he was given the diagnosis of psychopathic personality. The psychiatrist noted that the soldier had no insight into his problems and that he saw himself as a victim of fate. I was surprised to note, when I saw him, that he had only two weeks to go on his year's tour of duty in Vietnam and that his record had been clean during the fifty weeks he had served in the division.

I called his commanding officer in an effort to learn what rehabilitative techniques he had employed to salvage this young man. The CO said, "I didn't do anything in particular, Doc—he seems like a good kid to me. Heck, I got into a few scrapes myself as a youngster, and the military straightened me out." Apparently the CO identified with the young man and liked him. He saw him as a "good kid" and expected that he was going to do fine and make it through the year as everyone else would. The enlisted man recognized the respect and positive feelings from his CO and didn't exhibit his usual pattern of rebellious, provocative behavior. In addition, the enlisted man was a little older, more mature, and possibly wiser.

His DEROS (date expected to return from overseas) was only two weeks away, and we believed that his anxiety and mild depression were related to his being short. He met with Zecchinelli a couple of times to talk about the experience of being short in Vietnam. He was able to leave country two weeks later and functioned adequately in his unit until his departure.

THE TECHNICIANS KNEW the importance of a mental status examination. They were to alert a doctor if there were any signs of disorientation, memory difficulties, dizziness, blurred or double vision, or lack of coordination. The reason was that some physical ailments vividly express themselves in the form of psychological symptoms and can be overlooked if not considered properly.

For example, an infantryman from the 2nd Battalion, 33rd Artillery, was referred by his unit commander because he was behaving strangely. Specialist Falzone saw the young man, who appeared to be delirious. At times he would appear to be briefly in touch with his surroundings, but then he would lapse into a state of confusion. He was unable to give a logical history and appeared mixed up and disoriented. He couldn't give the date, identify his unit, or describe where he was at the time. He was sweating profusely and had a low-grade temperature. I asked the internists to look at him and work him up for the cause of what appeared to be an organic brain syndrome. Subsequent testing of his blood showed the presence of malaria parasites, and he was evacuated out of country with cerebral malaria. We saw additional cases of cerebral malaria over the year's tour of duty. Even though the base camps were fogged for mosquitoes and orders were to take antimalarial drugs, about 75,000 servicemen contracted malaria in Vietnam and 120 of them died.

On occasion we saw soldiers who initially appeared to be depressed but who were also disoriented and unable to calculate simple problems, and who suffered memory difficulties and volatile emotional states. Again, workup by specialists in internal medicine and neurology at the evacuation hospital demonstrated slow brain waves, elevated liver-function studies, and sometimes elevated renal-function studies. These symptoms were caused by exposure to the toxic fumes from burning C-4 explosive. Soldiers in the field, despite repeated warnings from medical officers, would use C-4 as a cooking fuel. The fumes from the explosive are extremely toxic, and exposure can damage the brain, liver, and kidneys. I believe that this provides an important lesson for those who advocate having nonmedically trained professionals evaluate new patients, much less prescribe medications for them. Even in the medically screened, relatively healthy, young population of the military, it is necessary to have a medically trained psychiatrist available who can diagnose the possible physical causes of the patient's symptoms. We saw confusion and disorientation due to physical causes such as low blood sugar, thyroid problems, dehydration and electrolyte imbalance, anemia, drug and alcohol toxicity, and head trauma. The prevalence of underlying medical causes of seemingly mental symptoms is much higher in the unscreened, older, civilian medical population.

PROBLEMS THAT WERE INITIALLY PERCEIVED as psychological sometimes had no medical basis at all. In one memorable matter, the CO of the "Black Lions" (2nd Battalion, 28th Infantry) called to say that he was sending one of his men to us for evaluation. It was possible to communicate with virtually any unit in the division by a combination of phone and radio patches. The process was very frustrating and time consuming, however. Typically, we would spend half an hour getting patched through to some commander in the field who would then be cut off, and we would have to start the whole process over again. The soldier the CO was referring had told his sergeant that he had been hearing voices.

The soldier arrived later in the day accompanied by his sergeant. He was a good-looking young man of average height. He was wearing a steel pot and had a layer of red dust on his fatigues and boots, indicative of field duty. He seemed to interact well with his sergeant and cooperated during the interviews with us. Falzone took an initial history, and then I interviewed him. We were unable to find much in the way of psychopathology other than his description of hearing voices and scraping noises at night. He had a normal range of emotional expression, and his thoughts appeared to be logical and appropriate. He just seemed to be an average, pleasant kid. He couldn't make out what the voices were saying, but the situation bothered him and interfered with his ability to sleep. We returned him to his unit, reporting that we had found nothing to treat, but they should keep an eye on him and send him back if they noticed anything further.

A few weeks later I ran into his company commander and asked how the soldier was doing. "Oh, don't worry about him, Doc," the commander replied. "We found a tunnel under his tent." The soldier had been hearing Viet Cong digging and talking in the tunnel at night when he was trying to sleep.

AS I BECAME ORIENTED to my new surroundings, my first professional activity involved organizing my treatment team and starting to provide direct patient services. We all wanted to be busy, and this was a familiar, comfortable endeavor that we could immediately become involved with in the division. Once we were "in business" taking care of patients in the division, we could then think about looking for trends, noting stresses that were unique to Vietnam, and trying to figure out ways to prevent some of the psychiatric casualties we were treating.

The Viet Cong's Perception of Mental Illness

Mental illness is seen as spiritual possession by many Vietnamese, who have specialists in the magico-religious realm who will exorcize a bad force. Depression and anxiety were considered to be spiritual in nature. Sometimes an amulet of cloth containing a Buddhist verse is worn around the wrist or the neck. In October 1994 a delegation of psychiatrists and mental health workers traveled to Vietnam to study post-traumatic stress disorder among the Vietnamese. They noted that medicine was at a third-world level. There were 360 psychiatrists in country and a few psychologists. Psychiatric facilities were very primitive. Medical professionals in Vietnam tend to view PTSD as a physical condition caused by trauma, such as the concussion of artillery shells or bombs. Treatment tended to be somatic, utilizing Russian techniques such as behavioral modification, *dauerschlaft* (sleep therapy), and electroconvulsive therapy.

DURING MY TOUR I was interested in learning more about the psychiatric treatment among the Vietnamese. We arranged to visit the Nguyen Van Hoai Mental Hospital in Bien Hoa near Saigon. On the scheduled day we donned our gear, grabbed our cameras, and then headed out in two jeeps for Bien Hoa. The hospital was in an area close to the airport where I had come into country. By now the scenery was familiar because I had driven by the same rice paddies and the same villages several times. Although I was acclimated to the temperatures and felt comfortable, I remembered how my clothing had been soaked with sweat and how foreign everything had looked the first time I traveled this road.

The hospital, built by the French in 1919, was surrounded by a stone wall that screened the grounds and the main building from public view. The wall and the hospital were painted a light yellow. The gate was covered with a tiled roof and an arched sign written in Vietnamese. It was largely a custodial institution until 1950, when Nguyen Van Hoai established a more humanitarian approach to care by removing the patients from chains and permitting open units for the patients who were less severely ill. The only other civilian care facilities in Vietnam were the Cho Quan Hospital in Saigon, with approximately 150 psychiatric beds, and a general hospital in Hue, which had a few psychiatric beds.

We drove through the gate and parked in the large courtyard in front of the hospital. The institution, like the civilian medical hospitals, was an open structure. There were large, open windows and open patio areas. Unlike the Vietnamese medical hospitals, there were no families camping outside the hospital buildings to supply nursing and housekeeping assistance. In addition, there were no food vendors selling provisions for families and patients.

Drs. To Duong Hiep and Nguyen Tuan Ahn, wearing long white coats, came out to greet us warmly. They were accompanied by a Vietnamese nurse dressed in a white uniform with a traditional nursing cap. They told us that American psychiatrists had worked at the hospital over the years as volunteers and had helped develop the treatment programs. Dr. Ahn was stockier than Dr. Hiep. Both were polite and spoke excellent English.

The doctors told us that they had about two thousand patients in the hospital with severe chronic mental illnesses and that most of these patients would remain at the hospital for several months. The medicines they used were primarily chlorpromazine (Thorazine) and thioridazine (Mellaril). These were two of the first major tranquilizers available to treat psychiatric disorders. At Di An, we used Thorazine to produce the *dauerschlaft* induced for the treatment of acute psychosis. The doctors also used amitriptyline (Elavil) and imipramine (Tofranil), which are two first-generation antidepressants. Our impression in 1969 was that Dr. Ahn and Dr. Hiep were very knowledgeable about the use and side effects of the medicines they were using.

Dr. Ahn excused himself and his nurse to care for patients while Dr. Hiep led the tour of the facility. He told us that Dr. Ahn had trained in France, whereas he had been trained on the job in Vietnam. He said that he would love to go to France or the United States for formal training in psychiatry, but he couldn't leave the country because he and the other psychiatrists were employed by the government for the duration of the war. This impressed us. Most of us were required to serve two years in the army, but these doctors were required to serve as long as the war lasted. They did not comment on the war, nor did they complain about their patient load or their indefinite servitude. Like most Vietnamese, they were soft spoken, humble, and polite.

Dr. Hiep showed us plastic, color-coded medication cups lined up on trays for the patients taking medicines in the hospital. He said that they had only one nurse in the hospital. Each morning, she would set up all of the patient's medications for the day in color-coded cups so the aides would know which cup to give at noon, supper, and bedtime.

As we walked through the grounds, we tried to guess the patients' diagnoses based on their appearance and behavior. Many of the symptoms were so severe that this was fairly easy. A suspicious, hyperalert patient who kept to himself was identified as being paranoid and confirmed by Dr. Hiep. A disheveled female patient who was talking out loud to the voices in her head was diagnosed as hebephrenic. An immobile patient who demonstrated waxy flexibility (when the patient's hand was elevated, she kept it in this position) was observed to be catatonic. We saw euphoric, hyperactive, manic patients as well as some who appeared severely depressed.

Dr. Hiep showed us one of the occupational therapy programs. Some patients were squatting on the hospital patio preparing vegetables and cooking a meal for the general population of patients under the supervision of hospital aides. These were duties we had seen performed by patients' families in the general medical hospital. Operant conditioning, a form of behavioral therapy, was used with some patients. The occupational therapy program was instituted in 1963 by the wives of the diplomatic corps. Up to one hundred patients were involved in tasks such as weaving, furniture making, and painting. Dr. Peter Bourne noted in 1966 that their most economically successful projects were making crossbows and punji stakes to sell as souvenirs to Americans.

While we were touring the hospital, some nearby explosions caused our group to become noticeably tense. We were in an unfamiliar area and did not have a military escort. In addition, we were unsure how safe or secure the area was. Dr. Hiep sensed our anxiety and said, "Don't worry. This is a very safe place. The Viet Cong are afraid of mental illness." He explained that during the entire time that he had been on the staff, the hospital had never been bothered by the VC because they were afraid of psychiatric patients and psychiatric illness. When he explained that there was a stigma associated with psychiatric illness in Vietnam, we told him that the same was true in the United States.

I DID HAVE A CHANCE to visit with a few Vietnamese throughout the year and was able to learn something about their social structures. My general impression is that the Vietnamese are a very gentle, kind people who are very much oriented toward their families and share many of the same concerns and interests in life that Americans have. I had several lengthy conversations with the Vietnamese woman who served as a translator during MEDCAP visits. Once, while talking about the difficulty that parents have with teenagers, she said that the Vietnamese have a saying that the baby is heavy on the mother's lap while the teenager is heavy on her heart. I told her it was the same in my home country. She also said that the war had cost many lives, the bombing had destroyed much of the land, but the biggest and most prolonged damage was the disruption of families.

There were Vietnamese workers in nearly every base camp who were Viet Cong. When the B-52s would bomb tunnels near the base camps, some Vietnamese workers would cry because they feared that their friends and family were being killed. Sappers were explosive experts who would crawl through the perimeter defenses of base camps and throw satchel charges into hootches to blow up U.S. and South Vietnamese personnel. Prior to my arrival in Vietnam, the Vietnamese barber in Lai Khe had been killed trying to get through the concertina wire at night with a satchel charge. He was said to be a funny, likable guy who joked with his GI customers. He was held up as an example of a popular Vietnamese civilian working in the base camp who was intent on killing as many GIs as he could.

MANY VIETNAMESE BELIEVED in the supernatural. They felt that they could be possessed by a spirit because of their own errors or neglect of their ancestors, or by not being buried in their homeland. These beliefs were exploited by the psychological operations units (PSYOPS or PSYWAR) during the war in Vietnam. Psychological operations were conducted by several organizations operating under the control of the Joint United States Public Affairs Office.

During one of my visits to Saigon, Al Breeland, a Special Forces doctor, asked me if I would be interested in visiting the PSYOPS people, who distributed propaganda and were headquartered in Saigon. I very much wanted to meet them and see what they were doing. The U.S. psychological operations personnel in Vietnam were referred to as "mind benders." Their motto was "Capture their minds, and their hearts and souls will follow." This was an offshoot of the campaign to "Win the hearts and minds of the people," which was modified by the troops to "Grab 'em by the balls, and their hearts will follow." Most of the men conducting these operations in Vietnam had been Madison Avenue advertising types in civilian life. Their purpose was to (1) reduce the morale and combat efficiency of the enemy; (2) provoke mass dissension within and defection from enemy combat units; (3) support our own cover and deception operations; and (4) promote cooperation, unity, and morale within our own units.

I did not work with psychological operations professionally but was curious about what sort of people were involved in PSYWAR and how they were conducting it. Al Breeland and I stopped by their headquarters. There were several young officers in starched and creased fatigues, spit-shined boots, and ascots, making chilled martinis in a shaker. They spoke in Madison Avenue phrases:

"Let's toss this one on the water and see if it floats"; "Just for ducks"; "Get our ducks in a row." They welcomed us and poured martinis, although it was early in the day. They were glad to have a psychiatrist and a Special Forces doctor visit them and willingly described their various projects.

They exploited the Vietnamese fear of the supernatural by having helicopters fly over the VC and NVA troops at night with flashing lights and loudspeakers broadcasting recordings in Vietnamese of a spirit wailing and moaning that he could never be at rest because he had been killed in South Vietnam and couldn't be buried in his homeland in the North. This was consistent with what I had heard about the Vietnamese believing in spirits and the need to be buried in their home ground to put their spirits at rest. Sometimes we heard these activities being conducted near our base camp. Theoretically, this should have been frightening to the Vietnamese enemy troops. Even though we could not understand the words and did not share in the superstitions about spirits, we found it to be rather scary.

The PSYOPS guys told us that they had intelligence that one NVA unit brought their wives and children with them, resulting in a lot of problems. PSYOPS flew helicopters over the unit, dropped leaflets, and broadcast this message over the speakers: "Women of the NVA division, your husbands are neglecting you. They will die in a strange land, and their souls will never be at peace." Then they dropped leaflets and broadcast this message: "Men of the NVA division, your women are unfaithful to you while you are in the field. They are having sex with your commanding officers while you are away." Finally, they made another pass with leaflets and this broadcast: "Commanders of the NVA division—look how screwed up your units are!"

The PSYOPS people would drop leaflets offering a safe-conduct pass, money, medical care, and food to individuals who defected from the NVA and VC. If they knew the troops were hungry, they would soak the leaflets in Nuoc Mam (a fermented fish sauce that is a staple of the Vietnamese diet) to appeal to their stomachs as well as their minds. They also had leaflets describing the mighty B-52, which couldn't be seen or heard in advance of bomb drops, and a leaflet with pictures of Maj. Gen. Tran Do alive and dead. He had been killed in the Cholon suburb of Saigon. This was part of the Chieu Hoi "open arms" amnesty program to encourage defection among the North Vietnamese and Viet Cong. In 1968 about 13 percent of the Viet Cong who were neutralized rallied to the government side. PSYOPS let the enemy know that amnesty was available through their leaflets and broadcasts, but a good many of the VC who took advantage of the program were responding to the heavy losses sustained by the NVA and the increasing government control of the villages throughout South Vietnam. We did see some kids on a MEDCAP who wore Chieu Hoi ("I surrender") T-shirts that someone had made as a joke. It didn't occur to the PSYOPS people to ask for any ideas from me as a psychiatrist, nor did I feel the urge to offer any suggestions. Propaganda is related to psychiatry and psychology in that psychology is utilized to understand the enemy and to develop strategies to influence them as a group. However, it is not an area in which I felt competent to make any suggestions. Similarly, Madison Avenue advertising firms do not, to my knowledge, seek input from psychiatrists on how to motivate buyers or improve company images.

Propaganda is a fascinating topic. In the base camp at night I occasionally listened to the Chinese Communist radio propaganda broadcasts. I could not understand their purpose. The messages were so boring, monotone, and self-serving that they would never persuade anyone to adopt their way of thinking. A typical broadcast would begin with the Chinese national anthem followed by a woman's voice reciting slogans such as "The Chinese textile workers, armed with the word of Mao, achieved 125 percent of their yearly production goals" and "The Chinese steel workers, armed with the word of Mao, increased their production by 100 percent." If I had wanted to produce a broadcast that would encourage people to dislike the Chinese, I could not have done much better.

CHAPTER 6

Drugs and Alcohol

O ne morning, a couple of weeks after arriving in Vietnam, I went through my usual wake-up constitutional routine, had breakfast in the mess hall, saluted the technicians, and was sitting at my desk having my coffee and staring out the back of the psychiatric hootch. Zecchinelli walked over to my desk and asked, "Sir?"

"Yeah, what is it?"

"Did you know that you are a part of the division drug education team?"

"No, I didn't even know we had a drug education team."

"Well we do, and you're on it."

Zecchinelli then presented me with a file put together by my predecessor that contained regulations, articles, and a prepared speech by the former division psychiatrist on the evils and consequences of drug use. The folder contained Regulation 190-3, titled "On the Detection and Suppression of Marijuana and Illegal Drugs," which ordered a program for suppressing drug use. The supposedly comprehensive program included orientation, education, monthly inspections in unit areas, and the reporting of drug abuse.

DRUG USAGE BECAME RAMPANT in the United States during the psychedelic era of the 1960s, and draftees assigned to Vietnam brought their habits with them. The combination of previous drug use in the States, stress, and easy access to inexpensive drugs ensured their continued use in Vietnam. The military tended to identify drug use as a serious problem, although the alcohol abuse by many officers and NCOs was generally accepted. Neither alcohol nor drugs had been identified as major problems by military psychiatrists prior to the Vietnam War. Self-medication with drugs and alcohol, along with racism, were among the new problems confronting us in Vietnam.

In 1969 the armed forces increased emphasis on apprehending and punishing drug users. Undesirable discharges and long prison sentences were recommended. Drug education programs were implemented, and articles warning about the dangers of drugs were common in the military media; for example, an article from *Stars and Stripes* titled "Say Pot Causes Psychosis among Viet-G.I.s"; and a December 1969 article in *Inside the Turret,* published at Fort Knox and reprinted from the *First Army Voice,* titled "Can Damage Mind, No Medical Benefits, Drug Abuse Doesn't Make Sense." This article cautioned that even mild forms of marijuana were not totally safe and that the stronger forms could cause psychotic reactions in almost anyone. These media stated that the use of marijuana was particularly hazardous, emphasizing that its use could cause concepts of time and space to be radically distorted and could impair the ability to respond to emergencies. They also advised that using pot violated federal law and the penalties could be as high as ten years in the penitentiary and a twenty-thousand-dollar fine for the first offense. Media directed toward officers asserted that marijuana was a dangerous drug that produced mental and physical effects and was associated with a notable increase in crime.

I knew that drug use was rampant in the United States. Most of the men coming into Vietnam had already experimented with drugs, and some were regular users. Enlisted men were not permitted to buy hard liquor in Vietnam. They could buy beer for ten cents a can, but drugs were cheap and readily available. Alcohol was the intoxicant of choice for the officers. This resulted in a division between the officers and NCOs, who were "juicers," and the enlisted men, who were "heads." Up until about 1968, alcohol use was also high among enlisted men. Clubs for enlisted men had been established in the base-camp areas, and beer was shipped to the troops in the field. By 1969 marijuana was ubiquitous in

Vietnam and was potent and cheap. You could buy a six-pound sandwich bag full of very pure "rope" for fifty dollars. A kid on the side of the road would sell you a joint for fifty cents in our area. In Saigon you could get a joint for twenty cents. It was estimated that 25 percent of the soldiers in Vietnam used marijuana. There were reports by some psychiatrists that men in the field used marijuana to reduce their anxiety but that support troops seemed to use larger quantities and were more likely to develop toxic psychoses.

Opium and heroin were easy to obtain, and by 1970 the latter had become a significant problem. Heroin that was nearly 100 percent pure was available for two to three dollars per dose, opium at one dollar per dose, and morphine at five dollars per dose. A survey of two divisions in 1970 revealed that 11 to 14 percent of the men had used heroin since their arrival in Vietnam. A subsequent survey in 1974 suggested that 34 percent of the troops in Vietnam had commonly used heroin. At that time the number of reported American heroin users in Vietnam exceeded the number of reported heroin users in the United States (81,300 users in Vietnam compared to 68,000 in the United States). LSD and mushrooms were also used by troops in Vietnam.

Binoctal was sold in civilian pharmacies in Vietnam as a headache remedy. It was a potent barbiturate produced by ISH Laboratories in Paris, France. The tablets looked like aspirin and contained fifty milligrams of Amytal and seventy milligrams of Seconal. These pills could be purchased over the counter in any Vietnamese drugstore without a prescription. While I was in Nha Trang for the USARV Psychiatric Conference, I went to a local pharmacy in the village and bought a package of twenty Binoctal tablets in a round plastic case for one dollar. There was no hesitation on the part of the pharmacist during the sale.

The Vietnamese peasants chewed betel nut, which stained their lips cherry red and blackened their teeth. It had a narcotic effect similar to that of opium. It never caught on with the GIs but was available to be picked by the peasants. As far as I know, the Vietnamese had no laws against using or selling drugs. The kids who sold pot openly approached soldiers to offer their wares, and opium dens operated publicly. To my knowledge, the use of marijuana, opium, heroin, Binoctal, and alcohol was not a major health problem among the Vietnamese civilian population.

EACH DIVISION HAD a drug education team. In the 1st Infantry Division, the team consisted of the division surgeon, the division psychiatrist, the division chaplain, a lawyer from the JAG office, and a Criminal Investigation Division (CID) officer. The premise was that the division surgeon would talk about the medical problems associated with drug use, the lawyer would describe the legal penalties for using drugs, and the chaplain would talk about drug use as a sin. The CID officer talked about the various drugs that were being used in Vietnam, described how they were used, and presented a display board showing the drugs and drug paraphernalia commonly used by the troops in Vietnam. My assignment was to explain that drugs made you crazy.

The overall approach reminded me of the venereal disease lectures in high school that relied on films and pictures of the most severe cases of venereal disease to frighten young people from having premarital sex. I knew that this approach was not very effective at controlling the spread of sexually transmitted diseases and did not expect it to work much better when applied to drug education. My predecessor left before I arrived in the division and was not available to brief me about his experience with the program. His drug program file contained a speech that he gave at the educational sessions and essentially said that drugs could make you paranoid, psychotic, depressed, and manic. Apparently the team went to a different unit in the division each month to put on a prevention program, and I was expected to attend and participate. The next program was in a few days, so I reviewed the material in the file to try to prepare myself for the presentation.

On the appointed day I met with the other team members outside the clearing station to board the helicopters. Because this was my first time with the team and I had not been oriented by my predecessor, I was not required to speak. The enlisted men had been assembled in the company area and were sitting on the ground, as ordered, to "learn about drugs." The various team members stood in front of the assembly and gave their presentations. As the CID officer presented his display board with the various drugs and paraphernalia, I thought—what if he had different brands of booze and martini glasses, old-fashioned glasses, highball glasses, shakers, stirrers, olives, cherries (i.e., alcohol paraphernalia) and showed these to a group of officers while telling them that some of the drinkers use this type of glass while others use this and some put cherries in their drinks but that other use olives. The enlisted men's faces expressed their boredom. Some smirked and whispered how stupid this was. I made up my mind I wasn't going to give the same type of canned speech.

I spoke the following month at the next educational program. I told the enlisted men that we knew that many of them used marijuana and noted that drugs were plentiful, accessible, and cheap. I mentioned that alcohol was the drug of choice for the officers and NCOs, partly as a generational thing and partly because alcohol was inexpensive and readily available to this group. I told the men that we were not expecting everyone to come in and ask for help with drugs or alcohol. If a person used either in moderation and it didn't impair their functioning on the job, we didn't see it as a problem. However, we had found that in every unit there were a few men with serious psychiatric problems who often presented as the unit "heads." These men flaunted their drug use by wearing marijuana leaf badges and peace emblems, putting "FTA" on their helmets, and talking "drug talk." When they were disciplined, they blamed the fact that they were being picked on because of their drug use. I suggested that it might be helpful to encourage this group of individuals to see us so that we could address the problems underlying their behavior. I could see that the majority of the enlisted men were nodding and understood that flaunting drug use typically reflected other problems.

I wasn't asked to participate in the next educational consultation because my talk was considered unacceptable by some of the other team members. It did not conform to the division policy on drug use and was inconsistent with the scare approach to drug prevention. Lieutenant Colonel Hefner, who served as both the division surgeon and the medical battalion commander, understood my position on the matter and agreed with it. He was in the minority, and when I discussed it, he didn't want to make an issue of it. He told me about the army general who was the head of medicine in Vietnam a few years before who had suggested that prostitutes be evaluated and treated by army doctors as a way of preventing venereal disease among the troops. The newspapers in the United States picked up on this, and there was a huge outcry from mothers back home who felt that the army was trying to corrupt their

CHAPTER 6

young, innocent sons. In response to the negative publicity, the general was relieved of his command. I got the point. The official policy was that drugs were bad, and we were supposed to pretend that only a few bad eggs used them. The official military position on drugs and public opinion at home could not be bucked, and being kicked off the team just meant I didn't have to do something I didn't want to do anyway. Personally, I did not believe that drug use significantly diminished the military effectiveness of the division in Vietnam. I was aware that all of my technicians, except Walt Smith, used marijuana. They functioned well in their jobs, and there was never a reason to bring the subject up. They knew that I drank booze with the officers.

WE SAW A FEW drug-precipitated psychoses and a few soldiers with toxic psychosis. It seemed to me that most serious drug reactions occurred among support troops, an observation consistent with the findings of other military psychiatrists in Vietnam. I remember one soldier who came in for a forensic examination escorted by two MP guards from the LBJ. He was a strange-looking person with hair that stood up like a blond lion's mane. His eyes were red and squinted, and he gestured in a manner similar to Dennis Hopper's hand movements in *Apocalypse Now.* He reported that he had been in country for three years. He had deserted from his unit during his first year to stay in Saigon, where he obtained money through illegal activities and spent his time in opium dens. According to him, there were a number of American soldiers who chose to remain in country in order to continue their drug use. He turned himself in, so he was entitled to amnesty as far as his drug use was concerned. However, since he had also been AWOL for an extended period of time, he was serving time in LBJ.

When we saw a patient who was addicted to Binoctal, we would admit him to the clearing station and give him two hundred milligrams of pentobarbital by mouth. If he showed symptoms of toxicity, such as slurred speech, loss of coordination, difficulty with his balance, side-to-side eye movements, or "drugginess," we would assume that the patient could tolerate no more than the equivalent of eight hundred milligrams of pentobarbital per day. If the patient perked up with two hundred milligrams and showed no signs of toxicity, we assumed he could tolerate more. On the basis of the response to the pentobarbital test dose, we determined an appropriate pentobarbital withdrawal schedule.

I was asked by Lieutenant Colonel Hefner, the division surgeon, to look into the death in the division of a nineteen-year-old E-4 cook who had been in Vietnam for three months. He was from a small town and described as being quiet, religious, and hardworking. He had never used drugs or alcohol until the night before he was to leave for R&R. At that time his friends persuaded him to have a beer. He had two beers and appeared intoxicated when he returned to his quarters. Before going to bed, he took two chloroquine/primaquine tablets instead of the recommended one tablet for the prevention of malaria. He died in his sleep from the slowing of his heart produced by the medication. We were involved in the investigation because of the question of possible suicide. Following this event, a warning was issued at all levels of the division regarding the potential cardio-toxic effects of the malaria tablets.

MANY RESEARCHERS BELIEVED that drug and alcohol abuse in Vietnam was a means of self-medication to cope with the stress of the tour. From my own experience I would agree with this speculation, but it was difficult to obtain accurate data. In 1971 all troops had to pass a drug test before leaving country. Drug users who were short would detoxify themselves through alcohol binges and self-induced vomiting. They also obtained clean urine specimens from buddies that they put in the specimen tubes in place of their own. As a result, only 5 percent of men came up positive, and most of these were clean when retested later.

For officers and NCOs, drug of choice was alcohol. It was inexpensive, readily available, and encouraged by the military. Every "hail and farewell" celebration, every TGIF, every change of command was associated with alcohol. We had regular parties with steaks and booze. The medical officers had an officers' club and bartender. Medical and medical support officers could also go to the support command's and headquarters' officers' clubs. Officers could purchase inexpensive liquor at the PX and drink it in their hootches. The military encouraged drinking—to a point. However, if drinking led to problems with performance or discipline, the army would come down hard, punish the drinker, and end his career.

During the year we saw cases of explosive violence in which alcohol played a role in loosening the individual's controls and impairing his judgment. We saw cases of alcoholic paranoia and acute alcohol hallucinosis. The hallucinations were usually auditory, frequently in one ear only, and the voices would tell the patient that he was "queer." The paranoia was typically of infidelity of a spouse, but in another type the patient believed that men in his unit were accusing him of being homosexual. Both of these symptoms accompanied chronic alcoholism, and neither responded well to short-term treatment. It was possible to evacuate men to a chemical-dependency treatment facility in the States, and we did evacuate a few over a year's time. While I was in Vietnam, there were no organized chemical-dependency treatment programs in country.

A middle-aged E-6 cook with fifteen years of active duty was referred after he went to his commanding officer complaining that he couldn't stand the persecution of his unit any longer. If something wasn't done about it, he was going to take matters into his own hands and kill the man whom he saw as the instigator of the plot against him. The sergeant was a stocky, white man in his thirties who had the standard crew cut with white "sidewalls" characteristic of many of the Regular Army NCOs at that time. He appeared to be hyperalert and suspicious during the interview. According to his CO, the patient had always been distant and was described by his unit as a loner. His IQ was low; in fact, he was rated in the bottom category of the Armed Forces Qualification Test (AFQT) scale, and his performance in the military had been marginal. He had grown up in an orphanage and enlisted in the military after quitting high school. He had a history of heavy drinking. He had had few heterosexual relationships in his life and no close male friends in the unit. In Vietnam he met a prostitute who spoke little English, and after spending one night with her, he attempted to go through channels to legally marry her. This produced some teasing by his unit, much of it on a very crude level. In the chow line, a number of men commented that they had sex with his "fiancée." The sergeant became extremely upset by these remarks and threatened to kill the men who made them.

After several talks with his CO, it was felt he might be better off transferring to another unit.

In the new unit the sergeant began to feel that the men were watching him and talking behind his back. He thought that the men from the previous unit had tampered with his records and told the men of his new unit that he was homosexual. I hospitalized him in the clearing station briefly and treated him with major tranquilizers, allowing him to vent his emotions. His ideas of reference continued ("ideas of reference" are thoughts that people were looking at him and referring to him as being homosexual), and it was felt that he was at risk to harm himself or others in his unit because he had acted on his delusional thinking in the past. He was medically evacuated to the 93rd Evacuation Hospital for further evaluation and treatment.

We saw a supply sergeant who complained of hearing voices that told him he was "queer." These voices caused him considerable anxiety. He consulted with his battalion surgeon and was referred to us. From the history we learned that he had experienced ringing (tinnitus) in his left ear prior to the onset of the hallucinations and that he heard the voices only in that ear. The battalion surgeon told us that there was a history of heavy drinking and he was probably a chronic alcoholic. We recommended abstinence from alcohol, fifty milligrams of Thorazine four times a day, and B vitamins (niacin and thiamine). The sergeant was not able to stop drinking, and the medication did not appear to dampen the hallucinations. We referred him to the 93rd Evacuation Hospital in Long Binh and learned later that they had evacuated him back to the States.

The vast majority of individuals who had problems with alcohol did not come to our attention. In addition to the usual denial that accompanies alcohol addiction, there was concern that medical attention and the mention of alcoholism on their medical records would adversely affect their careers in the military. Full-blown alcoholics were nearly always men who were Regular Army and did not want to identify themselves by asking for help. In addition, their units tended to cover up the problems until they got in trouble and at that point would punish them. We did try to pass on our observations about this situation when we saw the new battalion surgeons and when we went to the units for consultations.

Not drinking in Vietnam could also get a person in trouble. The docs used to go to the support command officers' club to play liar's dice and to rub elbows with the support command officers. (Liar's dice was popular at the bar. The first person would shake the cup full of dice and then look at it without showing anyone else. He would announce the total and pass the cup to the next person, who would repeat the performance and announce a higher total. Anyone could challenge this total. If you challenged and it turned out the shaker had lied, the shaker had to buy a round of drinks. If the shaker didn't lie, then you, the challenger, had to buy a round.) It was a larger and nicer club than the little hootch at 1st Medical Battalion. One night we were in there drinking and playing dice when the support command chaplain (aka sky pilot, padre, or sheepherder) walked around in the bar area, speaking out loud in a voice that was overheard by everyone around him: "Tsk, tsk. I don't know why they feel they have to drink." He then began to pray in a loud voice: "O Lord, help these men control their habits and abstain from alcohol." It didn't slow anyone down, but it was annoying when you were trying to do some serious drinking. The support command general came over to me and asked, "Hey Wizard—what do you think of that chaplain?" I responded, "I think he is a ding-a-ling, sir." The general leaned down, squinting one eye shut, nodded, and responded, "That's what I think."

I returned a few days later and found the same loud music, same loud drunk talk, but no "tsk, tsking" sky pilot. I summoned the bartender and asked him what had happened to the padre. "The general had him transferred to a unit within walking distance of Cambodia," he replied, smiling. "Meet the new sheepherder," he said, gesturing down the bar to a ruddy-faced chaplain who was slapping guys on the back with one hand and holding a drink in the other.

DRUGS BECAME A MAJOR PROBLEM in Vietnam. The number of men using drugs, as well as the amount and potency of the drugs used increased as the war continued. Alcohol consumption was high as well but did not receive the publicity, concern, or public response that drug use engendered.

Self-medication with booze was one of our ways of escaping the day-to-day boredom and stress. The superego is the alcohol-soluble portion of the personality, and for me, drinking carried the additional benefit of relieving some of my chronic burden of guilt.

Work was a healthier escape. Caring for our fellow soldiers was a loving activity. Another healthy outlet was our efforts to medically evaluate and treat the Vietnamese citizens in our area of operations.

CHAPTER 7

Civilian Health Care

Men in support areas sought to escape from the tedious routine of their day-to-day existence in Vietnam. MEDCAP visits to villages and orphanages provided the docs with a change of scenery, different medical challenges, and photographic opportunities. I joined my medical buddies in the battalion on many of these excursions. During a year's time the 1st Infantry Division made 549 MEDCAP visits and saw more than one hundred thousand patients.

NEARLY EVERY WEEK we conducted a MEDCAP visit at a village within the division's area of operation. Usually Lieutenant Colonel Hefner would mention at dinner the previous evening that a MEDCAP was scheduled and that those who were interested should report to the clearing station in the morning. We were never told where the MEDCAP was going to be conducted because this information could enable the enemy to set up an ambush or booby-trap the area. During a MEDCAP, we went to a village and set up our clinic in a public building—typically a temple or a school.

One morning I woke to the sound of the others talking as they shaved and cleaned up on their porches. John's stereo was booming the song "The Friendship Train" by Gladys Knight and the Pips, an appropriate choice as we were about to extend our hands in friendship in the middle of the fighting and killing.

I got cleaned up and trudged over to the mess hall with John and Malcolm. After breakfast we met near the clearing station. Zecchinelli drove the jeep, and Falzone and Smith rode in the back. We had our usual gear plus extra film. We joined the MEDCAP convoy consisting of two more jeeps, the pharmacy truck, an ambulance, an APC (armored personnel carrier), and a deuce-and-a-half. The deuce-and-a-half (aka M-35 truck, 6 × 6, and six-by) was the standard truck, which held two and a half tons of cargo. Used to ferry supplies and troops, it could be fitted with mounts for M60 or .50-caliber machine guns. In addition to the docs and the medics, we took along Mrs. Thu, a Vietnamese translator and practical nurse; and Sergeant Wu, an NCO with the Vietnamese army who also served as a translator; and several intelligence officers. Mrs. Thu wore the traditional ao dai (a dress with a split skirt) over black trousers, and Sergeant Wu wore tiger-striped fatigues and a cap. They rode with the Vietnamese pharmacist in the pharmacy truck.

The infantry escort led the column in the APC. We traveled on unfamiliar, secondary dirt roads. It was extremely dusty, especially traveling behind the heavy truck and the APC. We passed a Buddhist temple where we saw monks with close-cut hair who wore colored robes. On the temple were reversed swastikas. We passed several "prayer boxes," ancient, small, carved stone boxes on pedestals, sometimes covered by a roof, where Buddhist travelers could stop to worship.

The Vietnamese farmers wore conical straw hats and black outfits that looked like pajamas. They were working in their rice paddies, using water buffalo to pull their plows. I had an image in my mind of what the Viet Cong would look like, and to me, they all looked like Viet Cong. Later I learned that there were VC in the area, including some that worked at the military installations. One of the missions of the 1st Infantry Division at that time was to secure and pacify the villages in the area to free them from VC intimidation. Another mission was to interdict the NVA supply routes coming down from the Parrot's Beak and Angel's Wing areas of Cambodia. The local Viet Cong infrastructure (VCI) provided intelligence and stored food, weapons, and equipment for the NVA coming from North Vietnam. The NVA sent the supplies to an area under VC control, where it would be hidden for the troops who would follow. A third mission of the division was to locate and destroy the cached supplies. A two-thousand-bed tunnel hospital with blood and refrigeration was uncovered in our area. Some of the tunnel complexes were eight stories deep.

My jeep had "Division Psychiatrist" painted on the front beneath the windshield. When we passed tanks and tracks in the boonies, the soldiers would see the sign and start jumping around acting crazy. I'd give them a "thumbs down" and yelled that they couldn't go home until I did. They responded with laughter and profane comments.

As we approached the destination, Sergeant Wu and Mrs. Thu announced in Vietnamese through the loudspeakers on the pharmacy truck that we were setting up a medical clinic. We hauled our equipment into a schoolhouse and set up our clinic.

As we started setting up, some entrepreneurs arrived. A thin, elfin Vietnamese man pedaled in on his bike. He was wearing an army green shirt and floppy hat, loose blue trousers, and yellow flip-flops. The children ran out to meet him. He had two thick aluminum, insulated saddlebags on the bike. The bike was like one I had as a kid in the 1950s. The tires were covered with red dirt. He reached into a saddlebag and brought out blocks of ice cream, which he cut into cubes and inserted toothpicks. He began selling ice cream to the kids, to the American soldiers, and to the soldiers who were buying for the kids. Some of the kids wore T-shirts that said "Chieu Hoi," or "I surrender," on the backs.

ABOUT THIS TIME a couple of young "boom-boom" girls pedaled in on their bikes and began bargaining with the infantry escorts. The women were young and rather plain in appearance (which was "outstanding" to the generally sex-starved standards of the soldiers serving in Vietnam). They wore loose-fitting, flowered white blouses, black pants, and flip-flops. "Number-one boom boom" was very good, but if the soldier would not agree to pay enough, he was called "number ten," or even worse, "number ten thousand."

The girls were experienced at bargaining and seemed to enjoy haggling with the infantrymen. The interaction was something like this, with a good deal of giggling by the girls and laughing by the grunts.

"You souvenir me cigarette?" resulted in the GIs giving them American cigarettes.

"Twenty dolla for beaucoup boom boom" was the offer.

The soldiers tried to lower the price. "Sin loi [sorry about that]; you probably have the clap. How about ten dollars?"

"No way; we be clean girl. You pay twenty dolla cheap Charlie."

"How about all of us for twenty dollars?"

"You dinky dau [crazy]."

Eventually ten dollars per man with no extras was agreed upon.

One of the girls went into the back of the APC while about eight of the GIs lined up, eating ice cream as they waited their turn. The other woman stood outside to collect the money and relieve her partner. I didn't time the sessions inside the APC, but the line appeared to move along speedily, and the women finished their "clinic" long before we completed ours. The satisfied customers lay around and had a cigarette on the top of the APC.

Sex was as available as drugs in Vietnam and for a fairly reasonable price. Prostitutes bicycled out to the field to do business with the troops out in the rice paddies. There were signs that said "Car Wash" along the roads where kids would wash your vehicle while mama and sister serviced the driver inside their hootch. Every village bar had barmaids who would grab the customer's crotch and ask him to buy tea. Every steam bath (including the one in Long Binh) provided sexual services for an extra fee. There were call girls and brothels available in Saigon. Oral sex was not a common practice by Vietnamese prostitutes in the boondocks. Buddhists didn't practice oral sex, and 90 percent of the rural population were Buddhists. Oral sex could be readily obtained in Saigon but for an extra fee. Another resource for sex was available in base camps that permitted hootch girls, who cleaned the hootches and did domestic chores such as shining boots.

We didn't have hootch girls or doughnut dollies in Di An. The only females were those that burned the GI's feces and a few translators, such as Mrs. Thu. The only women who weren't Vietnamese that we saw there during the year were entertainers with the USO shows once or twice over a year's time. For the camps that had hootch girls, extra services were usually provided for an additional fee. In terms of looks and fees the hierarchy was Saigon call girl, Saigon barmaid, Saigon whorehouse, Saigon steam bath, village barmaid, village steam bath, car wash mama, prostitute on a bike, hootch girl, and finally, toothless Vietnamese women who burned feces (although I never ran into anyone who admitted to having sex with one of these women, but I imagine that someone probably got drunk enough or horny enough to do so). Masturbation was even rated above them.

The majority of enlisted men purchased sex somewhere, and everybody masturbated. Some men had "Vietnamese marriages" and lived with their "wives" in country. Some fell in love with bar girls and had children with them, and a few arranged for their Vietnamese girlfriends to fly to the United States.

There were a few naive soldiers who wanted to marry prostitutes because they had sex with them and fell in love. This was a problem in Korea, where a number of men did marry prostitutes. While stationed at Fort Knox, I saw many of these wives as patients, because in Korea many of the prostitutes were psychotic. The soldiers who had sex with them didn't understand the language or the culture well enough to realize that these girls were mentally ill. Several of the Korean wives on the inpatient psychiatric unit at Fort Knox were severely ill. All had been prostitutes in Korea when their Regular Army husbands had met and married them. Most of the enlisted men in Vietnam regarded the prostitutes as less-than-human conveniences who were providing a service. These women were hardened professionals who made sure that they were paid for their services and did not become emotionally involved with their customers. Commanders were not upset with their men for buying sex. Of course, officially they had to be against it.

Sexually transmitted disease was a major medical treatment problem in Vietnam both in terms of the number of soldiers infected and the resistance of the gonorrhea to antibiotics. The medical officers attempted to lecture their infected patients about the dangers of repeated infection. Men were cautioned in lectures before going on R&R and advised on how to recognize symptoms and to seek treatment when they returned from R&R.

Blacks were discriminated against by the pimps and prostitutes in Vietnam. There were a few brothels or steam baths that catered to them, and the working girls there were bigger, uglier, and often mentally challenged or psychotic. These girls were generally considered the least desirable prostitutes available. When approached by a black man, a prostitute would often refer him elsewhere. Pimps would approach white soldiers to describe the services available but indicate that their black friends were unwelcome.

I LOOKED THROUGH THE SCHOOLHOUSE window and thought, "We're in here giving the Vietnamese civilians medicine while outside our soldiers are having sex with them"—somehow this seemed to capture the essence of our presence in Vietnam at the time. We—the Vietnamese patients, Mrs. Thu, Sergeant Wu, the medics, and the doctors— pretended not to notice the activities going on outside the school. Surreptitiously, we all checked it out, and some of us photographed the event (there was very little we didn't photograph in Vietnam). It was fortunate that we were never attacked on these missions of mercy because our protectors were preoccupied with sex or they were engaged in postcoital recovery on top of the APC. The intelligence officers were busy walking through the village with Sergeant Wu and didn't seem to care about the platoon's recreational activities.

We were busy inside the school setting up our medical clinic. We had stethoscopes and blood pressure cuffs, and several doctors set up at different stations in the building. Mrs. Thu and, when present, Sergeant Wu, would take the initial information from the patients and relay this to the doctor. The doctor would examine the patient, focus on the particular complaint, and give a prescription to Mrs. Wu, who would in turn explain it to the patient along with a prescription to be filled from the pharmacy truck outside. The pharmacy truck was stocked with medicines, bandages, and ointments and was staffed by a Vietnamese "pharmacist." He wore a white intern's tunic, remained inside the truck, and passed out medicines through the side panel of the vehicle.

The patients lined up at the door to the classroom. They consisted mostly of children and elderly civilians. When Mrs. Thu told one of us what their complaints were, she often offered her own diagnosis as well. Translating the medical history for us, she would say, "She say she have beaucoup diarrhea."

"Any pain?" asked the doc.

"No, no pain—beaucoup diarrhea."

"Any fever?"

"No, no fever, she need medicine for dysentery."

The patients typically had tuberculosis, dysentery, and malaria. We once saw a small boy who had been burned from an explosion. Usually we arrived in the late morning and left by 3 or 4 P.M. By early afternoon we started closing up. As we passed through the village gate on our way back to the division, we saw our patients squatting in the dirt trading pills (one red one for two blues, etc.).

When medical supplies were captured from the Viet Cong, they typically contained medicines that were obtained from our MEDCAP operations. In reality, the primary medical need in the rural villages was public health. The Vietnamese cooked, bathed, and defecated in the same source of water. Giving out pills for dysentery did not address the real problem. Improved nutrition, antimalarial pills, and sanitation would have resulted in better civilian health. So, from a medical standpoint, the clinics were not nearly as effective as a preventive approach would have been.

Apparently the MEDCAPs were helpful to the military in that they gave the intelligence personnel good access to the villages. In addition, the doctors got a break from their routines and were able to take some good pictures. The infantry platoon got laid, and the prostitutes and ice-cream vendor made money. The medical value was questionable.

THE WAR IN VIETNAM had been going for so long that millions had been killed and millions of children were orphaned. Vietnam was known as the land of cemeteries and orphanages. One kind of MEDCAP operation that probably did substantial good was the Dong Hoa Orphanage that our division had "adopted." The orphanage was operated by the Catholic Church, but we provided it with linens, food, medical supplies, medical examinations, affection, and attention. We looked forward to going there and seeing the children and nuns. There were several hundred orphans, ranging from three to twelve years of age, who were always excited to see us. They piled on Szentpetery, who they thought was a giant. The game was to see how many kids could get on him each visit.

There were about a dozen Vietnamese nuns who fed, disciplined, and taught the children. Four of the nuns spoke some English. They would line up the children to be examined and explain their problems. The children typically had dysentery, colds, flu, and minor injuries. The nuns served us Vietnamese soft drinks.

On one occasion they invited the medical battalion for Children's Day. A stage was set up, and the kids put on a show with costumes, singing, and dancing. The girls danced separately from the boys and giggled as the boys performed. We brought party hats and toys for the occasion. The nuns were assertive in asking for food, linens, and other necessities for the orphanage. When we played with particular kids, they would ask if we might not want to take them home with us. Many kids had been fathered by black or white Americans who were looked down on as *bui doi,* or the "dust of life." One albino girl in the orphanage was an outcast among outcasts. The kids were starved for attention and affection, but we were also. We may have done some limited good medically, but certainly our visits provided emotional benefits for the children and for ourselves as well.

ONE MEDICAL OFFICER, Denny Beaumont, conducted his own MEDCAP. He went into a local village, where he examined and treated civilians. In the course of his work there he found a young boy who had a congenital ventricular septal defect (a hole between the large chambers of his heart). Denny had a colleague at home who was a heart surgeon and made arrangements for the boy to be flown to the States, have surgery, and stay at the surgeon's home until he recovered and could be flown back to the village. This was done, and Denny was featured on the cover of a national magazine and became a hero to the local village. We accompanied him to the village on occasion. Each time the villagers would insist on killing a chicken and making a special meal for Denny. They offered some of the food to us, but we politely refused, pointing out that Denny was the hero and should receive this special recognition. Each time he would eat the meal and thank the villagers profusely for what he knew was a great sacrifice on their part. Later he would end up in the hospital with dysentery and would be put on intravenous fluids.

I VISITED ED COLBACH in Qui Nhon on one occasion. Ed gave me a tour of his medical facility and briefed me on his experience as a psychiatrist there. While in Qui Nhon I visited the Red Beach and took pictures of American nurses in bikinis to show the guys in the division. The boys drooled over the pictures, but when I looked at the photos years later, I was struck by how plain and relatively unattractive the girls really were. With nearly six hundred thousand sexually deprived men in country, it was no wonder that the handful of American women were perceived as objects of lust. Even Ruby Begonia was achieving a degree of attractiveness by this time in the tour.

We were always looking for places to visit that would provide a change of scenery and a break in the routine. Sergeant Wu had contacts at the Vietnamese civilian medical hospital in Bien Hoa, and we were invited to tour their facility. The hospital was staffed by Vietnamese civilian physicians, six or seven volunteer Australian nurses, and a few Vietnamese nurses. They had six hundred beds and performed two thousand deliveries per year. It was an open-air structure, typical for a country with a tropical climate. The nursing support available was inadequate by the standards in the United States. Food and basic nursing care were not provided by the medical staff. The patients' families came to the hospital with the patients and provided the food, change of linens, and general nursing. The families squatted in the courtyard of the hospital, where they cooked on charcoal grills, visited with one another, changed linens, and washed them. (Hopefully, the managed-care groups won't learn about this!) In addition, there were vendors selling cooked rice, lemon-pepper crabs, noodles, and other food to the patients' relatives.

I read a few facts about the medical care in Vietnam. In 1945 there were forty-seven hospitals with three thousand beds, one doctor for every 180,000 patients, and the life expectancy was thirty-four years. By the time I was in Vietnam there were more than seven hundred hospitals and two hundred thousand beds. There was one doctor for every 1,000 patients, and the life expectancy had risen to sixty-three years. Malaria, tuberculosis, trachoma, dysentery, leprosy, and tetanus were the most common illnesses.

PSYCHOANALYSIS WAS AT ITS ZENITH in the United States. It was being applied to hospital treatment, business organizations, literature, physical illnesses, political figures, and social problems. Community psychiatry was the latest trend in the psychiatric field. I had taken community psychiatry courses during residency and worked with Dr. Harry Levinson on the industrial psychiatry faculty at Menninger's. We evaluated and treated business organizations using applied psychoanalytic techniques. My recent training in these areas resulted in my efforts to monitor organizational stress levels within the division and to identify high-risk individuals and organizational stress periods as well.

High-Risk Individuals
and REMFs

O nce we established what I felt was good-quality direct service within the division, I began to focus on using the data we were collecting to identify individuals within the division who appeared to be at higher risk for psychiatric stress. Once these individuals were identified, we could recommend measures to protect them from stress and perhaps reduce the need for psychiatric referral for direct service. We were able to determine several categories of individuals who were more likely to develop debilitating stress. We communicated these findings to commanders and battalion surgeons within the division and published them in the USARV medical bulletin for distribution among the medical officers in Vietnam. We also noted that the vast majority of the men in Vietnam functioned in a support capacity, and although combat troops faced obvious stresses, there were stresses uniquely experienced by the support troops as well. We were beginning to see that the psychiatric experience in Vietnam was different from what had been described by military psychiatrists in previous wars. There were fewer classic cases of combat exhaustion or gross stress reactions, but more problems with race relations, drug and alcohol abuse, and morale.

An initial task in our efforts to study and reduce organizational stress in the division was educating the units about what circumstances warranted a psychiatric referral. We had an incident in the 1st Infantry Division in which a soldier in a fire support base walked into a bunker and, without provocation, shot all six of the occupants, killing two and seriously wounding the other four. Subsequent evaluation of the individual determined that he was psychotic. In retrospect, his behavior had been quite bizarre for several days before the shooting. His commander and NCOs recognized this, counseled him, and attempted to obtain the assistance of a chaplain. However, before any additional corrective action was taken, the tragic incident took place. I prepared a talking paper for the division surgeon to present to the commanding general, who, in turn, issued a memo to all division commanders based on the information he received from Lieutenant Colonel Hefner. The essence of the communication was to alert commanders to the signs and symptoms of mental illness and to encourage them to refer these individuals to psychiatry for evaluation rather than try to manage them within their own units. Some commanders had been hesitant to refer men, thinking that this would reflect on their command abilities and be a black mark on their own performance evaluations. The memo by the general directed them not to try to handle these problems themselves and caused commanders to look more closely at changes in the behavior of their men.

The public health model was popular in the community psychiatry movement in the late 1960s and early 1970s. In public health, primary prevention is the elimination of a disease in the community through measures such as sanitation and vaccination; secondary prevention is the early detection and prompt treatment of illness; and tertiary prevention is the prevention, through physical rehabilitation and prosthetic aids, of disability that may be caused by the illness. Primary prevention in psychiatry is aimed at promoting activities that tend to reduce psychiatric illness in the community. For example, improving prenatal care might reduce the number of individuals who suffer postpartum depression. Secondary prevention is the early identification of psychiatric disorders, a prerequisite for prompt treatment—for example, spotting the development of psychiatric illness in young children when it is more treatable. Tertiary prevention addresses itself to the task of reducing the rate of defective functioning caused by the mental disorders. In addition to the course work on primary, secondary, and tertiary prevention in residency training at Menninger's, I had served as a member of Dr. Harry Levinson's industrial psychiatry faculty and had written my third-year paper on a study of a large organization under his supervision.

My previous training in preventive psychiatry and my new role as a mental health adviser to division command made it logical to look for tendencies that might be useful in preventing psychiatric casualties. I kept detailed records of the soldiers we treated throughout the division and then evaluated these records, looking for trends. I looked to see if there were certain categories of jobs or particular periods during a tour of duty that seemed to contribute to the development of psychiatric symptoms.

In civilian practice we know that individuals who were abused as kids or had an alcoholic parent will develop certain predictable patterns of behavior that may lead to difficulties with trust, intimacy, control, and stable relationships in adult life. Although we took lengthy histories of patients in Vietnam, early childhood behaviors did not correlate with the particular job stresses that seemed to lead individuals to develop psychiatric symptoms. This might be an area for future study in the military.

FNGs were at high risk to develop symptoms if they failed to make the transition from "the world" to the existence in Vietnam. Most of us stopped thinking about "the world" and adapted the language and lifestyle of the veterans stationed in Vietnam. Those individuals who could not develop the counterphobic defenses encouraged by their new units, were unable to give up their hold on "the world," or could not identify with the language and habits of their new peer group developed symptoms and often did not make it in Vietnam.

An extreme example of this was Private First Class François (pseudonym), a nineteen-year-old draftee of French extraction. He was a thin kid covered with acne and had bad body odor. He spoke haltingly with a strong French accent. He was obsessed with thoughts of dying in Vietnam and was referred to us after asking that a priest be called to administer the last rites. He felt that Americans could not understand him and regarded the technicians and me with suspicion. We were unable to collect an accurate, chronological history but discovered from his medical records and reports by his unit members that he was born and raised in

France, where he had been employed as a carpenter. Six months after moving to the United States with his parents, he had been drafted. He was initially frightened at the prospect of serving in the army but agreed with his father that he could earn good wages and would quickly learn about Americans in the military. When ordered to Vietnam, he felt he had been tricked by the official at the induction station, who had allegedly told him that there was no chance of his going overseas. He worried about his own safety and the impending separation from his family. When he arrived at his field unit in Vietnam, he kept to himself and believed that he could not communicate because of language difficulties. His main contact with other people was through lengthy letters sent home.

His naïveté and overreaction to war stories made him a natural target for jokes and teasing in the unit. He was told, and believed, that the NVA were going to launch an attack that would overrun and destroy his unit. His apprehension and isolation increased. He refused to eat, failed to attend to his personal hygiene, lost sleep, and stopped writing home. He gave away his money and his possessions and spoke of his impending death. The unit became concerned, and his sergeants tried to dissuade him from the conviction that he was about to die, but he was certain that his death was imminent.

When he was brought to us for treatment, he regarded the clearing station as a prison ward where he would be punished. It was obvious that he hadn't bathed in some time. He smelled of sweat and urine. François was seated beside a steel desk, where Specialist Zecchinelli was attempting to take an initial history from him. Suddenly, he rocked back and forth in his chair to beat his head on the edge of the desk and inflicted deep lacerations on his forehead that exposed his skull. We restrained him, applied a compression bandage to his head, and medically evacuated him to the 93rd Evacuation Hospital in Long Binh with instructions to place him on maximum suicide precautions. His lacerations required multiple layers of sutures. At the 93rd he later evaded the medics, climbed a sixty-foot tower, and jumped headfirst to the sidewalk below. He sustained serious injuries, including a broken neck. He miraculously survived his injuries and was evacuated back to the United States for further surgical and psychiatric treatment.

Soldiers who were able to take on the counterphobic defenses needed to survive in Vietnam sometimes went through a period of unnecessary risk taking after their arrival. Although excessive counterphobia put these soldiers at risk, they were not seen by the psychiatric unit. In most instances, guidance from personnel in their units cautioned them to behave more prudently. For example, I had the usual fears in the back of my mind when I first came into country. After the "veterans" confronted me with these fears and flooded me with war stories, I decided that if they could do it, then so could I and began imitating their language and behaviors. I forgot about "the world" or ever returning there. I focused on my day-to-day work and life in Vietnam.

Initially this process of adaptation was accompanied by a denial of the dangers that existed in Vietnam. My driver and I would take off and drive to Lai Khe in my jeep on the spur of the moment. Sometimes we returned after dusk. One night John straightened me out.

"Hey, Wizard, what do you think you are doing driving on Highway 13 after dark?"

"We got up there late, and the techs had lots of stuff for me to do."

"If it's starting to get dark, stay overnight."

"Yeah, whatever, it's no big deal. We didn't have any problems."

"The night belongs to Charlie, buddy. Nobody in their right mind drives on that road after dark."

"Yeah."

"I'm not joking around, Wizard. I don't want have to write a letter to your family explaining that you were killed because you couldn't get back to Di An before dark."

"Okay, Big John, you're probably right—there's no reason we can't do what we have to do during the daytime."

"I know I'm right. If you see it's getting late, then stay there until morning but call here so we know where you are."

"Yes, sir!"

"Don't be givin' me that 'Yes, sir' stuff—you just do it."

THE U.S. 67S were another high-risk group. In August 1966, Project 100,000 began. This was one of Secretary of Defense Robert

McNamara's ideas to bring opportunity to the 350,000 recruits who failed to meet normal IQ induction standards. Some of these recruits had IQs as low as 62 but were nonetheless brought into the army. More than 100,000 were trained for combat, and nearly half were African Americans. They were easily identified because their service numbers began with either U.S. 67 or R.A. 67, depending on whether they were drafted or enlisted. Sometimes they were referred to cruelly as "McNamara's morons."

The idea underlying the program was to train disadvantaged individuals to do simple, routine jobs in the military with the hope that they would develop improved self-esteem and self-confidence. Unfortunately, not everyone felt sympathetic or supportive toward this group of men. They were often the butt of jokes within their units. A high percentage of this group developed psychiatric symptoms and were referred to psychiatric services (this was noted and reported by psychiatrists across Vietnam). These were individuals who had limited intellectual and emotional coping skills. Although many were motivated for service in the military, the stresses of competing with others who were not disadvantaged, being asked to quickly learn to perform tasks they found difficult, and being scapegoated by their units overwhelmed many of them.

One example of this group was a young man, Private First Class White (pseudonym), who was brought to us for evaluation because he had developed psychotic symptoms while serving as a prisoner at the Long Binh Jail. He had been charged with the destruction of government property and attempted murder after blowing up a mess hall that was fortunately empty. He was brought to us in shackles by an MP escort. Clearly agitated, he appeared to be talking back to his own internal voices, had a speech impediment, and was shouting in an angry, fearful voice.

"Why are you hutting me?"

"We aren't going to hurt you. We are here to help you."

"Go way, go way, go waaay."

"We'll get you a nice hot meal, something to drink, and you can rest."

"I hate you! Go way! Leave me alone!"

White was a pudgy, disheveled, dull-eyed Caucasian, with streaks of tears on his face and a runny nose. The lack of sparkle in his eyes and his tendency to breathe through his mouth gave him the appearance of being dull. At first we were unable to take a history from him. He was talking to himself, grimacing, and fighting with the medics and technicians who were trying to settle him down. He was unable or unwilling to respond to our questions. We initially restrained him on one of the clearing station cots and sedated him with Thorazine. After being sedated for a day, he was able to eat and drink and responded positively to the nursing care provided by the technicians and medics. In two days he was feeling better and able to give me some historical information.

"How did you happen to go to LBJ?"

"Da cooks picked on me and beat me up and I got mad."

"What do you mean they picked on you?"

"Dey wouldn't give me my food, den dey gave me garbage, den dey spit on it. I got mad."

"What did you do when you became angry?"

"I yelled at dem—I told dem to give me my food! Dey pushed me outside and beat the crap outta me! Dey was very very mean to me."

"Then what did you do?"

"I tried to find my sergeant but he wadn't dere. I wad scared 'n mad. I picked up a grenade launcher, and I went back to da mess hall to kill da cooks, but no one was dere. So I blew up da mess hall."

I asked him if he tried to get away, but he said that he had just stayed there until he was taken away to LBJ, where the guards beat him up. He told me that he couldn't eat or sleep and had voices in his head that started yelling at him.

"What did the voices say to you?"

"Lots of scary stuff. You stupid. Kill yusself dummy. Nobuddy likes you."

I asked if the voices were still there, and he said no. I told him that his sergeant thought a lot of him, had come to see him once when he was sleeping, and was going to come again see him, to which he responded, "I love my sergeant! Don' make me go back to LBJ."

I let him know that we were going to send him home through medical channels and asked if he liked the medics and techs here. He said he did, and I told him that those were the kind of people who would be looking after him from now on and things were going to be better for him.

We learned from other sources that he had been a cook's assistant in a transportation unit. His first sergeant saw him as a good kid who was not very bright. The sergeant said White seemed generally happy around him and usually had a smile on his face. The NCO had looked after him in the unit. The young soldier talked to the sergeant and expressed a desire to make a career out of the army. The sergeant had protected him from being picked on and had encouraged him to remain in the service. The incident took place when the sergeant was away from the base camp. The sergeant's testimony and our report resulted in the legal charges being dropped. We arranged to have him medically evacuated back to the United States. I doubt that he remained in the army because he said that he hated the army when we last saw him.

The kindness of the first sergeant was a phenomenon I saw often during my military experience. Drill sergeants, for example, tend to appear very gruff and macho but actually are "motherly" in most cases. For example, if a kid told his sergeant, "Sarge, I messed up in high school, I got in trouble with the law, and I'm afraid I'm going to foul up in the military," the sergeant would do everything in his power to see that the kid made it in the army. Unfortunately, most young men don't approach their sergeants in that manner. Although it was the same message, the sergeants reacted negatively to enlisted men who griped about "lifers" and said they couldn't wait to get out of the army. The sergeants would react by coming down hard on these men, who would then end up failing in the army as they had in everything else in life. When we saw young men who had a pattern of failure prior to the military, we would counsel them to speak directly to their sergeant about their fears and to ask for his help. We also tried to help sergeants understand that seemingly rebellious, negative behavior by the trainees and enlisted men often a reflected their underlying insecurity and fear of failure.

OLD SERGEANTS were another high-risk group we identified. It was routine in the army at that time to send sergeants who had a year to go before retirement on a hardship tour. Many of these sergeants believed that the government wanted them to be killed to avoid paying for their retirement benefits. Some of these men had problems with alcohol. The sergeants' problems often worsened during a tour in Vietnam and sometimes led to their being administratively discharged.

One sergeant in the 1st Infantry Division committed suicide. He was married, the father of three children, and served as a supply sergeant in the medical battalion. During his tour he usually appeared anxious and tired. He was put up for court-martial after he had been arrested for sexually assaulting an enlisted man. He was intoxicated at the time and did not remember the event. Although he had been drinking heavily for several years and suffered blackout spells and withdrawal symptoms when he had been briefly abstinent, the alcohol problem was covered up rather than confronted by command. A commanding officer would become aware that the supply sergeant was an alcoholic. Instead of insisting that the sergeant get help, the CO would give the sergeant a glowing report and "sell him" to another unit. It would take a few months to discover the problem in the new company, and then they would do the same to another unit.

By the time the supply sergeant reached the medical battalion, he was a chronic alcoholic with one year left before retirement. The stress of Vietnam and the availability of inexpensive liquor led to the inevitable, and after a few months in country, the sergeant got into difficulty with the law for blacking out and making homosexual advances toward an enlisted man in the unit. He was arrested after he crawled in bed with the enlisted man and began fondling him. We didn't see the sergeant as a patient, but the situation was discussed at one of our evening sessions outside Lieutenant Colonel Hefner's hootch. Hefner drank heavily himself, although he denied it was a problem. It was obvious that the lieutenant colonel felt the sergeant was guilty of one of the worst things an NCO could do, and the supply sergeant was brought up on court-martial charges. The lieutenant colonel told the sergeant he was going to give him one more chance, but if he took another drink in Vietnam, he would see to it that he was court-martialed and kicked out of the army. I tried to persuade the lieutenant colonel to consider medically evacuating the sergeant for chemical-dependency treatment, but he denied the request. As would be expected with a chronic alcoholic, the sergeant could not control his drinking. A few nights later he started drinking and, thinking of the consequences of being kicked out of the army, shot himself with a .45. The lieutenant colonel didn't mention the event afterward, and I didn't bring it up to him.

SHORT TIMERS WERE GUYS who were getting close to their DEROS. Part of the process of adjusting to Vietnam involved forgetting about "the world," forgetting about making it back home, and focusing on day-to-day living in the bizarre existence in Vietnam. As the time to return approached, an individual began to think that maybe he would make it home after all and that "the world" was a real place where he might actually return and live. Once this process started, the soldier no longer wanted to take risks and became apprehensive about the inherent dangers that he had taken for granted prior to this time. Most short timers refused to travel and stayed close to their hootches. Soldiers in the field were allowed to stand down a couple of weeks prior to their DEROS.

There was a psychological ritual that took place between the short timer and his unit that helped him withdraw from them. He would shout "short" when he awakened and at frequent intervals throughout the day. He would tell his peers, "Just give me half a beer—I don't have time for a whole one—I'm short!" He checked off the days on his short-timer's calendar. He would hold a party for his buddies and give them his possessions. His peers would respond by talking about how great it would be without him in the unit. They would suggest that he might want to consider extending his tour in Vietnam because he was obviously going to be a misfit in "the world." The other guys would forget his name and talk about where "what's-his-name" used to sleep. They recounted stories of men who had been killed on their way to the departure airport.

The short timers themselves were anxious and fearful. We noted that many short timers were involved in accidents. Sometimes the injury delayed their return home, and we wondered if unconsciously this was a way to hang on to their units and their existence in Vietnam.

COMBAT ENGINEERS were at high risk because they worked on projects in the field, such as highway construction, where they were fired upon but could not fire back. There are some animal studies in psychiatry in which rats are placed on a grid that periodically gives them a shock. If they can access a lever that, when pressed, will block the electrical shock, they do not develop stress symptoms. If, on the other hand, they get a shock even if they press the lever, then they do develop stress symptoms. The combat engineers often operated in a similar situation of loss of control in that they didn't have rein over their exposure to fire and couldn't respond to the fire they received.

We saw Specialist 4 Williams (pseudonym) who had served on a road construction crew near Lai Khe. Near dusk his crew received fire, and he said that he felt helpless because he had no weapon or means to retaliate. He suffered from sleeping problems, diminished appetite, loss of energy, irritability, and depression, but denied being suicidal. He was apprehensive about returning to road construction. We talked with him about the possible reasons for the development of his symptoms and gave him antidepressant medication (one hundred milligrams of Tofranil two hours before bedtime), which seemed to improve his sleep and appetite. Nonetheless, he continued to become extremely anxious when return to his old unit was discussed. We tried to provide support by having members from his unit talk to him and encourage him as well. Finally, we concluded that we were not going to be able to return him to his old job. He was reassigned to a clerk's job in the division headquarters' base camp and was able to complete his tour in country with the division.

SERVING AS A COMBAT MEDIC was high-risk duty. Of the approximately 58,000 Americans killed in Vietnam, 1,349 of them were combat medics, and the 1st Infantry Division lost 113. Medics were expected to provide medical aid to anyone in their units who required it. They were frequently called upon to move under fire to retrieve and care for wounded soldiers.

Combat medics were attached to individual units and were extremely close to the men in their squads. Many medics felt that they were to blame if a man they tended to died and often believed that if they had been more skillful or more knowledgeable, or had acted more quickly, the man would have survived.

One of the technicians we recruited for our mental health team had been a combat medic who had suffered from guilt. Specialist Simon had gone to aid a wounded soldier under fire, put a pressure dressing on his chest wound, administered CPR, and performed a tracheotomy when he saw that the soldier wasn't able to pass air through his trachea to his lungs. Simon then inserted a chest tube to drain the blood from the wounded soldier's lungs and started an IV. Despite these heroic efforts the young soldier died from the wound. Simon saw me after becoming depressed. When I first spoke with him, he was crying, "I should have saved him. He was alive when I got to him."

"A chest surgeon couldn't have done more for your patient. The differences between you and a thoracic surgeon were he wouldn't have been as emotionally close to your patient as you were, he wouldn't have crawled out under fire to treat him, and he would have known that he did everything that could have been done for the patient."

"I still think it's my fault that he died."

"And I think you did everything anyone could have done and much more than most people would have done in your position. You are a hero, Simon. You risked your life to try to save your buddy. You did a tracheotomy, started an IV, put in a chest tube, and called in med evac, all while you were under fire."

Simon continued to cry. "That's my job. I'm no hero. He was a hero."

Simon had been in the field for eight months and would be getting short soon. He had symptoms of clinical depression, and I started him on an antidepressant (Tofranil). I felt that he would not be able to return to the field because of the severity of his symptoms. We made arrangements for him to work in our clearing station as our psychiatric hospital medic during the remainder of his tour. He was compassionate as well as skillful in his work with soldier inpatients.

Another case shows the survivor guilt many medics felt when they were unable to save a man. It also illustrates the skill of Walt Smith, the social work/psychology technician who treated the medic. Smith was bilingual and understood Hispanic culture. The following case is derived from his notes.

Gonzales (pseudonym) was a nineteen-year-old Puerto Rican combat medic. He was referred to Specialist Smith in Dau Tieng by his battalion surgeon because of his refusal to return to field duty. The medic had an excellent record during his seven months in the field and was admired by his company for his skill and dedication, but was now being considered for a court-martial.

During the initial interview and through consultations with his superiors and peers, it became apparent that Gonzales had been experiencing increasing internal and external stress for some time. Two months prior to the referral he had been wounded during an ambush in which his commanding officer was killed and several close friends were killed or wounded. During the confusion following a retrograde movement (retreat), several wounded men were apparently left briefly in the field. The medic returned under fire to aid them but was unable to save the life of one who was his friend. He attempted to carry his seriously wounded CO, whom he later said he admired and respected like a father, to safety but was unable to do so because of his small stature and his own wound. When ordered to the rear, he became hysterical and was evacuated by helicopter before some men whom he considered to be more seriously wounded and in greater need of surgical attention.

In the rear hospital he became depressed and self-critical. When he returned to his unit several weeks later, he refused to go to the field, indicating that he felt he was a proven failure as a medic and he did not want to cause further harm to his platoon because of his shortcomings. The unit was again attacked on a mission on which he had refused to participate. The battalion surgeon said he recognized that Gonzales was under stress but that he didn't appreciate the extent of the problem at the time. Another complication was that the medic's NCOIC (noncommissioned officer in charge) was an old-army Mexican American whose military experience had provided him with an opportunity for achievement and proof of manhood beyond that possible as a civilian in his home community. The NCOIC was angry and felt that the medic should be punished for what he perceived to be cowardly behavior. He was pushing the battalion surgeon and the new CO to give the medic the choice of returning to the field or being court-martialed. Smith handled the intake.

Gonzales felt that he had really messed up in the field. Smith said he had heard that Gonzales was trying to save his men and his CO even though seriously wounded himself. Gonzales replied that he should have stayed and might have saved some of the guys, but he was dusted off before guys that were a lot worse off than he was. Smith told him he was being very hard on himself and asked if he felt guilty for being alive. Gonzales didn't see why he was alive and they were dead. When asked if he was religious, he told Smith he was Catholic. Smith followed by saying that Gonzales knew then that he wasn't running things and didn't make those decisions. Gonzales started to sob, saying that they were his "bros," they were good guys, and he hadn't done enough to save them. Smith replied that he was just mourning their deaths, as he should, and that he wasn't powerful enough to save all of them. He did more than most guys would have been able to and called him a hero. Gonzales said he was no hero; his buddies were the heroes.

Smith saw Gonzales for several sessions in which he helped him mourn the loss of his friends and helped him reduce his guilt and self-criticism at not being able to save them. Gonzales returned to his unit and to the field. Smith also spoke with Gonzales's NCOIC to help him see that Gonzales was, indeed, a hero and that his earlier refusal to return to the field was not cowardice. Gonzales felt he had failed as a medic and did not want to endanger other men in his unit.

THE MP ROAD GUARDS were another group we saw frequently. These individuals were assigned to intersections in isolated areas to direct convoy traffic and provide security. It was sometimes dangerous to be alone in these areas, but the boredom and isolation that these men experienced were more stressful. Some appeared to suffer from a lack of outside stimulation and reality orientation. Some developed paranoid delusional thoughts or even auditory and sometimes visual hallucinations. For example, we saw a young MP who had been calling in reports of Viet Cong in his area. Repeated efforts to validate his observations had found no evidence of enemy presence near his station. It was eventually determined that his observations were hallucinations, and he was referred to us for evaluation and treatment. He came in the back of an ambulance to our clearing station. He responded to medication (Thorazine), rest, and the technician's efforts to help him recognize what was real and what was hallucinatory and delusional thinking. We recommended that he be restricted from isolated assignments when he returned to his unit.

RADIO OPERATORS WERE AT HIGH RISK for anxiety and made up a disproportionate number of our patients. Those in the field had long whip antennas that stuck up above the vegetation and made them more visible to the enemy. There were other factors that seemed to contribute to the development of anxiety symptoms. We were not able to determine why this particular group seemed at risk. Our impression was that as a group, these men seemed a little smarter and a little older than the typical infantrymen and were therefore more aware of the dangers they faced. They also had more to lose in terms of marriage and family and were more aware of their own mortality.

An example of the intelligence and maturity of this group was demonstrated by a young radio operator who came to us with his own workup and diagnosis, complaining that he thought he had hypoglycemia. It should be noted that many people "think" they have hypoglycemia. A few do have functional hypoglycemia caused by eating a large amount of sugar and then experiencing a drop in blood sugar when the pancreas excretes insulin in response to the elevated sugar in the bloodstream. Claims of hypoglycemia tend to be received skeptically by doctors. This man said that he experienced dizziness, confusional episodes, and tremors in the morning, but his symptoms cleared after drinking orange juice. He had been a premedical student in college before entering the service. He asked his parents to mail him a book on hypoglycemia and, after reading the book, concluded that hypoglycemia was causing his problems. We referred him to Malcolm Galen, who was an excellent internist. He agreed with the radio operator's self-diagnosis and sent him to Long Binh for additional testing. It was discovered that he had a benign pancreatic islet cell tumor that was secreting insulin. He was evacuated to Walter Reed Hospital for surgery.

A COMMON CATEGORY OF PATIENTS that could be called high risk for problems in the service were the immature young men whose parents had always run interference for them. This type of person usually entered the army with either his or his parents' hope that it would "make a man out of him." Frequently, when things became stressful, these individuals wanted to bail out and their parents supported them. A classic example was a young man in basic training who had acquired several Article 15s and ended up in the stockade for going AWOL. I had interviewed him as part of his Article 15 workup and had an opportunity to talk about him with his worried parents. They agreed that they had always babied him and bailed him out of trouble but now could no longer do so. They said they hoped he would mature in the military and agreed it was important for him to accept the consequences of his behavior. I sat in when they brought the young man out to meet with his parents. "Mom," he said tearfully, "I can't even take a walk outside." The mother turned to me and said, "Doctor, can he take a walk outside?" I reminded them of our discussion, but it was obvious that they couldn't tolerate his being unhappy in the stockade, and I went along with the recommendation for administrative discharge. This was the usual outcome. We used to return to duty most of the basic trainees who made suicidal gestures in the States, but a follow-up study showed that nearly all these individuals eventually were administratively discharged, so it was easier on them and on the organization just to go ahead and get them out.

On rare occasions we were able to help an immature young man with enabling parents succeed in the military. St. John (pseudonym), an E-4 infantryman with two months in country, came to our attention because of a congressional inquiry initiated by his parents. They felt that he should not have been sent to Vietnam, much less a combat division, because he was "mentally retarded and brain damaged." In reviewing this man's substantial medical record and taking his history, we found that he had always been overprotected by his parents, who early in his life became convinced that he was mentally handicapped. They were surprised that he was able to complete high school but would not permit him to apply for college because they believed it would be too much for him. The first congressional inquiry came when he was drafted into the army, and another followed during basic training and advanced infantry training. Another inquiry was received after he was given orders for service in Vietnam. Now he was being sent to us for evaluation.

His previous psychological testing revealed that his IQ was average and, other than mild apprehension, he had no symptoms of mental problems. When we discussed the findings and the situation with him, he admitted that his parents had overprotected him throughout his childhood. I sat down with him and discussed his situation.

"This is your fourth congressional inquiry—your parents must be quite worried about you."

"I wish they would just stay out of things. I wanted to go to college, and they were afraid to let me go. They didn't want me to go into the army, and they sure didn't want me to go to Vietnam."

"How did you feel about the army and Vietnam?"

"I was drafted, but so were a lot of guys. I figured it was something I had to do. I was scared when I got orders."

"Did you have a difficult time when you got here?"

"I was scared when I got to the unit, listening to all the war stories and everything."

"Do you think you were more scared than the other guys?"

"Probably not. We were all scared."

"How do you want me to answer the inquiry?"

"You're the doc, but you can tell them I'm doing okay and I want to finish my tour with my unit."

"Then that's what I'll say. What are your plans after you complete your tour?"

"I want to go to college. I figure with the GI Bill I'll be able to go whether my folks help out or not."

"Even though it bothers you that your folks are, as you said, somewhat overprotective, you must miss them and their support."

"Yeah, I'm homesick, but I try not to think about it. I really want to show them that I can make it on my own. If I can get through this year in Vietnam, they will see that I'm not handicapped and it will help my own self-confidence."

"I agree with you one hundred percent. Stop by and see me whenever you are in the base camp."

We informally checked on his performance in the unit. I wasn't going to intervene in any way that would make his assignment easier, as this could only undermine our effort to increase his self-confidence. St. John functioned in a combat unit throughout his tour and stopped by to see me once when his unit was in from the field. He did very well during a stressful tour of duty and was decorated for valor. At the completion of his tour, I enjoyed writing to his parents to detail the types of hazardous duty he had endured and repeated that his psychological testing and psychiatric consultations had shown no evidence of any mental handicap whatsoever. I ended by saying I hope that they shared our pride in his performance and courage in combat. I showed him the letter.

"Thanks, doc, I appreciate all the help you guys have given me."

"We appreciate your kind words, but we didn't do it—you did."

"Well, this is it. I'm going home next week."

"Hey, congratulations! I heard you did well in your unit and hung in there when the going got rough."

"It was the same for everybody."

"But you made it, and you made it in a combat unit."

"Yeah, I feel pretty good about it actually."

"You should, and you should know that if you had the courage and determination to stick it out through a year of combat, you can accomplish any goals you set in life."

"My goal is college."

"There is no doubt in my mind that you will do well in school."

St. John smiled. "What's even better, there's no doubt in mine either."

MEN WHO RETURNED from R&R or from hardship leave often had difficulty readjusting to Vietnam and their units. Everyone was entitled to one R&R during their tour, and many took more than one. Most of us felt down after returning to the same boring routine after a few days of luxury and overindulgence. However, some men became anxious for their own safety and were unable to function. Some would go AWOL instead of returning to Vietnam.

This was particularly frequent among those who returned to the United States for leave. The military offered thirty days of leave home near Christmastime for soldiers who would extend in Vietnam or in the military. Some homesick enlisted men would sign anything to be home for Christmas and then, near the end of the leave, realize that they had agreed to six more months in country or another year in the military. Rather than face this, they would go AWOL. We felt that the dynamics of this group were similar to that of the short timer. These men were confronted with the comfort and reality of "the world" and, as a result, could no longer maintain their counterphobic defenses. Therefore, they became too anxious for their personal safety to function well in Vietnam and, at the same time, they retained their attachment to the reality back home. Those who returned to their units in Vietnam were now preoccupied with missing "the world" and with fear for their own well-being in Vietnam.

Our approach was to talk to them about the reasons underlying their difficulties. Those who were psychologically minded enough to understand these dynamics were helped by this insight, but few were able to function as well as they had before R&R. When we explained the situation to their COs, some could empathize based on their own letdown after taking an R&R. Frequently, they were able to complete their tours of duty if they were assigned to the base camp. This approach was similar to giving routine assignments to short timers to allow them to stand down. Those who could not complete their tours of duty were either medically discharged or, more often, administratively discharged.

One such individual was Private First Class Wilkes (pseudonym). He was a nineteen-year-old, single Caucasian who served in the supply unit. He had taken advantage of the army's offer for a thirty-day leave home over the holidays with the stipulation that he would extend his tour in Vietnam by another three months. He returned to his unit on time but refused to leave his quarters, stopped eating, and appeared to be markedly depressed. He regretted his decision to accept the leave and regretted having returned to Vietnam. During the day, he was withdrawn and irritable and found it difficult to concentrate. At night, he had trouble sleeping. Although he admitted to having fleeting suicidal thoughts, they never evolved to planning to take his own life. We started him on an antidepressant (Tofranil) and talked to him about how he was reacting to the consequences of his impulsive decision. He met with Falzone.

Wilkes said that he had spent Christmas with his family and his girlfriend, but it was too short. It was really hard to come back. He thought about staying but would have ended up in the stockade or looking over his shoulder for the rest of his life. He didn't want to be in the army and didn't want to spend three more months here. He had really messed up by taking the deal to go home. He would have done anything to get home for Christmas, but now he was in a mess. Falzone responded that he had already made it through almost a year and could handle another three months. But Wilkes said that he couldn't eat or sleep and felt lousy.

Falzone told him that he had depression and that's why he was given Tofranil. He would feel better after it kicked in. Falzone asked Wilkes if he ever thought about suicide. Wilkes had, but he had not thought about how to do it, just that he would be better off dead. Falzone told him to come to the clearing station and have the technicians call him if Wilkes ever felt that he was in a corner and couldn't get out. He assured Wilkes that he should keep coming in and would start to feel better in a couple of weeks. He was scheduled to meet regularly with one of the technicians to vent his feelings.

SOME PSYCHIATRISTS DESCRIBED the middle months of the tour ("the hump") as a stressful period in which the individual soldier became bored and listless and increased his use of drugs and alcohol. Most of the troops in Vietnam were considered support troops. Even though we were assigned to a combat division, most of our patients were from support units or served in a support capacity. Obviously there were stresses in the field, but men serving in support areas had stresses as well.

Support troops had to deal with boredom. Every day involved the same routine. Drugs and alcohol were readily available and used much more extensively by support troops than those in the field. There was more tension between black and white troops. In addition, there was the REMF social order. This term was used to refer to anyone in a more desirable, comfortable, or safer assignment than your own. The men in combat units with the most dangerous duties, such as Rangers who were LRRPs (long-range reconnaissance patrol), were at one end of the continuum. Military personnel serving in the United States were at the other end. In between, the general hierarchy went from those at the fire support bases, those at base camps, and those assigned to large support areas such as Long Binh or Saigon. I was as far forward as a psychiatrist could be assigned, but I was an REMF to the combat troops who fought the enemy out in the paddies. Similarly, Dau Tieng and Lai Khe received rocket and mortar attacks more frequently than Di An; therefore, the men stationed at those bases regarded the men stationed at Di An as REMFs.

There was a kind of one-upmanship that took place when forward- and rear-assigned individuals interacted. Typically this occurred by subtly pointing out differences in hardships and risks faced by the men. For example, two infantrymen might talk with a mechanic at a base camp and express admiration of his relative comforts—in this case, an outhouse.

"How is the war going?"

"Okay, I guess—you guys ought to know."

"Hey, what is this?"

"Just a crapper."

"A what? Unbelievable! What do you do with it? It's fantastic, and it smells great too!"

"Hey, you remember—it's what people in the world dump in; you squat over this hole."

They would go on admiring his conveniences and then drop in a few war stories. This interaction allowed those with the more dangerous and primitive assignments to express some of the hostility they felt toward those with safer and more comfortable assignments.

Sometimes the anger toward REMFs produced explosive violence, especially when aggravated by factors such as the communication gap between white, inexperienced officers and black enlisted men from inner-city environments. I remember one morning when a short, thin, black enlisted man was escorted in handcuffs into the psychiatric hootch by two MPs from the LBJ. The enlisted man was to have a forensic psychiatric evaluation to determine his fitness to stand trial and to assess whether he was sane at the time he murdered an NCO. I took a detailed history and obtained the following information from him. The man had come from a single-parent home in a rough neighborhood in Detroit. His mother had lived with a series of men while he was growing up. As a small child, he had been frequently beaten up by bigger children until he started carrying a knife and established a reputation for being dangerous. He got into trouble with the law in high school after seriously injuring another student. When the court gave him the choice of going to jail or enlisting into the army, he opted for the army. At the graduation party at his advanced infantry training class, he attacked the sergeant. When the army gave him the choice of being court-martialed or sent to Vietnam, he chose Vietnam. His infantry unit in Vietnam made him a point man, hoping to get rid of him. Instead, his heightened alertness and street smarts enabled him to excel in the field, and he was decorated for valor. While at base camp during a stand down, he was berated by a white base camp officer for wearing nonregulation tiger-striped fatigues and then ordered to go to the supply sergeant to get a proper uniform. He went to the base camp supply sergeant, who swore at him and told him to go see his unit supply officer. Instead, he went to the nearby village, got drunk, smoked some dope, and had sex with one of the prostitutes. He returned to the base camp where the same officer spotted him and once more screamed at him to get a correct uniform. He returned to the same base supply sergeant, who again swore at him and told him to go see his unit supply officer. He returned with his M16 rifle and emptied a clip into the supply sergeant, killing him in front of several witnesses. Matthews, our tech in Lai Khe, backed up his story. We determined that he was fit to stand trial and that he was legally sane at the time of the incident. Nonetheless, his defense attorney was able to use our workup to help the court understand the factors that had contributed to the event. This was a person who developed a hair-trigger temper in childhood and whose controls had been further weakened by drugs and alcohol. His emotional state had deteriorated because he had been repeatedly frustrated by not being able to comply with what he was ordered to do. The REMF (white) officer in a base camp was jumping on him for not meeting a petty REMF rule about uniforms. Despite two attempts to comply with the officer's order, an REMF (white) supply sergeant refused to issue the uniform that he needed to avoid additional reprimands. The soldier was sentenced to prison, but the sentence was less than it would have been had his behavior not been explained.

This pattern of resentment toward REMFs occurred at all levels of the REMF social order. For example, during trips to Long Binh we would don our flak jackets, helmets, and weapons and then stand around admiring their air conditioning, running water, American nurses, and the amenities at the large base camp. Sometimes we directed our remarks to the staff, but we often would talk loudly among ourselves so that the staff could overhear.

Some men went further and used the guilt that many REMFs felt about being in a safer and more comfortable post to manipulate and control them. Each month the Psychiatric Department of the 93rd Evacuation Hospital held a case conference and invited the division psychiatrists and their staffs to attend. One morning we walked into a conference a little late. One of the evacuation hospital psychiatrists had been interviewing an enlisted man from the 1st Infantry Division in front of an audience of psychiatrists, psychiatric social workers, psychologists, nurses, medics, and technicians. The patient, Private First Class Walker (pseudonym), had identified himself as 11 Bravo (infantryman). He had been telling the audience and his interviewer that after seeing his best buddy killed before his eyes, he had started drinking to cope with the shock and grief he was experiencing. He told how his state of dysfunction had deteriorated to the point where he had been sent to the evacuation hospital. The audience was empathetic and wanted to medically evacuate him out of country, feeling that he had suffered enough. The interviewer saw us enter the room and asked me to take over the interview. I went up onstage, and Walker noted my 1st Infantry Division patch.

"What's your MOS [military occupational specialty]?"

"11 Bravo, sir."

"Where are you assigned?"

"Headquarters Company, sir."

"What do you do there?"

"Deliver mail, sir."

A murmur went through the audience at this point.

"How did you ever see anyone get killed while you were delivering mail at headquarters?"

"Well, no, sir, I didn't actually see anyone get killed—I just heard that he got killed."

By this time the audience realized that they had been duped and wanted to punish the soldier! Eventually they calmed down and sent him back to the division to continue delivering the mail.

This interview convinced me of the need to have psychiatrists in combat divisions. The REMFs in Long Binh believed the soldier's war stories. They were glad they weren't in the field but felt guilty about having a relatively safe assignment while others served in more dangerous and less comfortable settings. The soldier played on their guilt and controlled them in this way. By implicitly asserting that the audience members lived in comfortable surroundings and had no idea of what "hell" he had been through, he played on their sympathy to persuade them to send him home. It is similar to a panhandler with a disability confronting a passerby and playing on the person's guilt to get money.

If an REMF assigned to delivering mail at the 1st Infantry Division headquarters could do this to mental health professionals serving in Vietnam, one can only imagine how someone claiming to be a Vietnam veteran could manipulate mental health professionals back in the United States.

The ability to use guilt to manipulate others continues to this day in the legacy of impostors who claim to have been traumatized while serving in Vietnam. In their book *Stolen Valor,* B. G. Burkett and Glenna Whitley describe how men with long hair, fatigues, boots, and boonie hats portray themselves as the crazy, drugged-out, violent stereotype many people have of Vietnam veterans to garner sympathy, attention, and disability compensation. By researching government records, the authors show that many of these people either never served in Vietnam or served in a support capacity, such as a cook or clerk. I once saw a guy walking through a shopping mall at home with a jacket that read "When I die I will go to heaven because I spent a year in hell—Long Binh 1969–1970." To men in a combat division, Long Binh was considered pretty close to heaven.

My personal experience is that most people who tell war stories back in the United States are probably full of it. I have seen guys who start to tell war stories but then admit to serving as cooks or clerks and not having any direct combat experience once they learn that I had been in Vietnam. My father-in-law survived the Bataan Death March during World War II and was a Japanese prisoner of war for more than three years. He did not talk about his experiences. Typically, Vietnam veterans rarely mention that they served there. Some, if they know I was there, will talk about it a little. Over the years I've seen Vietnam "wannabes" who tell war stories about the trauma they experienced although they never served in Vietnam. One such case was the second husband of one of my patients. Her first husband had been killed tragically in an accident. She later met a man in a bar who almost immediately told her that he was a Vietnam veteran. She brought him to an appointment and introduced him to my head nurse and me. The man told us that he had been wounded when his helicopter was shot down and that he crawled to the edge of the jungle and watched the Viet Cong kill his crewmates. He had several other exciting adventures that he described in detail. After he left, I discussed the stories with my head nurse, Eric Traub RN, MSN, who served with the 82nd Airborne Division in Vietnam. At first we were sympathetic, but as the descriptions of his exploits continued and escalated, we began to suspect that the guy was full of it. A few months later, the fellow's wife noticed that he didn't have any scars although he described being wounded by bullets and shrapnel. He said that they had healed. She asked his mother when he was in Vietnam; she responded that he was never in Vietnam. Needless to say, it strains credibility to have someone brag about his war experience to women in bars and his therapist but never tell his mother. When his wife confronted him with his mother's statement, he replied that he had been on a secret mission and no one knew he was there. During our sympathetic phase we paid the man to serve as our office Santa Claus at our annual Christmas party. He arrived late, obviously intoxicated, but did a great job with the kids and played the part well—he was a good actor.

I think that the REMF phenomenon explains some of the provocative and negative reactions that veterans have toward those who did not serve in Vietnam or other combat areas. Their thinking is, "Where were you when I was over there?" It also explains why many veterans of the Vietnam War feel little respect for government officials, especially those who avoided service. This attitude has caused a few veterans to have problems interacting with civilian authority, difficulty maintaining employment, and troubled relationships. Vietnam veterans who remained in the military after their tour of duty often had trouble adjusting to stateside assignments. Most of us have gone on with our lives and tried to forget the experience and maintain some sort of acceptable social facade, but some of that feeling is present in all of us.

IDENTIFYING INDIVIDUALS who were likely to experience psychiatric symptoms enabled us to pass on this information to commanders and doctors within our division. At my request, Lieutenant Colonel Hefner had all new battalion surgeons stop by our office for orientation when they arrived in the division. This enabled me to meet them to explain what services we had to offer and pass on the information we were discovering. We discussed the problems faced by individuals at high risk for psychological problems and discussed issues such as drug and alcohol use, morale, and communication between newly trained officers and drafted high school dropouts. This information also went to the commanders throughout the division, the battalion surgeons, and the USARV medical bulletin for doctors in Vietnam. We later published our findings in psychiatric journals in order to share them with other military psychiatrists.

I found that monitoring events and studying our data helped me distance myself from the emotional trauma of the day-to-day events. I have always found that trying to study my clinical actions objectively has improved my clinical work. In addition, the clinical research aspects of our efforts made the work less tedious and more interesting for the social work/psychology technicians.

WE PROGRESSED BEYOND providing direct services, such as evaluating and treating soldiers, to providing preventive services. We identified groups of individuals who appeared to be at higher risk of developing psychiatric symptoms in Vietnam. The next step would be to identify stress periods within organizational units in the division and to intervene to try to reduce those stresses.

CHAPTER 9

High-Stress Periods

I started my work in the division by training and supervising the technicians to develop a uniform approach based on the Menninger case study method and to provide good direct service to our patients. This included having the technicians observe Captain Pabst and me interview patients and then observe each other work. We discussed treatment approaches as well. Once the direct services were up to par, we started looking at our data to try to identify high-risk individuals. When we felt we had identified soldiers who seemed to be at higher risk for psychiatric symptoms, we began to look at the individual units themselves. I was interested in attempting to apply the methods of organizational diagnosis and intervention developed by Harry Levinson. I shared what I had learned with the technicians and Captain Pabst, and we began to monitor stress indices for each unit in the division. When we observed a rise in a particular unit's level of stress, we would contact and usually visit the unit to try to determine what was causing the distress.

We kept records of our cases and noted that periodically we would receive several referrals from the same unit at approximately the same time. When this happened, we would go to the unit itself and try to determine what was causing the stress that led to these referrals. Specialist Smith, the applied anthropologist, was experienced at recording observations of human behavior and was comfortable going to units to try to ascertain the source of the stress. Sometimes the stress was due to factors we could do nothing about—when a unit was ambushed, for example. On the other hand, sometimes there were events such as a change of command that contributed to the stress. In order to improve our organizational consultation and to learn more about the types of stress that led to referrals, we began charting stress indicators for every unit in the division. We monitored the number of chaplain visits, accident rates, sick-call rates, mental health visits, inspector general complaints, Article 15s, court-martials, and malaria rates (this was a command indicator because it reflected unit discipline—if men didn't take their pills as ordered, they got malaria). It is easy to obtain this type of information in the military, so with Lieutenant Colonel Hefner's help, we got on the list to receive this data each month.

When the stress indicators for a unit increased, we contacted the battalion commander and battalion surgeon about the unit and made arrangements to meet and discuss our observations. If command concurred that there were problems in a specific company, we would meet with the company commander and the executive officer. If it appeared that further evaluation was warranted, we would interview members of command and assign a technician to the unit to live and work with the enlisted men while gathering information about the unit's stresses. Afterward we would report back to the unit, starting at the top, in written and oral form. Sometimes we could give specific recommendations to try to help reduce the unit's stress, and in other situations, the process itself seemed to help the unit focus on the emotional aspects of the organization and solve the problem.

By graphing the stress indicators for each unit and by going to units to discuss organizational factors that were producing stress within the units, we were able to identify a few organizational stress periods. For example, one unit that stood out was a dump-truck company that had a high incidence of drug-related problems, such as referrals to sick call, referrals to psychiatry, arrests, and Article 15s. We consulted with the key members of the company, and Specialist Smith stayed with the unit to gather information. He found that the company commander put his own promotion above the welfare of his men and refused to give the men breaks or even Christmas Day off. There was also a chronic shortage of tires and spare parts, motivating drivers to steal the needed equipment from neighboring units. The unit did not have safety cages to protect men working on high-pressure tires, and one driver was killed as a result. Armed guards were not provided to protect the truck convoys, and drivers had to keep their M16s in plastic bags to prevent them from getting jammed by dust. The AK-47s used by the Viet Cong did not jam with dust, and the VC would use the dust as cover when mounting ambushes. The drivers were frightened and jumpy and had killed some Vietnamese children who were digging into an old well near the road. Although the children were looking for food and salvageable items in the army trash, the drivers thought they were withdrawing hidden weapons from a cache. Another problem was that the first sergeant of the unit was a chronic alcoholic who was hard on drug users.

When the findings, largely obtained from Specialist Smith's investigation, were conveyed to command, some positive changes took place. New spare parts and a steel cage were ordered for the unit. The commanding officer was replaced, and the first sergeant was medically evacuated for chemical-dependency treatment. Specialist Smith was given his third Army Commendation Medal as a result of the consultation. He was also awarded a Bronze Star before leaving country.

THE COMBAT UNIT is a vitally interdependent group whose safety depends on the group integrity and its leadership. We know from studies of group and individual dynamics that change itself produces uncertainty and a basic fear of loss. The commander is responsible for the lives of his men. Not only is he responsible for their clothing, food, shelter, punishment, privileges, and discipline, but he must make the day-to-day decisions that will result in their survival or death on the battlefield. As a result, the unit regards the departure of its commander as a significant loss of an important figure. It also represents a loss of the identity of the unit, as developed under the commander's leadership. Strong negative as well as positive feelings toward the departing leader are evoked. The departure reminds individuals in the unit of their feelings toward loss in the past. The situation is similar to the termination of any close, significant relationship.

We found that in units that showed stress and difficulty in assimilating a new leader, the departing commander seemed to make an unconscious effort to deflect the angry feelings of the men in the unit. More specifically, the departing CO tended to loosen his controls and give additional privileges to the unit. The unit encouraged this tendency by praising him, joking about the extension of privileges, and expressing apprehension about the successor. These COs provided little opportunity for units to express their angry feelings about being abandoned. For example, hints by the unit members that they would forget him following his departure evoked further privileges from the commander. These commanders left the less agreeable disciplinary duties to their successors. Frequently, they excessively briefed their replacements and sometimes even bolstered the unit's apprehension about the successor.

One instance in the 1st Infantry Division happened while Captain Jones (pseudonym), the commander of a combat company, was preparing to leave Vietnam. He had become cynical and vocally criticized the battalion commander and the system in general. He became informal in his relationships with the enlisted men in his company. For example, he would drop in to their quarters and invite them to his hootch for bull sessions. These sessions centered on the ignorance and nit-picking of the battalion commander.

This company felt that he was a rare officer, who understood and sided with the men of the unit. The battalion commander was seen as the source of all the harassment suffered by the company. The enlisted men were apprehensive about who the battalion commander would select to replace Captain Jones. They feared he would select someone like himself who would act punitively toward them. Rumors began circulating that he was sending up a tough commander to shape up the unit.

The night on which the new company commander, Captain Brown (pseudonym), assumed command, a claymore mine was triggered in his hootch and a note was posted warning him not to mess around with the unit. For a turbulent period of several weeks, any order from Captain Brown was perceived to be harassment and was resisted by the company. The indicators of organizational stress for this unit showed an abrupt increase.

After a month or so the men were able to observe many of Captain Brown's good qualities, and the battalion commander again became the focus of angry comment. Captain Brown was seen as not being so bad but rather as having had the misfortune of being assigned to a bad commander. In a couple of months the unit was functioning at its previous level, and stress indicators had returned to normal.

During the replacement period we received several referrals from this company. We consulted because of the increased referrals and the elevated stress indicators associated with the company. We observed that Captain Jones had unconsciously avoided the negative feelings that his departure produced, and that by loosening his controls and befriending the men, he made it difficult for them to express any feelings other than positive ones for him. He also made the battalion commander into a scapegoat for their angry feelings. When Captain Brown replaced the idealized Captain Jones, he received the brunt of all the angry feelings the unit could not express toward Captain Jones.

We used this case as an example when we spoke with other units and with incoming battalion surgeons in the division to advise them about stress periods within the organization. We recommended that they follow the example of commanders who tightened their controls, took care of the disagreeable tasks (which some referred to as the "dirty laundry"), and were tougher on their units before the change of command. This permitted the men to be angry with them for leaving and made it much easier to accept the new commander.

These dynamics associated with changing command were portrayed in the CBS special "The World of Charlie Company" and in greater detail in John Laurence's book *The Cat from Hue.* The documentary, televised in April 1970, filmed the unit's reaction to the replacement of the popular Captain Bob Jackson by Captain Al Rice as the new CO of 2nd Battalion, 7th Cavalry, Company C. In a segment filmed after the popular company commander had finished his tour, the entire company refused to walk down a road in Tay Ninh province. The veteran foot soldiers complained that the new CO, Captain Rice, was too inexperienced; that walking on road exposed them to a probable ambush; and that there wasn't enough cover if they got into a firefight. Later, Maj. John H. Dorf of the Military Science Department at West Point requested a copy of the CBS film to help teach the cadets about the problems associated with change of command.

These same dynamics are within the experience of most civilians. I saw a doctor whose practice partner died suddenly and unexpectedly. The doctor tried to be nice to his partner's patients and to follow the same treatment approach his partner had used with them. Despite his best efforts, the patients seemed to be upset and angry with him. He came to see me because he was depressed about the loss of his partner and friend and because he felt he couldn't seem to do anything right in the eyes of his partner's patients. I explained to him that they weren't angry with him—they were angry with his partner for dying and leaving them. He was catching their anger because they couldn't direct it toward someone who died. Our favorite minister retired and died a year later. I gave his replacement my paper on change of command and discussed the difficulties he was likely to experience. Despite my efforts to help the new minister understand the dynamics of the situation, many people left the church, donations went down, and the new minister ended up taking an early retirement.

THE INFUSION PROGRAM, known by the troops as the "confusion program," created considerable organizational and individual stress in Vietnam. Men with more than two months remaining on their tour of duty in Vietnam were not allowed to return home with their departing units but were instead "infused" into other units. The soldier lost his close group ties with his unit and whatever sense of security he had. He also lost the benefits of having more time in country than many others in the unit. Seniority was important to individuals serving in Vietnam because it resulted in more comfortable and generally less risky assignments. For example, after gaining a certain level of seniority, the men in mechanized units were allowed to ride on the tracks (vehicles that move on treads) rather than walk. After having established himself in a former unit, the infused soldier was faced with being an FNG and starting at the bottom with regard to privileges. It was also difficult to put away the identity and allegiance to the prior unit and bind with a rival unit.

To make matters worse, the gaining units did not want these men. They didn't know them and didn't trust them. They were also offended by the negative comments that infused men would make about their unit and their typically poor attitude about being in a new unit. The infused soldiers were often ostracized or made scapegoats in the new unit. Thus, increased stress was felt by the soldier who was being infused as well as by the gaining unit.

In our consultation work we discussed this as a stress period with commanders and battalion surgeons. Discussion and understanding of the situation did help to some degree, but this remained a continual source of problems and stress within the division as units were withdrawn.

I WAS PLEASED that we attempted to apply Dr. Levinson's approach within the military organization. Our efforts were not very sophisticated and were limited by time constraints but did seem to yield promise in terms of reducing the stress within the units we studied. A good part of the success was due to encouraging people to look at problems within units and then discuss possible solutions. Another factor was the Hawthorne effect, which resulted from paying attention and listening to individual members of the unit. Some of the positive effects of our unit consultation may have been due to this phenomenon. We spoke with all levels of the unit to obtain information regarding stresses in the unit and then fed back our finding to unit members. Just the process of paying attention to individuals in the unit may have had a positive effect. We obtained information that helped commanders prevent problems in their units. The process of going to the source of the difficulty rather than treating individual soldiers referred to us from the units helped us understand the problems of racism and poor communication between officers and men within some of the units in the division. We were excited at trying some new approaches to the evaluation and intervention to alleviate stress in the military. This in turn raised our own morale and helped us pass the time more quickly.

The provision of direct mental health service in the division requires a medically trained psychiatric specialist because, as mentioned earlier, even in the young, medically screened population of the army, we found a number of soldiers whose mental symptoms were caused by underlying medical problems. In addition, treatment often involved the use of psychotropic medications. Organizational consultation, on the other hand, is an area in which a nonmedical consultant could do as well as or better than someone with psychiatric training. A higher-ranking individual with combat command experience who had additional training in organizational diagnosis and consultation would be excellent in this role. In my opinion, it would be advantageous if he or she were black or Hispanic.

Because individuals retire at a relatively young age in the military, I wonder if outstanding commanders and high-ranking NCOs could be utilized as consultants in this capacity after their retirement. They would be more likely to be welcomed and listened to by commanders as senior mentors. The consultant would not be consulting about strategy but about how to prevent or reduce organizational stress within individual units.

TRYING NEW APPROACHES to evaluate and reduce stress in the military organization had the added effect of boosting our own morale and energy. In addition to the uplifting effects of our work, we had opportunities to leave the country to look forward to during the year. My friends back at Fort Knox provided me with a special surprise at Christmas that made my tour more pleasant and less stressful.

CHAPTER 10

The First R&R

Rest and recuperation (R&R, also known as I&I, or intoxication and intercourse) was a break from the stifling routine of a tour in Vietnam. These leave periods gave us something to look forward to for months in advance and something to talk and think about for weeks afterward. It was a brief respite of indulgence and luxury.

THE MONSOON SEASON in our area was drawing to a close by October. The intense hour-long showers and the steamy mornings were about to end. In the Midwest we talked constantly about the weather because it was always changing and was important to the farmers. In Vietnam, we didn't talk much about the weather because it was pretty much the same—hot. The only change was that sometimes it was hot and steamy and sometimes it was hot and dry. When the temperature occasionally dropped to eighty-five degrees at night, we put on sweatshirts and complained about the cold. We didn't care about the weather. We were used to the heat, and our focus was on our R&R to Hong Kong, which we had been planning and preparing for since spring.

Capt. Ross Guarino had been one of the commanding officers of the basic medical officers' class at Fort Sam Houston when I attended. He had been in ROTC during college and had more military training than most new doctors. Ross was a trim, dark-haired,

Italian American from Buffalo, New York, whose father owned a body shop. He was hyperactive and also very intelligent. He later became one of the busiest and most successful cardiovascular surgeons in Buffalo. When he arrived in Vietnam, he was assigned as a battalion surgeon to one of the division combat units. After two months in the field he came to Di An, where he assumed command of Alpha Company.

All the doctors in the medical battalion had Nikon FTn Photomic cameras with 50-mm f/1.2 Nikkor lenses. They also had the same stereo equipment (Sansui 1000 tuners, TEAC tape decks, Fisher speakers). Later, as I traveled around the country, I found that other units had their own preferences. Some units, for example, favored Canon cameras and Fisher tuners. It was understood that whenever a member of the unit went to Hong Kong on R&R, he would buy whatever equipment other members of the unit wanted to order. I ordered my Nikon shortly after arriving in Vietnam and took photographs of just about everything I saw. We all said that we had the same images, the same banana trees, the same ox carts, the same lizards. I heard that some men in the field would take photographs during firefights. Looking back, I think I took pictures because the place was unique but even more because it helped me psychologically distance myself from my existence there. It made me feel more like an observer than a participant.

John was going to meet his wife in Hawaii for R&R. Because we were officially allowed one R&R (although most of us ended up with two), that was all he was going to take. Ross and I discussed going to Hong Kong together. We decided that if we went on R&R immediately, we wouldn't have much to look forward to for the rest of the year. So we scheduled our R&R in the fall. An R&R typically consisted of five days in Hong Kong, Bangkok, Australia, Hawaii, or Singapore, with the flight paid for by the government. The army recommended hotels, which in turn gave discounts to soldiers.

In preparation for the Hong Kong sojourn, we read about cameras and stereo equipment. I was the camera expert, and Ross, who had built a ham radio from scratch, concentrated on electronic equipment. We read brochures and travel books and talked to guys who had gone there on their R&Rs. By September we were familiar with the prices of the latest camera and stereo equipment and knew generally where we should shop and what we wanted to do in Hong Kong.

We picked a hotel that was attached to the largest shopping mall. Malcolm Galen was meeting his wife in Hong Kong, and we suggested that they might want to go shopping with us and take a few tours. Galen said he didn't think they would be shopping with us and if we didn't run into each other in Hong Kong, it would be fine with him. We packed our civilian clothing and headed to the airport at Bien Hoa for the relatively short flight. We arrived in Hong Kong and checked into our hotel. The room was modern, decorated with teak woodwork, and seemed luxurious to us. Air conditioning, flush toilets, running water, clean linens, room service, and a bright modern facility were all cause for excitement. The air in Hong Kong was cool, fresh, and clean.

The mixture of modern and ancient architecture, Victoria's Peak with its cogwheel train, and the busy harbor made Hong Kong a beautiful city day and night. We heard the bustling sounds of traffic but no helicopters or explosions. It was enjoyable to wear something other than fatigues and to visit a modern city.

We each had about ten thousand dollars of other people's cash and their orders for camera and stereo equipment. We also had a substantial supply of personal spending money. The first place we went was one of the recommended camera stores. The owner invited us to sit and have some tea and a bowl of rice. We complimented him on his hospitality and his establishment. He talked about the prosperity of the United States. We discussed China and its ancient history compared to our relatively new nation. We were following what we had read about the proper way to transact business in China. Although the Chinese probably appreciated our efforts, we were woefully outclassed by their negotiation skills. Although I don't think we came out ahead in the bargaining, we did avoid being cheated. Moreover, by our standards, we were able to get fantastically low prices on the items we purchased.

Eventually, I asked the proprietor for his price for a Nikon FTn Photomic camera. He quoted an unbelievably low price. I then asked him how much twenty cameras would cost. The owner clapped his hands together and sent two assistants running out of the store to find more cameras while the assistants in the store frantically piled them up for us. He named an even lower price because of the large-volume purchase. We went through the same process for the lenses. The prices were excellent, but as we had been cautioned, it was necessary to go through each box to make sure that all the equipment was there and was the particular product that had been specified. We found a camera with the light meter missing and a Nikon box that contained a Soligor lens instead of a Nikkor lens. On both occasions, the owner apologized profusely for the oversight and gave us a few inexpensive items to compensate for the alleged error. Once we had all the camera equipment, we took it to our hotel room. We then headed to the electronics store, where we went through the same procedure to purchase stereo equipment. We had the equipment shipped back to Vietnam rather than try to take it on the plane ourselves. Each soldier was permitted six hundred pounds of hold baggage that could be shipped to the United States for free. Shipping from Hong Kong to Vietnam was also free. Some guys wanted their stuff shipped directly home, but most set the stereo equipment up in their hootches and used it in Vietnam until they left country.

Even though we sent most of our paychecks home, we had a lot of spending money because there was little to buy in Vietnam. Money for booze went a long way because beer cost ten cents and mixed drinks cost twenty-five cents. Our only other expenses were for toiletries and occasional meals at restaurants in Saigon or Long Binh. In any event, we both had plenty of spending money and the prices were dirt cheap. On our next stop, we were measured for tailor-made suits. We selected fabrics and were measured for suits, vests, sport coats, pants, shirts, and accessories. We scheduled a time to return for the second fitting with the tailor and went to the specialty shops to look at jewelry, ivory, jade, furs, and other luxury items. I visited a furniture store that featured hand-carved teak furniture. I overheard an American tourist in the store who was ordering a custom-made yacht. I spotted a teak desk that had three-quarter carved figures that was priced at seventy-five dollars. I motioned to Ross to come over and check it out. We both were amazed at the price and were talking loudly about what an unbelievable deal this was. The shop owner thought that we felt it was priced too high. He came over to tell us that if we would bring a picture or describe a design, they would custom-carve it for us for the same price! We hadn't planned on buying furniture but couldn't resist having several pieces, including a desk, shipped back to the States. We purchased gifts to ship back to our families, such as ivory, jade, and Chinese dolls.

We decided to take a break from shopping and went to a bar in the mall. We overheard a Japanese man and Chinese man negotiating business with each other in English. The Chinese man went on and on about the efficiency and technological accomplishments of Japan. The Japanese man waxed on about the ancient history of China and the great wisdom of the Chinese people. They continued to compliment each other's country during the entire time we were there. We could not figure out who was selling and who was buying or what product was involved. We speculated that the actual business must have been brought up days later.

At the bar we met a stocky, blond American in his late thirties wearing an open Hawaiian sports shirt over a T-shirt, dark slacks, loafers, and aviator sunglasses. He was drinking alone. We struck up a conversation with him and learned that he had been a military pilot in Korea and later flew as a commercial pilot until he retired. He lived in Saigon and was flying "spooks" into Cambodia and Laos for Air America, which was owned and operated by the CIA. He co-owned a bar in Saigon with his "Vietnamese wife," explaining that he had married her in Saigon but that to him the marriage was good only while they lived in Vietnam. He also had a wife and children back in the States. He said he liked living in Saigon except that once when he was flying a mission, someone broke into his apartment and stole his television set. After this happened a second time, he booby-trapped the set so that an explosive inside the set would detonate thirty minutes after it was unplugged. He returned from a flight to find that his television had been stolen for the third time. The next morning he read in the paper that a taxi had blown up in the suburbs of Saigon. He laughed and said, "Haven't lost a TV since."

We actually did run into Malcolm Galen and his wife walking through the mall. They joined us for a drink, and we decided to have dinner together that night. We had the concierge at our hotel set up a dinner for four at the Mandarin Hotel. The huge doormen at the Mandarin looked even bigger with their turbans and scimitars. They bowed, held open the doors, and invited us to enter the five-star hotel. The lavishly appointed restaurant was filled with well-groomed cruise-ship passengers dressed in tuxedos, evening gowns, jewels, and furs. We felt shabby in our polyester civilian clothing. Both Ross and I sensed that the other customers were reacting negatively toward us. At first we thought that it was due to our cheaper clothing but later decided that the odor offended them. Our clothes reeked of the effluvia of the Sai Gon River where it had been washed, but we were used to the smell and it no longer bothered us. But what did we care what they thought? Where were these people when we were holding back the Communist hordes in Vietnam?

After a few martinis, our social concerns dissipated along with much of our social restraint. We had a great meal of vichyssoise, coquille Saint Jacques, filet de boeuf avec bordelaise, petits haricots verts, salade verte, and Irish coffee. The latter was served in glass cups set in a pewter bowl that steamed them so that they were hot. Fresh warmed cream was served as well. A live orchestra played during dinner and for dancing afterward. We bid the Galens goodnight and thought about hitting the hot night spots of Hong Kong. Unfortunately, the combination of age, travel, shopping, and martinis did us in, and we returned to the hotel to sack out for the evening.

The rest of R&R was spent going on photographic tours to the Forbidden City, the Communist border, and a classic grand resort hotel on Repose Bay. We also visited Tiger Balm Gardens, a Chinese version of Disneyland built by the wealthy owner of the Tiger Balm Company. We learned that the founder and owner had four wives and no sons. Tiger Balm was supposed to cure everything, but evidently not the inability to conceive male children or the heart attack that killed him.

A young female tour guide spoke of the shortage of living space in Hong Kong and pointed out the boat people who were born, lived, and died on boats in the harbor. She then showed us the lavish golf courses and commented that the Chinese don't play golf. We went up Victoria's Peak by cable car. There are two cars at a forty-five-degree angle that balance each other. We picked up our suits from the tailor and did more shopping. We thought the new clothing was high fashion and top quality but later found that it tended to come apart at the seams. We dined at the best restaurants we could find in Hong Kong, and the time passed quickly.

When we returned to Vietnam, we distributed the camera and stereo equipment to those who had ordered it, got our photographs developed, and shared our R&R experiences with the other docs. We experienced the typical post-R&R letdown as we returned to our hot, smelly, dusty, noisy surroundings and once again dined on imported army cuisine. We did, however, enjoy describing the wonders of civilization to our buddies.

SOON AFTER THE R&R, I had another opportunity to give my colleagues a hard time thanks to some friends at Fort Knox. My daughter Barby thought it was due to her magic—and maybe it was. As the holidays approached, our moods became more depressed. The Bob Hope Show was coming to Lai Khe, and we planned to attend. One day in December I received a copy of a letter from JAG (the lawyers at Fort Knox) addressed to USARV JAG (the lawyers in Vietnam) requesting that I be sent on temporary duty to conduct a forensic examination and testify at a sanity hearing for the black soldier (Private Brown) who had been charged with murdering another prisoner during the LBJ riot. They added that I had evaluated the prisoner when I was stationed at Fort Knox and was the only one who understood the matter well enough to testify. In reality, the other post psychiatrists had refused to evaluate the prisoner so the army would have to send me home for the holidays. Obviously, the soldier was still residing in the psychiatric ward at Ireland Army Hospital. I was excited at the prospect of returning home for Christmas. Then I received a copy of the USARV JAG response stating that I was serving in a combat unit, was indispensable, and could not leave the country. My hopes were as shattered as they had been when I learned the villa on the ocean was out.

A few days later I received a copy of a second request from the Fort Knox JAG office addressed to USARV JAG, which said that either I could return as a witness in the sanity hearing or they would have to send the soldier back so that USARV JAG could hold the hearing in Vietnam. A few days later I received temporary duty orders (TDY), meaning I would receive from USARV an additional daily stipend for expenses during the trip back to Fort Knox and orders to conduct a sanity hearing on the prisoner there. When I showed my orders to my peers, they became more depressed, and our conversation was similar to those held when someone becomes a short timer.

"I feel terrible. I wanted so much to be able to see the Bob Hope Show and just when I was about to realize my dream—I've been ordered to go home! Sure, the government is going to give me extra money for making the trip, but this will hardly compensate for leaving you guys over the holidays. I'll probably have to eat lobster, steak, and all that other stuff that they eat back there. I just know that they wouldn't have any moldy roast beef or chlorine-saturated Kool-Aid that I so dearly love."

"We won't be missing you," Guarino said.

"Did you hear about Dr. Remington [pseudonym]?" Guarino asked.

"Was he the psychiatrist who was going to leave country on R&R?" asked Zappia.

"Yeah, that's the one. His helicopter went down on the way to Bien Hoa and he was killed."

"Never made it to his plane—what a shame."

"Well, one good thing about all of this—they will probably send over a new wizard while what's-his-name is gone," said Guarino.

"Yeah, we could use some good psychiatric care around here."

"Not to mention some good companionship," said Galen.

I arrived at Ireland Army Hospital and reported to the hospital commander, who said that probably nothing could be done about setting up the sanity hearing until after Christmas and that I should just go home until after the New Year. I first went to Chicago, where my friend Gabriel Telot had purchased tickets to *Hair*. I sat in the audience in my uniform and enjoyed the musical, an antiestablishment, antiwar performance about hippies in the 1960s.

I spent Christmas at home. My youngest daughter, Barby, had "cast a spell" prior to my receiving orders to bring me home for Christmas. When I arrived, she was convinced she had magical powers. My older daughter, Cathy, was overjoyed to see me, and I had an opportunity to be with both girls for Christmas and to see what Santa brought them. It was great to spend Christmas at home and helped break up and ease the year's separation from the family.

After the New Year, I returned to Fort Knox, where I reevaluated the prisoner. I remembered how he had looked the previous December when he arrived from Vietnam with a tag around his neck. He was a big man who was quiet and docile. Before my orders to Vietnam, I had spoken with his mother, who was a psychiatric nurse in St. Louis and advised her to contact people who could put pressure on the military to resolve her son's legal situation. Now, a year later, her son looked better than he had when I last saw him on the unit. He was now on a lower dose of Thorazine (two hundred milligrams per day). He showed more emotional expression and was more spontaneous in his conversation. He smiled when he recognized me. He knew that he was stuck in the hospital under close observation until his legal situation was resolved. He also knew he had been charged with first-degree murder, and there was concern that he might end up in prison for an extended period of time. The other psychiatrists and his lawyers had told him that they were bringing me back to resolve the situation. He seemed happy and relieved to see me. The fact that I was now in Vietnam may have made him more comfortable as well.

He was cooperative as we went over his history but said that he had little recollection of what had happened in LBJ that had led to the charges. According to his psychiatric records, at the time of the incident he had acted on "command hallucinations" during which voices told him to kill the guard. He didn't remember hearing the voices or killing the white prisoner. He also denied having hallucinations at the time I was examining him. He hoped to return to his family in St. Louis and to get a job there. He was logical and appropriate in his thinking. His mother and extended family lived in East St. Louis and were eager to have him return. When I saw him, I was wearing my winter uniform with a chest full of ribbons and was now a major. Although he was glad to see me again and was hoping for the best, he was guarded because I looked like Regular Army to him, and those were the people who put him in LBJ in the first place, then charged him with murder. Paranoid schizophrenic patients tend to be very guarded under the best of circumstances.

From a practical standpoint, there was no way that he could be prosecuted for murder. It would be nearly impossible to locate the witnesses and to hold the trial after being away from Vietnam for two years. On the basis of his medical records and the history he was able to give me, I concluded that he was not guilty of the offense by reason of insanity. His mother had followed my recommendations and had the NAACP, the ACLU, and her congressmen putting pressure on the army to do something with him. The hospital was glad to release him and send him home. JAG was glad to be out from under the case. The patient was glad to be out of the hospital and to be free from the murder charges. His mother and family were happy to finally have him home with them. I was thankful to the guys at the post JAG and my old psychiatric buddies for their efforts to bring me home for Christmas.

Once the hearing was over, I headed back to Vietnam. By this time I had less than four months to go in country and had already scheduled another R&R during that time. I met the other medical officers at the mess in a reunion that was every bit as sentimental as I expected.

"Boy, it sure is great to be back!"

"Who the hell are you?" asked Galen.

"He looks vaguely familiar," said Zappia.

"It could be old what's-his-face who used to live on Broadway," said Guarino.

"There goes our good psychiatric care," sighed John.

"You got that right; Dr. Forrest was really a great psychiatrist," said Zappia.

Galen added, "And a wonderful person too—everyone seemed to like him."

"Let me tell you guys—it wasn't easy over there. I couldn't find this delicious steamed roast beef, and none of the beverages I tried had chlorine in them," I told them.

"We feel for you."

I had planned my R&Rs to break up the year but had not planned on being home for Christmas. This surprise visit home made the year go even faster.

AS THE YEAR went by, we began to look at problems that seemed to be more prevalent in the military than in civilian practice. The enlisted population seemed to be more suggestible, perhaps as a side effect of the training itself, and more amenable to Sodium Amytal interviews, suggestion, and hypnosis. Malingering is relatively rare in civilian populations but was commonplace in the military. Finally, we saw a rare case of *pseudologia fantastica* that caused quite a stir at division headquarters.

CHAPTER 11

Escaping from Stress

lthough racism, extensive drug and alcohol abuse, the education gap, and the antiwar movement distinguished Vietnam from prior wars, we did see a few classic cases of hysteria and conversion reactions in response to combat stress. Although there were very few cases of suicide and self-mutilation, we saw many individuals who feigned illness to avoid combat or to get out of the field. We saw another soldier who lived in a world of his own making.

ORAL ROBERTS typically included a hymn before healing individuals in his congregation that said everything is possible if you just believe. The history of hysteria, hypnotism, and suggestibility has always interested me. I read about hypnotism in high school and once, at a party, hypnotized a girl and told her that she was falling over backward. She did what she was told, some of the audience caught her, and everyone applauded. The party continued, and a few minutes later the same girl walked up the staircase and fell backward down the stairs and lay unconscious on the floor. Our family doctor, who lived across the street, came over and awakened her and then gave me a verbal thrashing for hypnotizing people without knowing what I was doing. This ended my experimentation in this area until I took two courses on hypnotism at Menninger's during my residency training.

My first contact with extreme suggestibility in the military was at the Ireland Army Hospital emergency room when a busload of basic trainees came in hyperventilating. Apparently one soldier had started hyperventilating, and before long, the entire barracks were breathing shallowly and rapidly and passing out. The treatment for hyperventilation is to have the patient breathe into a paper bag until the carbon dioxide level returns to normal, but we had a problem when we ran out of paper bags in the emergency room. Infectious hysteria was a huge problem when, for example, a case of bacterial meningitis was found in a basic training area. Hundreds of young men would show up for sick call complaining of severe headache, stiff neck, and sensitivity to light. The doctors would have to weed through the hysterics to find the few that were actually infected and try to isolate them.

Suggestibility also played a role in treating some disorders, especially conversion reactions in which unconscious psychological conflict caused physical disabilities, such as paralysis. Under Sergeant DeLeon's tutelage at Fort Knox, I conducted many successful sodium amytal interviews on evacuees from Vietnam with hysterical symptoms. He told me about his past work with Dr. Roy Grinker in World War II when he used sodium amytal interviews in the combat area. Sergeant DeLeon had been impressed by the technique and told me it was very effective in many cases. We tried this technique on patients from Vietnam who had been evacuated with hysterical symptoms. Some were paralyzed, some were blind, some couldn't hear, and some couldn't speak. The technicians prepared the patients for a week by describing how quickly others had been cured. We exposed the new arrivals to other patients who had experienced the treatment. We also told the patients that if they were cured, they would be given a thirty-day leave to visit their families; but if they didn't respond, then they would remain at the psychiatric unit for further evaluation and treatment. We did this because their symptoms had gotten them out of Vietnam and therefore had considerable secondary gain. By giving them a pass, we were providing secondary gain for recovery. By showing that others had recovered and by using a somatic treatment approach, we relieved their survival guilt for getting out while others remained. We had a 100 percent cure rate.

CHAPTER 11

While I was at Fort Knox, Barry Gault, a Harvard-trained psychiatrist assigned to the Mental Hygiene Clinic, had read about this technique and asked if he could observe a sodium amytal interview. I invited him to watch the treatment of a patient named Simpson (pseudonym) who had hysterical aphonia (he was mute). After being prepared by the positive suggestion of the staff for a week, the patient was brought into the darkened examination room we used for interviews. I entered in my starched, ankle-length, white lab coat. A goosenecked lamp was over the inside of the patient's elbow in the otherwise darkened room. I slowly injected sodium amytal in his vein.

"What happened in Vietnam that led up to you losing your voice?" I asked Simpson.

"My sergeant told us to move out, and when we did, all hell broke loose. Oh God! Medic! Oh God, oh God!"

"What's happening?"

"The dinks are killing us! Oh shit! Medic! Tommy's dead!" Simpson rambled on for a short while but then calmed himself.

"What happened after the ambush?" I asked.

"I ran up to my sergeant. I wanted to kill him—I wanted to scream at him, 'Look what you've done!' but nothing came out. I couldn't speak."

"You're speaking now."

Simpson look surprised, paused for a moment, then exclaimed, "I am speaking now. I'm speaking! Oh thank you, doc! I can speak!"

Dr. Gault was already impressed by the amount of emotion expressed by the patient and the fact that he had witnessed this dramatic cure, but I decided to try to go a little further and asked Simpson if he had ever had a similar experience. The patient thought for a second, then told me that his mom was a single parent and he never knew his dad. His mom always had guys up to the apartment, and when they were there, he had to go to the park. One day in the park a man molested him. He wanted to call his mom, but he couldn't speak. Simpson began to sob convulsively as he related this incident. I asked him whether the experience in Vietnam reopened the wound he had as a child. Simpson responded, "I guess—I felt the same then."

I told him, "Now you are an adult, and no one can hurt you

the way the man in the park hurt you. Some of the anger you felt for your sergeant probably came from the rage you had as a child toward the man who hurt you. Now that you are talking and you realize what was behind your inability to speak, you will be able to talk with one of the psychotherapists and figure out how the patterns you developed in your childhood are affecting you in adult life and change the ones that are getting in your way."

"Can I talk to you?"

"Yes, but I'd also like for you to work with one of the therapists as well."

"Okay, if you think that is the way to go."

Dr. Gault was very impressed by the drama and emotion of the interview and asked me whether this was a typical case.

"Pretty routine," I responded, trying to act cool.

"Wow, that was really great!"

"Good enough for government work," I calmly stated, trying to maintain a blasé facade.

"You trained in a psychoanalytically oriented program at Menninger's—why don't you want to see the patient for therapy? Apparently he wants you to be his therapist."

"Two reasons. First, I don't have time since running the inpatient service is a full-time job, and second, I won't be here much longer because I have orders for Vietnam."

Another, less important, reason for wanting another therapist to treat him was that he idealized me because of the sodium amytal procedure. This would become a resistance in therapy because he would expect me to actively cure him while he remained passive.

I conducted several sodium amytal interviews on soldiers with hysterical symptoms in Vietnam. Early in my tour, a nineteen-year-old infantryman named Wilson (pseudonym) from the 1st Brigade was brought to our clearing station by helicopter. He was paralyzed, unable to use his lower extremities, but the medical officers could not find a physical reason for his disability. He had slumped to the ground during a firefight and was unable to walk. The medic had him dusted off to the nearest clearing station. When we interviewed him, he said that he could neither feel nor move his legs. He related this in a very calm, matter-of-fact manner (*la belle indifference*), which is characteristic of a conversion reaction. In fact, he didn't mention his disability unless directly asked.

His history was pretty much unremarkable. He had been treated for an episode of hyperventilation during basic training. He had been drafted into the military, gone through basic and advanced infantry training, and then been sent to Vietnam. He had been with his unit for about one month. This was his first firefight.

The technicians had been anxious to see a sodium amytal interview. We decided to conduct the interview in the psychiatric hootch rather than the clearing station because it was more private. The technicians spent a couple of days talking to Wilson about the technique. They explained how "truth serum" would be slowly injected into his vein, making him able to remember what had led to his disability, and afterward he would no longer be paralyzed. When he recovered, they told him, he would not return to the field. After two days of positive suggestion and reinforcement, the day of treatment arrived. The soldier was brought over from the clearing station and placed on a cot the technicians had set up in the psychiatric hootch. Sheets had been draped around the cubicle to reduce the light and to provide an unanticipated and unusual treatment environment (part of the "magic" of the procedure). I sat down in the cubicle and again explained what we were going to do. I told him that he would be able to walk but assured him that he would not be returning directly to the field. During the injection, I had him count backward by threes. When his speech became slurred and he began to have difficulty counting, I stopped injecting the amytal.

"It is the day of the firefight. You are with your patrol walking down the trail. Describe what you see, hear, smell, and feel," I told Wilson.

He responded, "It is hot, we are walking along a trail, there were rubber trees to the left of us; all of a sudden we hear AK-47s and hit the deck." Wilson became increasingly agitated and appeared to believe he was back in the combat situation. He reared up on the cot and shouted, "Oh, noooo!! Fuck!"

"What is happening now?"

"Medic! Somebody help him! Medic!

"Was your buddy shot?"

"Yeah. Oh God. Medic help him. You've got to help him!"

"Where are you now?"

"I'm lying on the ground."

I asked Wilson if he could move his legs, and he responded that he couldn't. When asked what he wanted to do, he said, "Get out of here!"

I told him, "But you can't move your legs," and he agreed. We discussed how the medics were evaluating him and were having him dusted off by helicopter. I brought him back to the present by telling him that he would be able to move his legs and to walk just as he had before the firefight. He said that he understood.

"What you had was a common reaction to combat. You wanted to run and get away from the danger in the field, but you knew that you would get in trouble if you did and you would be letting your buddies down. The problem was solved by the unconscious part of your brain by paralyzing your legs. You didn't get in trouble, but you were taken away from the danger in the field."

"It was real!"

"We know that. But now that you are out of danger, there is no reason for your brain to keep your legs paralyzed. You will be able to move them and to walk. Go ahead and move them."

"Yeah—I can move them!"

"Yes, you are going to be fine. You are waking up from the medication now; you will be wide awake, alert, and feel refreshed. You will be able to move your legs and to walk as you did before the firefight."

I motioned for the medics to get him up. When they stood him up, he was able to start walking. We had him lie down again and then told him that he was now cured and able to walk. The technicians continued to reinforce that the cause of his paralysis was a psychological conflict between his wish to run from the field and his knowledge that he had to stay there. Now that he was aware of the cause of the problem, he was able to walk and would continue to be able to walk.

The technicians also told Wilson that he would not be returning to the field. We had found from previous experience with cases of this type that nearly all the soldiers who had recovered from conversion reactions relapsed when they returned to field duty. We restricted Wilson to an assignment in the base camp. When he came in for follow-up, we asked him about returning to his original unit. We asked him about his friends in the unit and attempted to evoke those bonds as a motivation to return, but to no avail. He became visibly anxious and agitated when we discussed returning to the field.

During the year we did several sodium amytal interviews on patients with hysterical symptoms. In each case the symptoms were quickly alleviated by suggestion, but none of the patients were able to return to the environment where they had the conversion reaction. This had been Dr. Roy Grinker's experience in World War II as well. I think that the primary factor was that the patients' symptoms had gotten them out of the field, and removing the symptoms was not a big problem as long as they did not have to return to battle. Failure to remove the symptoms could produce a problem in some soldiers—their survivor guilt might cause them to maintain their disabilities to justify their release from hazardous duty. Another factor was that the fear of dying in the field outweighed any motivation to return to the field. This particular patient had been in his unit for only a month and had not formed bonds strong enough to make him want to go back for the sake of his buddies. It was the bonds with fellow unit members that were cited as the primary motivating factor for returning soldiers to combat duty in World War II.

The sodium amytal interviews we did were, for the most part, quite dramatic in terms of the outpouring of emotion by the patients and quick recoveries. However, most cases of conversion reactions in the 1st Infantry Division were cured by medics and battalion surgeons without any specialized techniques. For example, a young enlisted man from the 2nd Battalion, 16th Infantry, was air-evacuated to our clearing station after a firefight in which he had fallen off a track and been unable to move. Neurological examinations failed to elicit an organic cause for his paralysis, and he was referred to us for further evaluation and treatment. The technician asked the battalion surgeon to sedate the soldier. After the patient had a night's rest and some food, the technician encouraged the patient to exercise his lower extremities, assuring him that his injury was temporary and that he would be able to walk and run as he did before. After a day or so in the clearing station with food, drink, exercise, and reassurance that his problem was a normal reaction to combat, the soldier was able to walk on his own.

MOST YOUNG MEN are raised being told that it is wrong to harm others. In a relatively brief period of time, the military must teach them that it is justifiable to kill other people when ordered to do so. The process of inculcating this concept is accomplished by replacing the individual's conscience with a group conscience. This is done by breaking down individuality through regulation haircuts and uniforms and disaffecting people from their emotions by adopting dry, objective language and performing actions "by the numbers" and on command. The individual becomes a cog in the military machine. The army lists the number of individuals of each rank and each occupational description for each unit in a table of equipment (TOE) as if they are replaceable parts of a machine.

This training process adds to the general suggestibility of the basic-trainee population. I was amazed at Fort Knox that an enlisted man would be running across the grounds, spot my captain's bars when I was in my car driving to the hospital, and then come to a full halt and snap to attention. This discipline and respect for rank were deeply indoctrinated into their psyches. I remember severely psychotic patients on the psychiatric unit in seclusion who would nonetheless snap to attention and salute when I opened the door to their rooms.

The suggestibility of this young, largely uneducated, anxious military population has long been recognized by military psychiatry. The three principles of military psychiatry of immediacy, proximity, and expectancy reflect this knowledge. In the field, psychological stress can cause a soldier to develop symptoms almost immediately, and it is also possible to mistreat these symptoms so that they become permanent. If you examine an average man in the field and start focusing on some bodily function or anatomical feature—looking in his ear, for example—he will become anxious and start imagining symptoms. The symptoms will decrease if you remove him from the field and recur if you attempt to return him to the field. This doesn't mean that the individual is cowardly or feigning illness. His unconscious reptilian brain is telling him that this is a dangerous place and to get out any way he can. When an acceptable route out of the field appears, the brain seizes on it to ensure the individual's survival. The longer the soldier is out of the field, the harder it becomes to return to the combat area.

WE DID NOT HEAR OF MANY CASES of men who shot or injured themselves to be medically evacuated out of a combat area. The "million-dollar injury" and the "ticket home" were described during World War II but were not seen (or perhaps recognized as such) in Vietnam. There was a case reported in which a soldier persuaded a medic to anesthetize his foot with Xylocaine and shoot him so he could avoid duty in Vietnam. We heard about another soldier who had shot himself in the foot and destroyed the arch. His foot was eventually amputated.

One case that did come to our attention had been followed by Specialist Smith when he was assigned to a combat unit to evaluate the organizational stresses within the unit. The specialist had noted in his report that a particular NCO was at risk for self-inflicting an injury, but his warning was not heeded by the command. The NCO complained to Specialist Smith that instead of being assigned work commensurate with his training, he was assigned the most undesirable jobs in the unit. One night, the technician saw him carrying a 60-mm mortar shell while drunk. The NCO said it was disarmed and bragged about the other explosives and weapons he had accumulated. He visited the tech informally and told him he stayed in the military for security. He also said the enlisted men made fun of him for being a career soldier. One night, while drinking heavily, he revealed to the technician that his wife was expecting their second baby and there was a possibility of complications due to the Rh factor. He said he hadn't heard from his wife for ten days because she didn't want to upset him. He told the tech he was thinking of rolling a truck over his leg so he could get evacuated back to the States. He claimed that he couldn't request emergency leave because of financial problems.

The NCO continued to drink heavily and displayed behavior that made Specialist Smith think that the NCO should be referred to me for evaluation. The NCO was restricted to quarters one evening after he threatened the bartender at the NCO club when refused an additional beer. The next morning, the company commander talked with the NCO, thinking the problem could be handled within the unit. Specialist Smith strongly recommended that the NCO be referred to psychiatry in the support command base camp and that the NCO be restricted from retaining explosives or weapons. A few nights later, the tech saw the NCO drinking in the NCO club and then smoking alone outside the club at 9:30 P.M. About thirty minutes later, the NCO was wounded in the upper leg while allegedly cleaning his M16 rifle. There were no witnesses to the incident.

IN A HOSTILE COMBAT ENVIRONMENT where death is feared, self-inflicted death seems more shocking and incomprehensible than in a civilian setting. Suicide has been the leading cause of death in the peacetime army. Apparently this was the case in the ancient as well as modern armies. The Romans imposed the death penalty for soldiers who attempted suicide, and Napoleon regarded suicide as desertion in the field.

I had been taught at Fort Sam Houston and at Fort Knox to evaluate and, in most cases, return to their units the basic trainees who made suicidal gestures and not to hospitalize them or discharge them. The idea was that if you went along with this manipulation, the person would become an emotional cripple and would continue to try to threaten suicide as a means of blackmailing his way out of situations later in life. However, a later study concluded that nearly all the individuals who had made a suicidal gesture during basic training eventually got out of the military prematurely—usually by administrative discharge. These findings changed my later approach, and that of most military psychiatrists, to patients who made suicidal gestures. We immediately processed them out of the service to save the army time, energy, and money.

Individuals who express suicidal thoughts, display self-destructive behavior, or attempt suicide in a combat area are different from those who do so in a civilian or training environment. If you want to die in a combat zone, all that is usually required is that you stand up and the enemy will do it for you. Suicidal threats don't have the escape value in a combat area that they do in a stateside military setting. In addition, the outlet of going AWOL was not considered a viable option by most soldiers in Vietnam. Suicide is one means of getting out of an intolerable situation if a person feels cornered. Individuals who are clinically depressed often dwell on the negative aspects of the present and past and cannot see their quality of life improving in the future. It is as though they have on negative filters. If you try to cheer up clinically depressed individuals, they usually screen out anything positive you have to say or interpret your comments as babying them. On the other hand, they can be extremely sensitive, and even slightly negative comments can be misinterpreted and lead to severe self-chastisement.

During my tour in Vietnam, only one individual in the division came to our attention who committed suicide (the alcoholic sergeant who relapsed and was facing a court-martial that would end his army career), and we did not see him as a patient. The French draftee who was psychotically depressed also seriously attempted suicide. He failed to adjust psychologically to service in Vietnam and was convinced that he was about to be killed. The suicide attempts reflected a desire to have some control over his destiny. The previous year, three individuals had killed themselves, and there were thirty-one suicides among the seven army divisions (about 140,000 men) in our area.

WE SAW MANY PATIENTS in Vietnam who were trying to get out of a particular situation or the military by feigning illness. Malingering is the voluntary fabrication or exaggeration of physical or psychological symptoms in order to achieve a tangible goal distinct from the gain of being in a patient role. The malingerer pretends to be ill or incapacitated to escape duty or work. The Greeks around 500 B.C. considered malingering in the military to be a serious offense punishable by death. In A.D. 2, Galen's treatise *How to Detect Malingerers* tells of Roman troopers who would cut off their thumbs or fingers to escape military duty. They were called "Pathomimes."

Malingering, conscious or unconscious, is fairly common in the military. In private practice, we tend to believe our patients because they are making a sacrifice to come and talk to us and they don't achieve any gain by convincing us that they are ill. In the military during Vietnam, many men were trying to avoid military service and had plenty to gain by convincing a doctor that they were unfit or too ill to continue serving.

Sometimes malingering is expressed in an intimidating manner. One morning, there was a huge commotion in the reception area of the psychiatric headquarters. Specialist Falzone came back to tell me that we had a helicopter door gunner out there who was throwing a "jungle act." The gunner was a big, slightly overweight man who was shouting that he couldn't take it any more and he was going to turn his machine gun on his own men if we didn't get him reassigned. I had Falzone escort him back to my desk. "What's going on?" I asked.

"I can't take it anymore, sir. If I can't get another job I'm going to lose it—I'm going to turn my gun on our own men. I don't want to do it, but I think I'm having a nervous breakdown."

"First of all, this isn't personnel," I said. "We don't give people different jobs and couldn't give them different jobs if we wanted to. Second, if you do kill anyone, it will now be premeditated murder because you've told us you were going to do it."

"Okay. Well, it will be on your head when I start shooting. I told you I can't take it!"

He stomped out of the office still ranting and raving. I was not as certain in my diagnosis as I acted and asked one of the technicians to follow him and see how he behaved once he left our area. The tech returned and reported that the door gunner was playing pool with his buddies, drinking a beer, and laughing and joking. I felt better after hearing this report. A few weeks later, I was flying in a helicopter and looked back and saw that he was the door gunner. I hit him on the shoulder and asked him how he was doing. He wiggled his hand to indicate "so-so."

I discussed the case with the techs and told them I had learned something about this type of malingering by intimidation (which they referred to as a "jungle act") from my old army mentor at Fort Knox, the psychiatric ward master, Sergeant DeLeon. We were having a combined medical and psychiatric department conference at Ireland Army Hospital, discussing a patient who had thyroid disease and schizophrenia. Suddenly a patient began screaming and throwing furniture in the hall outside the conference room. The nurses, medics, and aides ran out of the room in response, and after a few minutes, the head nurse stuck her head in to tell the group, "That was the patient Captain Bey discharged this morning." Everyone laughed, and Sergeant DeLeon said he would take care of the problem. The patient in question was a skinny, small basic trainee who wanted out of the army. Sergeant DeLeon drilled the men on the psychiatric unit each morning. The schizophrenic patients who were awaiting discharge loved to drill and march, as it made them feel they were a part of the army. The patients with personality disorders who were trying to get out of the military griped and moaned that they were ill and shouldn't be expected to meet inspection or to march. This particular basic trainee was one of the gripers. His psychological testing, my interviews with him, and the observations of the unit staff all supported a personality disorder diagnosis, which meant he could be administratively discharged by his commanding officer, but he did not meet the criteria for medical discharge. I had given him the results of our evaluation that morning. He had thrown a "jungle act" when the men from his unit came to get him to return him to duty. We had a lieutenant named Purkinjee (pseudonym) in a locked seclusion room at the time. Purkinjee was six feet eight inches tall, about 260 pounds, and bore a resemblance to Lurch from the Addams Family. He had been medically evacuated from Vietnam after his unit was ambushed. He blamed himself for the deaths and injuries of his men. He became psychotically depressed, attempted suicide, and was smearing himself with his own feces when he first arrived on our unit. Sergeant DeLeon opened the seclusion room door and handed the frightened basic trainee to Purkinjee. Purkinjee picked up the recruit so that he could look directly into his eyes. He held him out at arm's length and then bent him down to the floor, keeping his own nose inches from the trainee's. The recruit started looking desperate and in a hoarse whisper said to Sergeant DeLeon, "Hey—what's going on? Get me out of here, man. Get me out."

Sergeant DeLeon said, "Purkinjee—give him to me." Purkinjee, with robotlike movements, lifted the recruit up and handed him to Sergeant DeLeon so that his feet remained two feet off the floor. The sergeant closed and locked the seclusion room door, to the relief of the trainee. He then said, "Purkinjee is mentally ill. If you are mentally ill, we will keep you up here with Purkinjee—if you aren't, I want you to sit over there in that chair and wait for your unit to pick you up. I don't want to hear another peep out of you." The recruit sat in the chair with his lips tightly closed and returned quietly to his unit.

The passive form of malingering is more common, in which the individual claims a problem that makes him inherently unsuitable for a particular duty. One morning, I was seated as usual at my desk drinking my coffee and reading *Stars and Stripes* when

I overheard a neatly groomed, anxious-appearing, young enlisted man tell Specialist Zecchinelli, "I think I can make it—if you give me a tranquilizer or something, I know I'll be able to make it." This was highly unusual. Most of the clients we saw tried to convince us that they couldn't make it. I hollered at Zak to bring the fellow back to my desk. He sat down on the edge of his chair and repeated his conviction that he could make it home with psychopharmacologic assistance. As I reviewed his medical chart, I learned that he had come to Vietnam a year before as an 11 Bravo. On the plane he learned that the 1st Infantry Division had a band. He had played the trumpet in high school, so as soon as he arrived at the division, he applied for a position with the band. It turned out that they needed a trumpet player, and he was transferred from a combat infantry unit to the 1st Infantry Division band.

What he didn't know was that the army doesn't let anyone off that easily. The band was flown regularly to the fire support bases in the division area of operations to play for and raise the morale of the men in the field. This meant that band members got rocketed and mortared just as everyone else did. After learning this, the trumpet player went to my predecessor to convince him that he had a fear of flying. He pled his case successfully, and the previous division psychiatrist had restricted him from flying. The rest of the band continued to fly to the fire support areas while the trumpet player remained in the relative safety of the base camp during the remainder of his tour. Now his tour had ended, but he was not able to fly home with the rest of the men because he was restricted from flying.

He pleaded plaintively, "I believe I can do it if you will give me a tranquilizer."

"No, I wouldn't want to risk it—it's a nineteen-hour flight, and you could lose control."

"No, I wouldn't!—if you just give me a tranquilizer I will be fine!"

Shaking my head from side to side, I reiterated that I was uncomfortable with prescribing a tranquilizer so the trumpet player could fly home. He asked me about how he would be able to return home, and I responded, "I don't know; this is the first case we've had of this type, but I'll check on ships leaving from Saigon. Get back to me in a month or so."

"A month! I'm supposed to go home Monday! Once I get a ship—how long does it take to get home?"

"Well, I don't really know—I think the ships go to Japan, then to the Philippines, probably Guam, maybe Wake, Hawaii—I'd guess five or six months."

"Five or six months—but I'm supposed to go home Monday."

"Well, that's the best we can do."

He left our office shaken and despondent. I called his commanding officer and told him what I'd done and that he could let him go with everyone else on Monday but that I just wanted to tweak him a little. The commander said, "Good enough—the little SOB deserves a good tweaking."

Sometimes malingering was done to evade a disciplinary situation. On a particularly hot, muggy day, we were seated in the psychiatric hootch fanning ourselves with magazines and drinking sodas we had scrounged from the clearing station. During the monsoon season, it would rain intensely for an hour and then stop. Whenever it rained at night, it became hot and muggy in the morning, and this was one of those mornings. Two MPs escorted a skinny, disheveled young enlisted man from the 1st Engineering Battalion to the clearing station. Simon and Specialist 4 Mike Weissman took the history and then came back to my desk to fill me in. "The story is that this guy shot off his weapon in the company area, and when he was arrested and questioned, said that he had no recollection of the incident." His history and mental status examination were unremarkable except for his amnesia of the shooting event. Weissman and I discussed the situation and decided on a course of action. We told the enlisted man that we would give him a sodium amytal interview later in the week. If he really had an unconscious conflict, he would be able to remember shooting the weapon and why he did it. If he didn't have a psychological problem, he wouldn't be able to remember. That night, he went AWOL from the clearing station, got drunk, and later reported that the alcohol restored his memory. This wasn't psychiatric treatment. We were sure that he was lying about not remembering the incident and put him in a double bind where he had to recover his memory. It worked except he decided to recover it on his own terms.

Malingering in civilian practice usually reflects more serious pathology. My friend and teacher Dr. Karl Menninger always had another slant on things. He made the following comments on malingering in *The Vital Balance* (New York: Viking Press, 1963, 208):

> There is another type of personality deformity which is so ancient and classical, so commonly assumed to be prevalent, and yet so rare, that we must list it out of sheer curiosity. It is the compulsive deception represented by the feigning of disease. Curiously enough, the individual who does this, the malingerer, does not himself believe that he is ill, but tries to persuade others that he is, and they discover, they think, that he is not ill, but the sum of all this, in the opinion of myself and my perverse minded colleagues, is precisely that he is ill, in spite of what others think. No healthy person, no healthy-minded person, would go to such extremes and take such devious and painful routes for minor gains that the invalid status brings to the malingerer.

Dr. Karl demonstrated this belief when we were making rounds with him one day in the Winter Veterans Administration Hospital in Topeka. The hospital was very modern and featured a theater, a swimming pool, a canteen, and comfortable furnishings. One of the psychiatric residents in our group commented, "Who wouldn't want to collect a pension and stay in a place like this?" Dr. Karl overheard the comment and responded, "I have some influence in this organization. Pack your things and report to the hospital, and I will see to it that you're given a bed." The resident protested, saying he had a family and he didn't mean that he personally would want to stay in the hospital—he was speaking in general. Dr. Karl insisted that since he made the statement, he should get his things and come to the hospital for immediate admission. The resident continued to back pedal until finally Dr. Karl let him off the hook, but said to all of us, "You see, no one who was not ill would really want to stay in the hospital."

WE SAW AN UNUSUAL CASE in which fantasy represented an escape from reality rather than from combat, the military, or Vietnam. Ford and Zecchinelli were doing paperwork at the psychiatric hootch one day when the bird colonel, who was the senior JAG officer of the 1st Infantry Division, brought in a thin, meek, sad-looking soldier and angrily ordered us to "medically evacuate him, give him a 212 administrative discharge, shoot him—do whatever you have to do, but get rid of him—I never want to see this SOB in the division again!" We wondered what this shy, unassuming, enlisted man had done to provoke the intense rage of the top legal person of the division.

The soldier's records had apparently been lost when he arrived in Vietnam, but the personnel staff were informed that the soldier had come for his second tour of duty and had served his prior tour with the 101st Airborne Division, where he had received many decorations, including a Silver Star for valor. His father had been an admiral who had been killed in World War II. The soldier had requested to be assigned to the 1st Infantry Division because he knew that it was a prestigious combat unit. When the senior JAG officer of the division learned about his heroic background, he asked to have the young hero assigned as his driver.

Soon after the soldier arrived at his post, a series of strange events occurred at division headquarters. The colonel's driver received a radio transmission that some prisoners had escaped from the Long Binh Jail. The 1st Military Police Company set up a roadblock on Highway 1 and manned it all night before learning that the report was false. Next, several of the colonel's personal items disappeared, and he ordered an investigation to find the thief and recover them. The final event occurred when the commanding general of the division had a birthday party and the cake was stolen. The MPs initiated a search and found the colonel's driver sitting in a CONEX box (a large corrugated metal shipping container) eating the general's birthday cake. It was then discovered that the soldier had not served previously in Vietnam, his father was neither deceased nor an admiral, he had called in the false reports regarding escaping prisoners, and he had stolen the colonel's personal items. The head legal officer was embarrassed and angry that he had been duped by the soldier's lies and wanted him drummed out of the division.

When we confronted the soldier about these events, he calmly reported that he had uncovered a large drug ring in the United States while working undercover for the federal narcotics bureau and had enlisted for duty in Vietnam to avoid retaliation from drug lords. He did not change expression or miss a beat while telling the story. He just went on to fabricate another tale. This was a case of *pseudologia fantastica,* which is considered to be a form of psychosis and possibly a variation of schizophrenia. The individual makes up his own reality and lives in it. We evacuated the patient through medical channels with a complete typed history. We hoped that he would provide an interesting clinical case for the psychiatric residents at Walter Reed.

IRONICALLY, THE VIETNAM CONFLICT has resulted in opportunities for malingering following the war. In particular, post-traumatic stress disorder is easily feigned by people looking to excuse themselves from responsibility. The PTSD diagnosis was pushed by the antiwar activists and adopted by the American Psychiatric Association in 1980. The book *Stolen Valor* suggests that the Veterans Administration supported and encouraged the PTSD notion, as it gave the VA a large patient population that justified its existence, expansion, and continued funding. The same book demonstrated that many of the individuals who have received compensation for disability for PTSD never served in Vietnam or, if they did, had REMF jobs as cooks and clerks with little or no opportunity for them to be traumatized by combat. The authors go on to note that this situation is costing taxpayers billions of dollars. It also encourages the image of Vietnam veterans as traumatized, messed-up individuals. I agree with the authors that individuals who were not in Vietnam should not receive benefits that should be going to real veterans. On the other hand, I've treated Vietnam veterans who I am certain suffered from bona fide PTSD symptoms resulting from their combat experiences. I've also had an opportunity to evaluate and treat several Special Forces troops who had the classic symptoms of PTSD as a result of their service in Afghanistan. I know that there are many dedicated VA counselors in our area who work with veterans with mental disorders. I feel that veterans who have mental problems, whether or not they were caused by the stress of war, should receive psychiatric attention. Veterans who have sacrificed for their country are entitled to some recognition and benefits. There are some recent positive-emission tomography

(PET) scan studies indicating that the primitive areas of the brain that control emotion (amygdala area of the limbic system) appear to be responsible for our reactions to severe stress and the memory of the trauma that produces the stress. It is possible that in the near future we will be able to objectively differentiate true victims of PTSD from individuals feigning war trauma.

Agent Orange exposure is another source of compensation and disability that is vulnerable to abuse by malingerers. There are recent studies showing that veterans from Vietnam who were exposed to Agent Orange show higher incidences of some illnesses (lymphoma, diabetes II, peripheral neuropathy) than matched individuals who were not exposed. In my opinion, we always need to give the benefit of the doubt to the veteran.

VIETNAM WAS UNIQUE from a psychiatric standpoint. We saw cases that were rare in civilian practice and were confronted with others that were unique in the military. Our own lives in Vietnam ground on as we plodded through the day to day of our one-year tour of duty. Our conversations and our ways of coping with the routine and boredom remained the same, and their predictability was boring as well. Anesthesiologists are said to have hours of boredom interspersed with moments of absolute terror. Our life in Vietnam was like that. Most of it was very routine and predictable, but occasionally we would have some excitement that was too scary to be enjoyable.

CHAPTER 12

Time Grinding On

During the year, we added some more men to our team who came to us as "walk-ons" rather than through regular military channels. Three of the men we added had been actual combatants.

Mike Weissman was a short, wiry, dark-haired, bright-eyed, Jewish man from New York City. He had been serving as a tunnel rat with the 1st Engineer Battalion's team of "Diehard Tunnel Rats." This group was based in Lai Khe and flew by helicopter to tunnel sites within the division's area of operations. The team was made up of an officer (Rat-6), an NCO, two or three enlisted men, a medic, a radio telephone operator (RTO), and two Kit Carson scouts. (Kit Carson scouts were former NVA/VC who had rallied to the government of Vietnam under the Chieu Hoi program and were encouraged to become scouts. They were usually assigned to U.S. troops in the area where they had surrendered. Some of these "recruits" were later found to be double agents working for the NVA.) The tunnel rats' motto was "*Non Gatum Anus Rodentum*" (not worth a rat's ass). The tunnel rats were given hazardous-duty pay. The Viet Cong had 125 miles of tunnels three feet high by two and one-half feet wide. These tunnels zigzagged to make them less vulnerable to attack by gas or explosives. The tunnel rats were the guys who went into the tunnels first, armed with hand grenades, flashlights, and pistols. Although crawling through a dark, narrow tunnel was bad enough, it could get worse. The VC would leave booby traps in the tunnels, such as poisonous snakes tied to the ceilings and punji stakes (sharpened bamboo) concealed in covered pits and tipped with poison or night soil (feces). Punji sticks were also rigged to swing down from the ceiling and impale whoever might enter the tunnel. Tunnels were sometimes rigged with explosives and trip wires and populated by scorpions and bats. The VC inside the tunnel were another danger. One tunnel complex discovered in the division was eight stories deep. A tunnel hospital discovered north of Saigon had two thousand hospital beds, fresh blood, intravenous fluids, and refrigeration.

Weissman walked into our hootch one morning and spoke with Zecchinelli and Smith. They listened to his story and then introduced him to me. Weissman's fatigues and boots were covered with red dust. His shirt was stained with dirt and perspiration. He certainly looked like a man who had been serving in the field. Weissman said he had been in country a little over three months and had been working as a tunnel rat the entire time. Typically, men worked as tunnel rats for no more than four months. Prior to being drafted, he had worked as a probation officer in New York City. He stopped by our area because he was wondering if we could use him as a social work/psychology technician. Lieutenant Colonel Hefner told me that if I could use Weissman, he would authorize the transfer. The technicians and Captain Pabst were in favor of having Mike join us, so he became one of the team. He functioned well and was able to quickly establish a relationship with the soldiers and patients who served as combatants. His civilian experience and training had prepared him to evaluate and counsel individuals, and he was able to learn new information quickly. Mike was a quiet, humble guy who didn't volunteer stories about his time as a tunnel rat. He said that they usually put explosives in the tunnel before he went in, but the tunnels were pitch black and narrow and you never knew what you were going to encounter.

Private First Class Pattburg was a different type of recruit. He had an awkwardness about him that stemmed partly from his having a prominent lumbar lordosis (swayback) that caused him to walk with a broad-based gait. His hair was shaved on the sides (whitewalls) but grown out on top and draped over his forehead on one side. Adding to the Hitleresque image, he had a small, square mustache. He appeared somewhat anxious and depressed. The

CO of a transportation company sent him to us to clear him for administrative discharge and described him as "completely useless." The CO had already given him an Article 15 and withheld promotion. The specific event that triggered the decision to kick him out of the military was rolling a new truck.

We evaluated him and found him to be a simple, nice guy who was remorseful about the accident with the truck. He was Regular Army and had enlisted with the hope of making a career in the military. He was upset by the prospect of being discharged. He had been a scapegoat in his unit, where his peers as well as the CO saw him as an accident-prone individual. Our technicians felt sorry for him. When asked, he said he could type. We had him type a couple of reports, and he was able to complete them at about thirty words per minute with many typos. I called the transportation company CO and asked him if it would be okay if we tried him out as our clerk typist/receptionist. The CO did not object as long as he was rid of him, but he once again cautioned me that he would be a problem. As it turned out, Private First Class Pattburg was pleased to stay in the army and to be assigned to a unit that treated him well. He contributed by typing reports and correspondence, acting as an office receptionist, and being a part of our mental health team. He and Simon frequently wore blue scrubs instead of the tropical fatigue tops, which was fine with everyone else as long as they wore regulation uniforms when we were inspected or visited by VIPs. Pattburg turned out to be an excellent receptionist and an adequate typist. His ability to get along with the team, be nice to patients, and be polite to Regular Army types was a significant asset.

Simon had come to us as a patient. He was a short, good-looking, Jewish man from New York. When he was not depressed, he had a cocky demeanor about him. He wore aviator glasses, a sign of some ability to "operate," because they were issued only to pilots. He had a thick, neatly trimmed mustache and black hair of medium length. He had been a 91B (combat medic) assigned to a combat infantry unit. We needed a medic to look after patients in the clearing station and arranged for a transfer. He was very gentle and kind with patients, and his knowledge of medicine was helpful in caring for the patients we admitted to the clearing station.

The final technician added to the unit was Spc.4 Louis Straka. He had a round face, prominent ears, and a goofy, elfin smile that reminded me of Alfred E. Newman of *Mad Magazine* fame. He was tall, thin, and lanky and wore the dirty, stained, worn fatigues of a field soldier. He walked in one day and introduced himself by asking, "Can you use someone with a Ph.D. in psychology?" Apparently he had been drafted, and rather than enlist as an MSC officer, he had opted to go in as an enlisted man and get out of the army in two years. Trained in artillery, he was serving as a forward artillery observer in Vietnam. His job was to identify enemy targets and call in artillery strikes. Once again, Lieutenant Colonel Hefner expedited the transfer. Louis was a good interviewer. He was capable of performing psychological testing, but we didn't have testing materials, and it was impractical and unnecessary for the type of work we were doing.

I DON'T KNOW IT IF WAS THE HEAT, a full bladder, or the bright sunlight that woke me one particular morning. I heard John stirring around through the plywood wall that separated us and then I heard his tape recorder playing Aretha Franklin's "Chain of Fools."

I threw off the poncho liner, slipped into flip-flops, and poured some water into my plastic wash basin, then carried the stuff to my porch and did my morning hygiene in the company of my neighbors on Broadway. The air was already hot and oppressive. Helicopters were up flying as they had been throughout the night. Malcolm stumbled out of his hootch across the street, and Ross appeared soon after. We took turns going to the outhouse and exchanged the usual morning feces reports.

Malcolm was just entering the outhouse when he yelled, "Hey, Wizard, could you go with me in the privy this morning?"

"Why would I want to go to the privy with you?"

"Well, I have this problem, and you are the Wizard, you know."

"What sort of problem?"

"I can't go unless someone is watching."

"Get out of here."

"That's the kind of psychiatric care and support we get around here."

We put on our fatigues, which looked good but smelled bad because they were washed in a river that was polluted with sewage. Eventually our olfactory senses adapted, and we no longer smelled them ourselves. We trudged down the gravel path to the mess hall where we lined up for a breakfast buffet.

My schedule was more varied than that of most of the other doctors, but it was still pretty routine and predictable on most days. We all did the same things each day, said the same things, ate the same food, played the same music, took the same pictures, wore the same clothes, and relaxed with the same activities each evening. Later that night, we had a little excitement that was a change for all of us.

At breakfast the conversation typically involved events in the division, such as rocket attacks. This particular morning, Guarino started off by asking, "Hey, did you hear about Lai Khe getting rocketed last night?"

Galen responded, "Yeah, the high-tech computerized counter-artillery gear they have there isn't much use."

Bob Anzinger joined in. "What do you mean?"

"Well, the radar picks up any mortar or rocket in the area, and the computer calculates where it came from and causes the artillery to shell that area, but, unfortunately, that doesn't do much good. A VC walks down from Cambodia in his underwear with a rocket, a couple of tin cans, and some wire on his back. He makes a tripod out of bamboo and sets up two cans, one with water inside of it and a small hole and the other can inside of the bigger can floating on the water. He wires it so that when the water leaks out of the bottom can, the other one makes contact with it, which sets off the rocket—a crude but effective timing mechanism. Anyway, he sets this up and starts walking back to Cambodia to get another one. Twenty minutes or so later the rocket goes off, our radar picks up the blip on the screen, the computer calculates where it came from, and alerts our artillery, which blows up the area where the Viet Cong had been and, at best, kills a couple of water buffalo."

We all agreed that the technology wasn't a match for VC ingenuity. John interjected, "Hey! That reminds me—do you remember when that plane went off the runway here in Di An and ended up in the mine field?" We all said we did. "Well, we sent ambulances and the explosive experts and, guess what?—there were no mines in the mine field! The Viet Cong had stolen them all and were using them on the highway to blow up our vehicles."

I added, "I saw a Viet Cong sapper demonstration in Lai Khe when we were there the other day. The sapper was a skinny little Vietnamese Kit Carson scout dressed in underwear shorts and flip-flops. He raised his hands so everyone could see him and then dropped to the ground, and a few minutes later stood up and raised his hands inside the base camp perimeter. He had gone through three sets of concertina wire, avoided the mines, and, on his way in, had turned the claymores around so that if they were triggered they would explode toward the base camp."

Galen responded, "So much for our perimeter defense."

John picked up the conversation. "Speaking of perimeter defense, they had a drill the other day to check our readiness. The perimeter guard was supposed to sound the alarm. He didn't know how to work the radio, so he tried to call headquarters on the land line. The land line was busy, so he waited until they got off the line. Needless to say, we flunked the test. We would have been overrun by the time the land line was free."

I responded, "Hey, I feel secure!"

We admired the cleverness of the NVA and VC for using our weapons against us and outwitting sophisticated counterartillery systems with primitive equipment. We weren't frightened by these events, nor did we doubt that we would prevail. I think our admiration for the skill of the VC was based on the tendency Americans have to cheer for the underdog and our own heritage as colonists using primitive techniques to defeat the more powerful British military.

We walked to our hootches. The sun was higher and the air temperature hotter by now. Malcolm was already sweating, and his fatigues showed perspiration. The morning contents of the privy pans was sautéing in kerosene. The constant "woomp woomp" of the helicopters overhead and sound of heavy vehicles seemed a natural part of our environment and were hardly noticed. We got cleaned up again. I wrote a letter. Then, I walked with the now sweat-soaked Malcolm back down the gravel path to the clearing station area. He was panting from the heat and exhaustion. I was glad that I didn't have his job. The thought of spending the rest of the day seeing guys with gonorrhea and dysentery wasn't very appealing. When I entered the psychiatric building, Pattburg greeted me while continuing to peck on the ancient upright typewriter. Captain Pabst was interviewing a soldier by his desk. Zecchinelli was putting data from the monthly reports on the chart of the division units hanging on the wall.

Our new corpsman, Simon, ran over from the clearing station, also in scrubs, to let us know that we would be getting a psychotic patient by medevac in the next few minutes. Shortly thereafter, we heard the helicopter approaching. The technicians and Simon retrieved the patient, who was cursing and screaming from within the stretchers. Once in the clearing station, they transferred him to a cot with restraints. He thrashed around on the bed and screamed about God, Adam and Eve, the serpent, the end of the world, and how he had sinned. He was too agitated to eat but was able to take some fluids. One of the division chaplains had visited us a few days earlier. He told us that he had had considerable training and experience in counseling, and if we had any patients he could work with, he would appreciate being called. I told Zecchinelli to reach the chaplain. Within a few minutes the chaplain arrived at the clearing station and thanked us for calling him. We left him at the bedside to counsel the new arrival.

We went back to our building and later to the mess hall for lunch. After lunch, we returned to our quarters and lay around writing letters, making tapes, reading magazines, and napping. When I returned to the psychiatric hootch, I shared the information I had received at breakfast about Viet Cong ingenuity. About three or four hours later, the chaplain came in and reported that he'd been attempting to counsel the patient. "What do you think his problem is?" I asked. "Well, he is very confused about Genesis," answered the padre. I told Zecchinelli to have Simon give the patient two hundred milligrams of Thorazine and then one hundred milligrams every four hours that he was awake. Simon reported that he was out after the first dose. We kept him asleep or in a twilight state for about twenty-four hours and then removed the restraints, stopped the medication, and gave him a good meal. His acute psychosis had cleared, and we were able to get a logical history. Simon spoke with the soldier, who said that the sack time had really helped.

Simon asked the soldier what had happened. He said he wasn't sure. They were on patrol and caught some fire. He was on the ground firing his M16 and remembered feeling hot and thirsty. The next thing he remembered was waking up this morning.

Simon told the patient that he was yelling about religion when he came in. Did he remember? He was raised as a pretty strict Pentecostal and was still religious, but he didn't remember thinking about religion before he blacked out.

Simon thought the soldier had probably been dehydrated and was delirious. The patient thought it was weird to lose a block of time like that and wondered if he seemed weird when he was brought in. Simon told him that he had seemed confused and was talking about the Bible. The chaplain came in and tried to talk to him, remarking that he was confused about Genesis. The soldier didn't remember any of this and hoped he hadn't upset the chaplain. Simon assured the patient that the chaplain was just worried about him. We kept him for another day at the clearing station. He saw the chaplain again and then returned to his unit.

After work on the day the patient was admitted, I went back to my hootch and changed into shorts and flip-flops. I sat in my car with the group having an early beer when Ross came out of his hootch with a towel wrapped around him carrying a bar of soap.

"Where are you going?" I asked.

"Gonna take my shower now."

"Gonna take your shower?" asked Anzinger.

"Yeah, I thought I'd get cleaned up."

"Let me know how the water is," said Galen.

After a short time Guarino returned from the shower and passed by on the way to his hootch. With great curiosity and interest, I asked, "How was it?" Ross responded, "Well, it started out cold, but then it got warmer." I thought back to my first day in the unit and how odd the doctors seemed when they asked Tony Columbo about his shower. I realized that I had crossed over into the parallel existence of Vietnam and had become one of those odd docs.

We spent the afternoon engaged in routine activities. We sat in our lawn chairs and on the stoops of our hootches using chopsticks to share a care package that Ross got from home. John brought some kim chee. We drank cold beer and listened to John's Motown blasting from his speakers. Then we donned our fatigues for dinner.

The discussion at dinner centered around the new psychiatric patient. Lieutenant Colonel Hefner repeated the story about how he liked having psychiatric patients at the clearing station. I'd heard the story before but didn't mind hearing it again—especially the part about the general getting a kick out of it. Everyone laughed, and the conversation turned to the night's movie. "What's the movie?" asked Ross. "Some beach-party movie with the Mouseketeer with big boobs," answered Anzinger. Because there wasn't any choice and we knew we were going to the movie, everyone agreed it sounded great.

About halfway into the movie, a huge explosion lit up the area and shook the ground. Then a second explosion shook the entire camp. We hit the deck and crawled into the ditch that ran along the movie area. As I lay with my face in the dirt feeling the ground shake beneath me, I recalled my first night in the division and the instructions I received on how to differentiate incoming from outgoing artillery. It did not seem all that difficult I thought as another shell exploded nearby. More explosions hit, and we started thinking—neither the VC nor the NVA had shells that large—at least not in our area. The artillerymen at the base camp quickly determined that the shells were coming from the South Vietnamese division north of us. Apparently it isn't uncommon in artillery to make a 180-degree error when calculating where to aim the guns. Our artillery tried to raise the South Vietnamese on the radio, but they couldn't understand us, so we continued to be shelled. Finally, our artillery in Di An lobbed a couple of shells into the Vietnamese compound, and the shelling stopped. Apparently they understood that message!

We'd had enough of the beach party for the evening. We headed for the officers' club to have a few drinks and talk about the evening's excitement. Drinking in Vietnam was a daily event, and when we had a party, we probably spilled more than we drank in medical school. When we weren't working or in the mess hall, we had a drink in our hands most of the time. If you were hungover, it was because Fremont banged your head around the night before. If you got sick, you called for "Ralph." The incoherent drunken talk went on and on—and frequently centered on the ongoing debate about whether to urinate on the fence or the bamboo near the officers' club. For instance, the bartender might inadvertently start the debate by asking Guarino if he wanted water in his scotch, and Guarino would respond, quoting W. C. Fields, "Water? Never touch the stuff—fish fornicate in it!" Zappia would then accuse Guarino of urinating on the fence.

"As a matter of fact, I do piss on the fence. I feel the fence is emblematic of the United States' presence in Vietnam, and I'm pleased to be able to piss on it," responded Guarino.

Galen interjected, "Au contraire, mon frère. You are merely micturating on some Vietnamese boards that were made into a fence by our own beloved Vietnamese carpenter. It would be much better to Abschlag on the bamboo as a symbol of ecology, the circle of life, and as a contribution to this piss-ant country."

To which I added, "I prefer hosing the fence myself. Or, as we say in psychiatry, 'wizzing' on the fence. For one thing, I can hit it. I find the bamboo to be elusive; bending in the wind, sometimes it flings my own urine back at me. There is also the danger of the dreaded bamboo snake lurking in the shadows of the plant waiting to strike or possibly mate with the one-eyed snake held in its presence."

John would add his practical wisdom to the debate: "You mothers are so full of crap. It's better to piss on the fence because you drunken dorks don't have as far to walk."

I felt at home with my technicians and my fellow medical officers. Almost all the doctors were putting in their obligatory time with the military and intended to go into private practice when we got out. In Vietnam we lived together, ate together, watched movies together, drank together, went to the privy together, listened to the same music on our Sansui 1000s, took the same pictures with our Nikons, and followed the same boring, routine, intimate, existence for a year. No one griped about his lot in life. We shared care packages from home, kidded each other in a supportive way, tried to practice good medicine in the situation we were in, and kept busy to make the time go faster. As a group we almost never talked about home, politics, religion, or the possible danger. We kept things positive and focused on the present. Since life in camp was pretty routine and boring, our conversations followed suit.

VIETNAM WAS A CRAZY ENVIRONMENT. Generals flew in their mistresses, and a colonel jerked a sampan out of a river as a souvenir. Beauty queens performed before thousands of sex-starved enlisted men and had to be evacuated to escape the troops who stormed the stage. I threw an optometrist through a door and nearly shot Big John during a red alert. Perhaps as an effort to raise morale, perhaps as a way of rewarding the guys who went to Vietnam and did their jobs, sometimes as a way of trying to entice reenlistment, whatever—medals were passed out liberally in Vietnam. As the war progressed and the morale went down, the number of medals awarded went up. I got my share but had a knee-jerk rebellion to what I felt was an effort to manipulate me into playing the role of a "hero."

Madness and Medals

I've always thought that *Apocalypse Now* was the best movie portrayal of the sounds, the surrealistic environment, and the crazy behavior that I remember from Vietnam. When I first watched *Apocalypse Now* and saw Martin Sheen lying on his bed in Saigon listening to the helicopters, it immediately brought back the memory of waking each morning and lying on my poncho liner, listening to the sound of helicopters passing to and fro overhead. I had read *Catch-22* before coming to Vietnam but didn't understand it. It made no sense to me. I read the book again in Vietnam and understood it completely. It described our lives in Vietnam.

My own method of dealing with Vietnam was to focus on my work and, to the extent possible, remain a detached observer of events. We did our best to help the individual soldiers we saw for evaluation and treatment. I saw patients and supervised my technicians throughout the division. We also tried to apply Dr. Harry Levinson's organizational consultation methods to our military setting. I recorded and kept track of my observations in the division, hoping to learn something, as Dr. Menninger had suggested I might. As I think now of Dr. Karl's attempt to explain dysfunctions in human behavior in terms of a lack of balance between eros and thanatos (love and hate), it seems to me that our loving activities (and a good deal of alcohol) got us through the year. When we focused on trying to help our soldier-patients individually or trying to reduce tension in the units, we felt and functioned optimally. Occasionally, my frustration and anger would surface through bouts of excessive drinking and aggressive outbursts, such as the night when I threw Beau through the door of the officers' club.

Unfortunately, this drunken evening was not a rare event. Periodically we would have a party at the club. We would cook steaks on the grill and drink ourselves into oblivion. My friend Bill Taylor in Chicago sent comedy tapes to cheer us up. He asked that I send him a tape in which I interviewed some of the guys for their views on Vietnam. I took my tape recorder to one of our drunken parties and interviewed my peers. When I later listened to the tape, it sounded completely insane. All you could hear was loud music in the background and men screaming profanities at the top of their lungs. I thought of the field trip to the back ward at the state mental hospital that traumatized me as a teenager. I remember the shock of walking into a ward where people were screaming and out of control. In retrospect, it was one of those "in-your-face" examples we liked to give people back home.

One night we were on red alert, which meant that Viet Cong had been spotted within the perimeter of the base camp. This was very scary because in past situations when base camps had been overrun, VC sappers tossed satchel charges into the buildings and caused many casualties. The alert came late at night when most of the docs were well into their cups. Someone said that if you wanted to inflict massive casualties, then fire a shot into the medical area. The heavily armed, intoxicated doctors would blow each other away! I stumbled into my hootch after an evening of heavy drinking and was having a paranoid nightmare involving sappers and red alerts when suddenly a figure burst through the door to my hootch shouting, "Red alert!" I pointed my .45 at the figure and pulled the trigger. Fortunately, the safety was on, because in the same instant I realized that it was John who had come in to warn me of the red alert. If the safety hadn't been on, John would have been dead, and I would have had to live with the fact that I had killed my buddy and neighbor.

Once in a while the support command would bring in live entertainment for the troops. This would usually consist of a Vietnamese rock band, who would play popular songs on a stage while stoned or drunk soldiers danced and screamed. If they played a song about home or going home, the troops would join in and scream the words along with the singers. The officers would sometimes drop in on these events but maintained control and sobriety because we didn't want to make fools of ourselves in front of the enlisted men. John would frequently dance to the music, and the enlisted men would form a circle around him and applaud his skill. He would start with one finger joint, then his wrist, then his forearm, then his whole arm and progress until his whole body was moving in time to the music. He said dancing was easy and that his sister had taught him to move on the beat. One USO show featured Miss America, Judith Anne Ford, from Belvidere, Illinois.

THE RED CROSS doughnut dollies passed out Kool-Aid to soldiers in the Lai Khe base camp on most mornings. When they appeared at a base camp, all eyes would follow their every move. Guys would take pictures of the women and ask to have their picture taken with them. They would be a topic of discussion for days afterward. Such talk would inevitably lead to stories and rumors that have become an established part of the lore of Vietnam. There was a rumor that if you had the money and the rank, you could have a doughnut dolly. Another story was that one of the generals had his American mistress flown in regularly and she stayed a few days at a time at the base camp. Apparently the relationship had been going on for a good many years, and she had flown into his headquarters when he was in the Korean War. I didn't pick up any resentment about this arrangement. The attitude seemed to be that he was the general and could do what he wanted.

Another subject of the lore of Vietnam was the interrogation of enemy prisoners. A rumor told by seemingly reliable sources was that the techniques were often unpleasant. They would put a VC prisoner in a helicopter and take him up to one thousand feet, question him, and threaten to throw him out. Sometimes they would blindfold him and then descend to two or three feet above the ground and push him out, which scared him but didn't hurt him. We heard rumors that in some instances several prisoners were taken up in a helicopter and one would be pushed out at one thousand feet. As I understood, they usually got the information they wanted from the remaining prisoners.

My personal experience with prisoners was limited. Once, after entering a clearing station, I accidentally got in on the interrogation of a wounded VC soldier and took a picture of the event. The American patients had been examined and treated, and the last patients to be seen were the Vietnamese prisoners. I saw a wounded Viet Cong on a cot surrounded by two American officers and a South Vietnamese officer who were questioning him. I started to take a picture when one of the Americans waved his hand and shook his head. "No pictures," he said. "Oh, sorry, I just got a new camera and wanted to try it out," I explained. The other intelligence officer asked what kind of camera I had. When I told him, the first intelligence officer said, "Oh, what the heck—go ahead and take the picture." I took the picture and have it framed at my house. This was the only interrogation I actually witnessed.

My other encounter with prisoners happened when I was in Lai Khe one morning in the outhouse. Suddenly, three Viet Cong prisoners walked in, hopped up on the bench, and squatted with their feet on each side of the other holes in the privy. Their guards outside had sent them in to the privy not knowing that I was inside. This was my most intimate contact with the Viet Cong.

The air cavalry division based near our division was like the unit featured in *Apocalypse Now*. These are the troops that used Cobra helicopters to attack with machine guns and rockets, often accompanied by music blasting over huge speakers on the copters. The officers wore cavalry hats, ascots, and boots and were portrayed accurately in the movie. There is a famous legend of an air cavalry bird colonel in our area who spotted a sampan. He called in a "Shit hook" (CH-47 Chinook—a large, two-bladed helicopter that could carry heavy loads), which dropped its hook and lifted the boat out of the water. As the boat started to go airborne, the occupants jumped into the river. The Chinook carried the sampan to Saigon where the air cavalry colonel had it shipped home as a souvenir.

APOCALYPSE NOW probably seems like a surrealistic fantasy to those who weren't in Vietnam. It was surrealistic, but it did portray the bizarre milieu of Vietnam. People did crazy things in that crazy environment. Part of my job was to help them make the adjustment. I threw myself into this task in my typically compulsive, type-A, workaholic style. In recognition of my efforts I was given two Army Commendation Medals, two Bronze Stars, two Air Medals, several Campaign Medals, Unit Citations, and a Vietnamese Civic Action Medal.

Lieutenant Colonel Hefner was very encouraging and supported our efforts. He also wanted me to stay in the army. He noted that the highest percentage of doctors who stayed on in the military were from the group who served in combat units. Because he liked me and my work and because he wanted me to stay in, he would regularly put me up for medals. Everyone in the division received the Vietnamese Civic Action Medal, and we got a new campaign ribbon every time the division had a campaign, which occurred frequently. I read somewhere that Napoleon once said you couldn't pay a man enough money to risk his life in battle, but he will gladly die for a ribbon.

People from other wars and civilians are sometimes impressed by the chest full of medals I received in Vietnam. My late father-in-law, having survived the Bataan Death March and a Japanese prison camp, was awarded one Bronze Star. I had two. He wasn't particularly impressed by my medals because we both knew that my experience was nothing compared to his. It isn't the medal; it's what you do to get the medal that means something. Anyone can go buy a martial arts black belt—but if you don't earn the black belt, it has no meaning. (As I've gotten older, I have been given awards and titles for merely staying alive.) I have come around to accepting the Bronze Stars and Army Commendation Medals as awards for our extra effort and the new programs we developed. My awards were for achievement and service; my father-in-law was decorated for valor. The Air Medals were automatically awarded based on the number of flights we flew to see the technicians at Lai Khe and Dau Tieng.

We were occasionally exposed to rocket and mortar attacks in the base camps, we flew constantly, and we did have Viet Cong inside the wire on one occasion—but my being in the division did not reflect any courage on my part. Like all officers I was a "volunteer," because officers cannot be drafted, but the alternative would have been to be drafted as an enlisted man and do the same work for less pay. The other alternatives were to go to Canada or Oxford or to break rocks with Dr. Levy. (Howard B. Levy was a physician and a captain in the U.S. Army who was court-martialed in 1967 for refusing to train Special Forces medics bound for Vietnam. He served twenty-seven months in prison before the Supreme Court ordered him released on bail in 1969.) I understood what Lieutenant Colonel Hefner was trying to do for me. I could see that if you were a career military person, then medals might be a good thing in your personnel file and would look impressive if you wore your uniform daily in a stateside military assignment. But I knew I wasn't going to stay in the army, and the medals I received did not mean much to me.

I wasn't the only one receiving decorations at the time. They were awarded liberally in Vietnam. Our division headquarters sign, "Danger Forward," was damaged in a rocket attack and was written up for a Purple Heart, which was pinned to the sign. The top brass were giving each other medals every day. Major Martinet had several, and as far as I or anyone else in the unit could see, his only contribution was to attempt to ingratiate himself to the colonel and bully the enlisted men. Lieutenant Colonel Hefner saw a helicopter go down while he was making rounds. He had his helicopter land, and he administered medical first aid to the injured pilot and crew. For this act he was awarded a Silver Star. When Lieutenant Colonel Hefner arrived in the division, he replaced Lieutenant Colonel Koberle, who was both division surgeon and CO of the 1st Medical Battalion. The previous division surgeon, Lieutenant Colonel Weinburg (pseudonym), had held only that office. I met him briefly, but he was leaving country when I arrived. Weinburg had been in Lai Khe during a rocket attack and had dived under his desk and discovered that he had a splinter in his finger when the attack was over. He went to the clearing station, had a medic remove the splinter, and then insisted that the medic write him up for a Purple Heart. The number of medals and awards in Vietnam increased during the latter half of the war. In 1968, the ratio of awards to combat deaths was 28 to 1. In 1970, the ratio was 132 to 1. Lowering the standards to receive awards diminished the value and true meaning of the medals. "Gongs" was a derogatory term used to refer to these cheapened awards.

The brass were constantly setting up opportunities to get more medals. For example, John and I were told that if we spent a few days in a combat unit and supervised the sandbagging of their medical facility, we would each get a Combat Medic Badge. John went and received the badge. I thought that was okay for him, as he was an administrative officer and was performing his management duties in the combat unit. I declined. I thought of how Simon had crawled out under fire to work on his dying friend. He truly deserved his Combat Medic Badge, and it would have been a farce for me, as a psychiatrist, to be awarded one for watching some guys fill sandbags. I believe this, but I think the real reason I did not go was that I knew Lieutenant Colonel Hefner wanted me to receive the badge. Ross had received a Combat Medic Badge for serving as the battalion surgeon in a combat armored unit for a couple of months when he first arrived. I think this was appropriate because he was living and functioning in the field.

Shortly after Lieutenant Colonel Hefner received his Silver Star, two of the medical company sergeants came to my hootch and said that the lieutenant colonel wanted me to know that there was a soldier in a unit who had threatened suicide and was asking for me. The soldier was sitting in his tent with his rifle. They wanted me to go and persuade him to come in for treatment. They were talking to me as if they were giving the orders and I was expected to get in the jeep and go. I knew at once that the command was setting me up to get a Silver Star. I also knew that if the word got out that the division psychiatrist made house calls on demand, I would be constantly traveling to see malingerers who wanted to get out of something. I declined and told them to bring the soldier to me. The sergeants appeared miffed that I refused to go. The unit chaplain did go. He talked with the soldier, who then came over to see me. The chaplain was given a Silver Star. Some of my peers pimped me for being a wimp and not going. John and Lieutenant Colonel Hefner were disappointed because they wanted me to get the award.

I sometimes think I should have just gone along with the program, gotten the medal, and enjoyed being a "hero"—but I just couldn't make myself do it. I wondered if I was kidding myself and that underneath I was afraid to go get a guy with a loaded rifle, but I knew that wasn't it. We frequently saw soldiers who arrived in the back of a meat wagon or a truck or walked in with loaded weapons, and since this guy was asking for me, I had no doubt he would come easily. It wasn't fear that caused me to turn it down, nor was it idealism on my part. It was my reaction against being manipulated. It was a decision point in my life that has continued to stick in my mind, and I am still a bit conflicted as to whether I did the right thing.

In Vietnam I was the division Wizard and could pretty much do things as I thought they should be done. Lieutenant Colonel Hefner gave me plenty of slack. My technicians would jump to attention and play military if any Regular Army officers were around, but otherwise we operated as any independent mental health facility might have in the States. My reaction to refuse the sergeants' request was based on my reaction to someone telling me what to do and my knowledge that the situation was contrived so that I would get the award, a sort of reflex reaction on my part. Although it was no big deal, I sometimes wonder how I would have felt if I had retrieved the patient and accepted the medal. Would I have felt like a phony having it, or would I have started thinking I was a stud and convinced myself I deserved it? I'm sure I would have felt I didn't deserve it.

Specialist Walt Smith was an intelligent and idealistic young man. Although he was a conscientious objector, he was courageous and would stay with combat units to talk with the men and observe their stresses. He was given several medals for his courage and his efforts above and beyond the normal in Vietnam. I put him in for the medals and felt he deserved them. He recently e-mailed me to say that he was planning to return his medals to the Pentagon along with a letter explaining his actions. When I returned from Vietnam, I had my medals framed and then put the framed awards in the back of the closet, where they have remained.

WE CONTINUED TO CHECK OFF THE DAYS and to try to find ways to break the routine and offset the boredom. In-country trips to Saigon were a relief. Ross and I arranged for a second R&R to Bangkok as another sojourn to look forward to near the end of the tour.

Getting Away to Saigon and the Second R&R

My monthly trips to Saigon had little to do with work. They were primarily a holiday for myself and the technicians. They provided a change of scenery, photograph opportunities, a chance to have a gourmet meal, and an opportunity to have a cocktail in the plush officers' club on top of the Hotel Rex. In the same way, my second R&R to Bangkok with Ross Guarino was another respite from the usual scenery and routine of Vietnam. We planned it to break up the remaining months in country and went through the usual pimping with our buddies that was our way of sharing the experience and their way of sharing their feelings about our indulgence.

As I entered the psychiatric hootch Zecchinelli jumped up to pour me a fresh cup of coffee. Captain Pabst and the other technicians were all smiles and gave me a warm greeting. The team was on its best behavior, as we were heading to Saigon for a vacation day away from Di An. We were supposed to be going to the 3rd Field Hospital. However, everyone knew that we were just having an in-country holiday.

Saigon was the capital of South Vietnam and the largest city in Indochina. It was located about twelve miles from our base camp in Di An. Tan Son Nhut Airport, Bien Hoa Airport, and Long Binh were some of the huge American installations near Saigon. Many apartments, offices, hospitals, and military installations for U.S. personnel, as well as the U.S. embassy, were located there.

We actually went to the field hospital once; the rest of the times were pure R&R. We put on our travel gear, loaded our cameras, gathered our weapons, and headed out by jeep to the "Paris of the Orient." Specialist Zecchinelli nearly always drove. We rotated technicians so that everyone got to go. John Hamilton joined some of our road trips as did Guarino, Pabst, Anzinger, and Galen. Traffic was usually heavy on Highway 1 and Highway 13.

There was safety in numbers, and convoys from Saigon to Lai Khe on Thunder Road sometimes contained as many as 150 vehicles accompanied by APCs and helicopter gunships. During our first trip to Saigon, we were passed by a giant flatbed truck carrying a damaged tank to Saigon to be shipped out for repairs. The flatbed bumped our jeep and flipped us into the ditch. The crew of the truck roared on, unaware that they had hit us. Although the jeep rolled and was wheels up in the ditch, we all jumped or fell free and avoided injury. It totaled the jeep, however, and I had to do some fast talking and a little manipulation with Lieutenant Colonel Koberle to get a replacement.

On another trip we came upon a large crowd of Vietnamese standing around the road. The expressions on their faces were a mixture of shock, sadness, horror, and anger. As we stopped, we saw the body of a young Vietnamese boy lying on the street next to a badly damaged bicycle. Two women who appeared to be close relatives of the child were embracing each other, sobbing, and wailing. An army truck had run over the boy. Again, the truck driver had not realized he hit anything and had gone on. The Vietnamese police arrived, cordoned off the area, and called for an ambulance. There were many accidents on this congested highway, and the victims were usually Vietnamese. I felt the anger and resentment from the onlookers and even from the police and thought it was justified. We were the foreign army whose truck had just run over and killed a young boy like a squirrel in the street with no recognition of the event, no remorse, and no apology. We were shocked and saddened by the scene, but the crowd looked at us in our military attire as if to say, "See what you are doing to our country and our people." Although we generally photographed anything out of the ordinary in Vietnam, none of us reached for a camera or took a picture.

As we approached Saigon, we were always overwhelmed by a terrible stench. The city garbage dump was located on the north side, and the odor of raw garbage baking in the 110-degree sun was choking. It was a large, open, unfenced field located about two hundred yards from the highway. Junk and garbage were mounded up, and fires were burning here and there. Some ragged Vietnamese were picking through the junk.

After the dump we passed by the huge Xa Loi Buddhist Pagoda. In 1963 the South Vietnamese government made it unlawful for Buddhists to carry flags on the birthday of Buddha. On June 11 a Buddhist bonze (monk) named Quang Duc set himself on fire in protest. That summer, six more bonzes died there by self-immolation. On June 11, 1970, another bonze set himself on fire on the anniversary of Quang Duc's death in protest of the U.S. incursion into Cambodia.

Traffic and noise increased as we entered Saigon. Buses, military vehicles, mopeds, Lambrettas with benches on the back, motorcycles, Renaults, Citroëns, rickshaws, cyclos, blue and yellow taxicabs, pedestrians, and cyclists were all crammed onto the road. Occasionally we would see one of the "white mice" directing traffic. These were local Vietnamese police officers who wore white gloves, white shirts, gray pants, and white or blue helmets with "QC" on the sides (Quoc Canh, or National Police). We were a little apprehensive about anyone being next to our jeep because the Vietnamese "cowboys" (teenagers on mopeds) were known to drop grenades wrapped with natural rubber into military gas tanks. The rubber would dissolve in the gasoline and set off the grenade. They also put grenades on the canvas roof of jeeps. I pointed my .45 at anyone pulling too close and motioned with the gun while telling them "di di mau" (move quickly), which gave us some breathing room in the congestion. We passed by some large houses covered with white stucco and topped by red-tiled roofs. Through the gates we could see groomed lawns and gardens and expensive cars sitting in the driveways.

We went on to Thong Nhut Boulevard where the Independence Palace was located and passed the U.S. embassy. It was a large, white structure with narrow windows fortified with barbed wire and sandbags and guarded by MPs in a pillbox at the gate in front. We drove on and entered the Lam Son Square in the high-rent district of the downtown area. The continental hotels were located there. A large statue of two soldiers—the Vietnamese marine monument of the unknown soldier—dominated the square. It was one of the first statues the Communists destroyed when they took over in 1975. The ten-story Caravelle Hotel was near Le Loi Square and located on Tu Do Street (Freedom Street). We drove by John F. Kennedy Square and the red-bricked, twin-spired basilica. We passed the large, yellow Post Telegram and Telephone building.

Nguyen Hue Street was known as the "street of flowers" because of the many flower stalls along the way. We drove to the USO to check our weapons and flak jackets. The only times we did not check our equipment at the USO were when we stayed overnight with the Special Forces. Then we headed for the Caruso, one of the best French-Italian restaurants in the city. The center of the city was built during the 1930s by French architects who attempted to duplicate the atmosphere of Paris streets (hence the "Paris of the Orient" nickname).

The Caruso was paneled in dark wood, and crystal chandeliers hung from the ceiling. The tables were set with starched, white linen tablecloths and napkins. Crystal glasses and silverware were set on the tables. Thick carpeting added to the rich ambience and to the stillness of the room. Soft French and Vietnamese music played in the background. The seated patrons wore suits and attractive dresses, and the waiters wore black tuxedos. Our contingent was the incongruous element in the room. We entered wearing sweaty, dusty tropical fatigues, dusty boots, and steel helmets. We had plenty of money and ordered the best wines and the best of the excellent menu. The total tab was about what you would pay for a nice meal in San Francisco at that time. While sitting in the opulent room, sipping a fine French red from a crystal goblet, enjoying the crusty bread and the gourmet meal, it was hard to remember that we were soldiers in a combat zone. The patrons and the waiters looked at us with sad, helpless expressions. I often thought afterward that we must have appeared to them the same as the Nazis appeared to the Parisians during World War II.

After the Caruso, we usually stopped at the officers' club at the top of the Hotel Rex, which was used as a field-grade bachelor officers' quarters. This was a popular gathering place for journalists and "Saigon warriors." The journalists were friendly and enjoyed our stories. This bar was decorated inside with heavy, dark wood paneling and had a patio area under an awning with a view overlooking downtown Saigon. We enjoyed having a cocktail and relaxing in the plush surroundings.

I once met a reporter for a major magazine at the Rex who later came to visit me at the division. The technicians and Captain Pabst gave him a tour, and I showed him what we were attempting to do in our division. He seemed very interested in the organizational consultations and our work in monitoring stress in units. Unfortunately, I expressed some of my conservative political views and told a few war stories that may have grossed him out. When the article came out in the magazine, it contained the information about high-risk individuals and high-stress periods in the units but featured another psychiatrist's name with no mention of me or the 1st Infantry Division. It was another lesson in life for me. If I had shared the reporter's liberal views and laid off the grossness, our work likely would have received national publicity. I subsequently learned that enlisted men in the division were sometimes interviewed by journalists who tended to select the men who had peace sign medals or "FTA" written on their helmets. If their views supported the military or the war in Vietnam, they did not make it into print. If they griped about either, they were featured.

Sometimes we would head for a steam bath. John was with us on several of our Saigon trips. When he was along, it changed the complexion, so to speak, of our interaction with the Vietnamese. The hustlers would approach the rest of us regarding steam baths, boom-boom girls, or "number-one virgin" but ignore John. They would sometimes whisper to the rest of us: "Number-one girls—no black GI." They would try to get us to go and leave John. We refused to go to places that refused John so sometimes ended up in places that catered mostly to black soldiers. The women working in these places tended to be mentally defective, unattractive, psychotic, or social outcasts. We usually left Saigon before dusk because night travel invited ambush. The saying was "The night belongs to Charlie." By 1970 the city and surrounding areas were actually pretty secure. One visitor at that time described Saigon and the surrounding territory as safer than the major cities in the United States after dark.

I STILL BROOD about the horror of the boy who was run over in the street. I think of our MEDCAPs, where we passed out useless pills while our grunt escort paid a few dollars to the young Vietnamese "boom-boom" girls in the back of the APC. These were young farm girls who left their families to sell their bodies for money from the GIs. Then we barge into their best restaurants in our grubby fatigues, throw down a few dollars, and enjoy their best food and wine. Perhaps this was a personal experience with the "rape and pillage" that goes with war, but it makes me sad and guilty to think what we were doing to the Vietnamese people and their culture.

AT FORT SAM HOUSTON I met a neurologist named Al Breeland who had previously served in the military and had airborne training. He and Ross Guarino were the commanding officers of our training class. Al told Ross that he was practicing neurology when a female patient entered his office and said, "I have a headache." Al said he picked up the phone and called the army recruiter and enlisted on the spot. I thought he looked pretty sharp in his tiger-striped fatigues, red beret, jump boots, aviator-style dark glasses, and airborne badge. He had requested to be assigned to Special Forces in Vietnam and was told that there were no slots for a neurologist but could go if he was willing to serve as a general medical officer. He accepted the assignment. His headquarters was in Saigon, but he went into the field with the Special Forces troops and sustained a shrapnel wound during his tour of duty.

When Al first arrived in Vietnam in May 1969, he stopped by our division to check on me and to let me know where he was and how to reach him. I received a phone message that I was to come right away to deal with a psychiatric emergency in Bravo Company. I replied that I did not make house calls. I then got a message that Capt. Ray Troop, the CO of Bravo Company, needed to see me and I should immediately go to his office. I responded that Ray could trot over to my office if he needed to see me. Finally, I got the message that Major Breeland was at Troop's office trying to surprise me with a visit.

I went to Saigon at Al's invitation to attend a Special Forces party. The event was held in the Special Forces housing unit, a modern apartment complex. The rooms were new with spotless white walls, full kitchens and baths, and comfortable furnishings. The men had just returned from the field, which was the reason for the celebration. They were young, clean-cut kids who looked muscular and fit. They reminded me of a group of college football players and wrestlers. Al introduced me to some of the troops and to the sergeant major. About forty-five men were partying. The men began drinking in the afternoon. Their voices became louder as the day progressed, as did their irritability. They began punching one another and wrestling about, and the situation turned into a brawl. One soldier was thrown through a second-story window. Fortunately, the bushes and his state of inebriation protected him from serious injury. Al and I continued to smoke our pipes and remained on the periphery. "Happens every time," he explained. "Pretty soon they'll quit and go out and get laid." Sure enough, they quit fighting and headed off to the city.

Al said he wanted to take me to an interesting bar in Saigon. We drove to a low building with a sign written in Vietnamese above the door. He explained that this was the Vietnamese Air Force officers' club, also known as "the snake pit." He was allowed to go there because the Special Forces helped train the Vietnamese military forces. It took awhile for my eyes to adjust to the extremely dark bar. I noted that we were two of the very few non-Vietnamese in the place. Some patrons looked at me initially in a questioning, hostile way, but the questioning looks ended when they saw Al in his Special Forces uniform (the hostility didn't). We headed directly to the bar and, figuring "when in Rome, do as the Romans do," ordered Ba Mi Ba beer. The room was filled with Vietnamese pilots, who were small, thin, young men who looked very sharp in their starched jungle fatigues. Most had standard caps, but a few had berets, and several had ascots around their necks. Some wore dark glasses even though the place was very dark and smoky. There were many attractive Vietnamese girls who would approach officers by putting a hand on the "gentleman's" crotch and asking if he would buy them a drink. The Vietnamese pilots appeared cocky and reacted as if the girls should be thrilled to be in the same room with them. The scantily clad young women wore heavy makeup, short skirts, plunging necklines, and high heels.

Al pointed out a table of seven or eight Vietnamese officers play-ing cards. Three of them appeared to be older, a little stockier, and, I assumed, higher ranking than the other officers in the bar. "Look under the table," he said. Beneath the table, two prostitutes were performing fellatio on the players. Al explained that there were two games going on: the card game and a variation of liar's dice in which the men at the table would try to guess who was getting a blow job. If they guessed correctly, that person bought the drinks. If they were wrong, they bought. In addition, they were playing some type of card game for money. Oral sex was available more readily in Saigon than in the rural areas. Al said that any kind of sex imaginable was available in "the snake pit." From what I saw, I have no reason to doubt him.

We had another round of drinks, fended off a couple of the girls, and left after an hour or so. We talked about the place while sitting at the bar. I said I didn't think we were too popular and wouldn't win any friends if we started getting friendly with the girls. Al agreed. He said the Vietnamese were coming along and would probably end up becoming good soldiers, but this was their club and their girls and we should keep a low profile. We both felt that the pilots had little regard for the prostitutes as individuals, but the idea of a foreigner fooling around with a Vietnamese woman who worked in their club would probably offend many of them. I did not think too deeply about this at the time, but I later learned that Vietnamese men were worried that their women would be less interested in them sexually once they discovered that American "birds" (penises) were larger than Vietnamese "birds." To save face, a rumor was started that Americans had given the Vietnamese men the "shrinking bird disease." They also said that the Americans had been immunized against the disease and therefore weren't affected by the disease's shrinking effects.

John joined me on one trip to the Special Forces in Saigon. Major Breeland accompanied us to the Caruso and the Rex. We looked out over the city from the roof of the hotel and photographed downtown Saigon from above. Then Al took us on a sightseeing tour that included the Saigon zoo. The buildings and animal cages were ancient, but the animals appeared to be healthy. We saw troops of Vietnamese Boy Scouts and girls in blue and white school uniforms who were accompanied by teachers and scout leaders.

They behaved like kids on a field trip at home. Al then led us to a French patisserie, which had crusty French bread, croissants, and delicious desserts. We ended up spending the night at the Special Forces quarters and visiting several nightclubs in violation of the curfew for the U.S. military. The curfew ran from 11 P.M. to 5 A.M. on weeknights and from 1 A.M. to 5 A.M. on the weekends. The Special Forces made their own rules, and we were armed and partying with them. The patrons were about two-thirds Vietnamese civilians and one-third civilian and military Americans who were also violating the curfew. The first smoke-filled club had a Vietnamese rock group for entertainment. We got a table, but no one came to wait on us. After a prolonged period of being ignored, we caught on that they didn't want to wait on us because John was part of our group. John had recognized the problem immediately. We told the proprietor that we were together, and if John did not get served, we weren't buying. He relented and had the waitress take our orders, but we moved on to another nightclub. We were all wearing our .45s. John and I retained ours since we were staying with the Special Forces; Al and his Special Forces buddies always wore theirs. The weapons were noticed immediately and garnered a little additional fear and respect. As Al Capone once said, "A kind word with a gun in your hand will accomplish more than a kind word alone."

My relationship with the Special Forces apparently got around the division. One day I received a call from a lieutenant who was the executive officer of Alpha Company in an armored battalion. "Major, I've got a problem—I need an M55 Quad [a motorized gun mount fitted with simultaneously fired and parallel-aimed .50-caliber machine guns] that I can mount on a track and I can't get them through channels."

I responded, "I'm the division psychiatrist."

"I know that, but I heard you knew people."

"What have you got to trade?"

"Captured weapons."

"Okay, I'll see what I can do."

I then called the Special Forces sergeant major and explained the situation to him. He asked me what the unit had to trade and told me to have the lieutenant call him. The Special Forces then ripped the M55 Quads from a vehicle that had recently been loaded off a ship and delivered them to the armored unit. In exchange, they received captured weapons that they sold as souvenirs to guys leaving the country.

Talking with Al, it seemed the Special Forces had few psychiatric casualties. Like the LRRPs, they were volunteers, well trained, and highly motivated. In 1966 a group of researchers from Walter Reed Army Hospital measured the cortisol in these men to assess their degree of stress and were surprised to find low levels. The low psychiatric referral rate might also be attributed to their having their own ways of coping with stress, such as the drinking, fighting, and sex noted earlier. They were a macho group, and seeking psychiatric help was probably contrary to their self-image as well.

ON ONE OF OUR TRIPS TO SAIGON, we had stopped at the USO to drop off our weapons, then dined at a French restaurant, and were walking around downtown. We stopped in the Caravelle Hotel to look around, and I took a photograph of the glass spiral staircase. We strolled along Tu Do Street, which was Saigon's Fifth Avenue, in the downtown area to do some window-shopping. Next we walked to the market at the end of Le Loi Street to observe the various vendors who displayed their wares. Many of the products had obviously come from U.S. inventories either stolen from PX supplies or purchased illegally from some profit-minded supply sergeant. Vietnamese lacquerware was very attractive. I bought a black photo album with goldfish swimming on it that is still on my coffee table at home. Other goods offered included Day-Glo pictures painted on black velvet that looked as ugly as those in the States, Vietnamese dolls, nons (conical straw hats), traditional ao dai slit dresses with trousers, and ceramic elephant end tables. Crossbows and punji sticks were also popular, and no doubt some were made by the patients in the mental hospital we visited in Bien Hoa.

We were frequently solicited by beggars who were amputees, beggars holding up sick babies, and beggars who appeared to be blind. Rickshaw drivers would pull up offering a ride to a "number-one girl." Young women squatted by pots where they cooked deep-fried foods. Old peasant men and women squatted by their don ganhs, with baskets filled with fruits and vegetables. The don ganhs were poles with baskets on each end that they would carry into Saigon in hopes of selling their produce. A young boy was sitting in a chair getting a haircut.

As we walked back to the shops on Tu Do, we saw a crowd in front of an electronics store looking at a television in the window. We looked in and saw that it was a live broadcast of the astronauts landing on the moon. We were excited and awed by the sight. We all agreed that the United States must be in pretty good shape as a country to be able to land men on the moon while conducting the war in Vietnam.

Looking back, our trips into Saigon were a needed break for our team. We worked hard, but we needed a break periodically to reduce our own stress. I sometimes got drunk with the other medical officers as a way of letting off steam and reducing my own stress—the trips to Saigon served the same purpose and were probably a healthier way of coping with the stress of our work.

GUARINO AND I DECIDED to take the second R&R after the New Year. The army tried to deter men from two R&Rs by stamping "R&R" on their shot cards. Since we were in the medical battalion, we simply made ourselves new shot cards. In fact, this was the medical battalion's main "currency" in the division. If we wanted a case of steaks for a cookout, for example, we would merely dry-lab some new shot cards for the supply company.

Ross and I prepared for our trip to Bangkok. We called directly from Di An to the Oriental Hotel in Bangkok and made our reservations. We each had our own jeeps and drivers and knew a lot of pilots. We could drive or fly pretty much anywhere in country whenever we wanted to go. We became a little grandiose about our abilities and decided that it was beneath us to simply be driven to the airport for R&R. We thought it would be "one up" to have a helicopter fly us to the airport. We spoke with our pilot buddies, who said this wasn't a problem. The morning of our R&R we were picked up by helicopter at the clearing station and flown to Saigon. The pilot, who had been told that we were going to Bangkok on R&R, landed in a large compound and yelled, "This is it." We jumped out with our luggage, and the helicopter took off. We found ourselves on a large parade ground filled with Asian troops in unusual uniforms. No one seemed to speak English, and we didn't recognize their language. Eventually we figured out that we were at the Thai army division headquarters in Saigon. We had to be at the R&R briefing when it started, or we would not be allowed to board the plane to Bangkok. We grabbed our suitcases, ran outside the compound, and located a taxicab. The cab drove us to the airport, where we arrived a few minutes after the briefing had started. After considerable whining and begging from us, the officer-in-charge felt sorry for us and allowed us to attend the rest of the briefing and board the plane. The briefing was primarily a presentation of the various types of sexually transmitted diseases that could be contracted in Bangkok, which establishments were known to be infected and should be avoided, how to prevent STD infection, and how to get treated if you contracted a disease.

From the Bangkok airport we took a cab to the Oriental Hotel, an old, five-star hotel on the Chao Phya River where Somerset Maugham wrote some of his books. It had open halls where attendants would stand waiting to be of service. When you pushed the room-service button, an attendant would ring the doorbell to the room and, when you opened the door, would throw himself prostrate on the floor in front of you. If you requested ice, he would hold up the ice bucket while lying flat on the floor. Thai dancers and musicians performed on the lush lawn that lay between the hotel and the river. It was an amazing contrast to be in an army base camp in Vietnam in the morning and to be waited on like royalty that same afternoon. We watched Thai dancers, saw kickboxing, took the river tours, visited the famous Buddhist temples in the area, and shopped for opals, star sapphires, and celadon pottery. We also dined at the best restaurants. We had Kobe steak at a Japanese restaurant, great food at an Indian restaurant, and some excellent Thai meals. Some of my father's former Thai mathematics students met us and took us to their favorite Thai restaurant. The Thai people were very soft-spoken and gentle. Sometimes a Thai citizen would stop us in the street in order to visit and practice speaking English.

It was expected that we would bargain for everything. For example, a cab ride across town was fifty Baht ($2.50 at that time). The driver knew it, most riders knew it, but you still had to bargain. There were exceptions. One occurred when Ross was walking down

CHAPTER 14

a street loaded down with packages when a cab stopped to offer him a ride for fifty Baht. Ross was so into bargaining that he said, "I'll give you twenty-five Baht," and the cab took off and left him.

When we left Thailand to return to Vietnam, we attended the mandatory debriefing prior to boarding the plane. We were told the symptoms of the various venereal diseases indigenous to Bangkok and ordered to report to our medical units if we observed any sign of infection. The officer conducting the debriefing added, "And for those of you who went to the Thai Heaven nightclub, step up and get your shots now because you are infected." We returned to our base camp in Vietnam and had the usual post-R&R letdown.

WE WERE CLOSE to getting short by now. We noted several coping devices that seemed to be employed in Vietnam. Counterphobia was used by all of us. Extreme cases led to bizarre behavior and unnecessary risk taking. Homosexuality existed in the military, although it was officially taboo. Homophobia was definitely present. Passive aggression was common in the authoritarian military organization, frequently with humorous results. It also provided just consequences for Major Martinet.

CHAPTER 15

Coping with Vietnam

B eing stuck in a potentially dangerous environment, having to balance between meeting the moral obligation of being effective and conforming to seemingly useless bureaucratic requirements, is stressful. Counterphobia was an important defense mechanism we employed to deal with the fear we experienced about being assigned to duty in Vietnam. Passive aggression was a common way to handle anger in an organization where the muck flowed in one direction only.

COUNTERPHOBIA IS A REVERSAL of a situation in which one is the passive victim of external circumstances to a position of attempting to actively confront and master what one fears. A child who has had a shot may play doctor and pretend to give a doll a shot. A person who is afraid of heights may take up mountain climbing. A coward becomes a bully. These are all examples of counterphobic behavior. Old guys who take up martial arts, ride motorcycles, and marry younger women are showing counterphobic behavior in response to the fear of their own mortality. Of course, my reasons for doing these things are more logical.

Counterphobia was used to some degree by most of us to adjust to Vietnam. We were all afraid of going home in a body bag when we arrived, and the veteran soldiers in Vietnam welcomed us by telling us war stories that suggested we were likely to go home that way. This "flooded us," as the behaviorists would say, with the things we feared most and helped us deny our anxieties, forget "the world," and focus on our assignments. The greeting to the FNGs by the soldiers leaving Vietnam was a way of reinforcing the new guys' counterphobic defenses. As soon as you deplaned, you were inundated with what you most feared—going home in a body bag. Veteran soldiers would tell you war stories and initiate you into your new unit. Soon you figured that if they can do it, so could you, and you stopped thinking about getting home or staying alive and focused on the day-to-day activities you had to deal with in Vietnam.

IN MOST INSTANCES, facing the phobic situation should be considered a healthy desire to put the phobia to the test in hopes of mastering the fear. To some extent it is the stuff that heroes are made of—but when medical personnel become killers, something has gone awry.

Rich D'Angelo (pseudonym) was a dentist I knew from Fort Knox. He was married and had two young daughters. He was usually present at our Friday TGIFs at the officers' club. He knew that although I might be socially liberal in many ways, my politics were generally to the right of Genghis Khan's. After I had been in Vietnam for a few weeks, I received a letter from Rich reporting that he had also received orders for Vietnam and wanted to be assigned to the 1st Infantry Division. He asked that those in command be told that "I am a God-fearing, John Birch–sympathizing, Goldwater-supporting, Oriental-hating, churchgoing, all-around swell fellow, looking for a job drilling teeth." I passed the request to Lieutenant Colonel Hefner, who thought he must be our kind of guy, and thus Rich was assigned to the 1st Infantry. Actually, it wasn't hard to be assigned to a division—it was hard to get out of being assigned to a division.

When Rich arrived, he passed his initiation with flying colors and was accepted by the group. He was very outgoing and funny. In a short time, however, he started creating dangerous missions for himself in Vietnam. He had himself inserted by cable into an area that was too hot for helicopters to land so that he could drill teeth under fire. He started hanging around with the LRRPs. The Rangers let him fire a case of light antitank weapons (LAWs) into the jungle during one of their evening drinking sessions. One evening as he was sitting around with a group of LRRPs, one of the Rangers noted that Rich seemed depressed. The Ranger asked Rich what was wrong. Rich responded that he had been here for over three months and hadn't yet killed anyone. He said he didn't come all the way over here just to drill teeth. According to the word among the doctors, the Rangers took D'Angelo, combat dentist, to a nearby village and let him shoot a Vietnamese.

I met a stocky battalion surgeon assigned to one of the field units who swaggered around with crossed bandoliers of ammunition over his flak jacket as if he were Pancho Villa. He carried grenades and a grease gun (aka M3A1 SMG, or burp gun, a U.S.-made .45-caliber submachine gun that used a thirty-round magazine; called a "grease gun" because it resembled a tool used for injecting grease into vehicle axles and a "burp gun" because of its distinctive noise) and had "Kill a Commie for Christ" written on his helmet. Battalion surgeons were more exposed to rocket and mortar attacks and were farther out in the field than the medical officers in the base camps, but primarily they treated the same kinds of problems we saw, such as clap, foot rot, and dysentery. The wounded were given primary attention by the medics and then medically evacuated by helicopter to evacuation hospitals or MUST (medical unit, self-transportable) units that could do surgery. There were no medical or military reasons for a doctor to be armed to the teeth or to have slogans about "killing commies" on his helmet.

The counterphobic dentist and battalion surgeon were extreme and exceptions to the norm. Most of the doctors I knew functioned compassionately as physicians and tried to help their soldier-patients to the best of their ability. They were good doctors before they came into the military and continued to be good doctors in the military.

ONE MORNING AT BREAKFAST, Ross Guarino turned to Bob Anzinger and announced that there was a new assignment for a doctor that seemed to be sort of hairy: "This assignment doesn't look too good. We have a policy that the newest doc in the unit gets the next assignment. You are the newest, so you get it."

Anzinger responded, "Uh, okay—what is it?"

"One of the units is requesting a doc. Their LZ [landing zone] is too hot to land a helicopter, so the doc will have to be inserted by cable."

"When is it?"

"Right away—get your stuff."

There was silence around the table. Anzinger looked tense and gray. He got up and headed for his hootch, and the rest of us followed. We stood around him in a circle as he jammed his things into his duffel bag. He looked like he could cry. The rest of us were thinking that we were glad we didn't get the assignment but also that we felt sorry for Bob. You could cut the tension with a knife. No one seemed to know what to say to Bob. Finally, I spoke. The rest of the docs looked up expectantly, thinking that I would know the right things to say.

"Bob?" I said.

"Yeah?"

"If anything happens to you—can I have your Nikon?"

"What! You SOB!" and Anzinger started laughing.

This was an example of boosting Anzinger's counterphobic defenses. This kind of pimping went on all the time.

ONE OF THE MOST CHARMING "counterphobes" I had a chance to meet in Vietnam was Maj. Michael Downey of the Australian army. We have remained friends over the years, and he has continued to be consistently fearless.

At one of our in-country R&R trips to the 93rd Evacuation Hospital, I had spotted an unusual-looking military officer. He was gray haired, well built, with a rather dignified look—he was a handsome fellow, but his physical appearance wasn't as distinguishing as his dress. The rest of us had on our green tropical fatigues and boots. He was dressed in a khaki uniform with gold insignias, brown brogan dress shoes, and a matching "digger" hat. As I approached him, I realized that he had an Australian accent and that his uniform must be what Aussie officers wore in Vietnam. We started visiting, and I learned that he was Maj. Michael Downey, a psychiatrist from Adelaide, and had volunteered for Vietnam out of curiosity. He said that the Australians had nearly 8,000 men in Vietnam (I later read that it was 7,672, which was the peak of their involvement).

It was my habit to invite people to our division to visit (they rarely took me up on it), so I asked him to come out and visit and we would show him around the division. He immediately said he would like that very much and would be out to see us the next day.

When we returned to Di An, I had a beer with Lieutenant Colonel Hefner and the rest of the medical officers. I told them the Australian psychiatrist would be visiting the next day and said that this was the first person who had accepted my invitation to visit. Lieutenant Colonel Hefner suggested that I might want to accompany him on his rounds of the fire support bases in the morning, as this would give Major Downey a better picture of the division's area of operations. Major Downey arrived early the next morning to begin his tour. I took him to our psychiatric headquarters, where the techs and I briefed him on the types of individual patients we were seeing and showed him our graphs of unit stress and our efforts to develop an organizational consultation program. We discussed drug use in country, and he shared examples of his work in the Australian division. He told us that initially the Australian troop morale had been a problem because there were a number of horrendous injuries from land mines in their area. Once those were cleared out and the danger removed, the morale improved considerably. Also, they sustained a number of injuries from animal bites (monkeys, lizards, and so on), but once "pets" were outlawed by command, these injuries were also eliminated. Major Downey said that the Australian army worked closely with the New Zealand troops in Vietnam. He told us that the New Zealanders were fierce fighters but were a problem when they came out of the field—much like our Special Forces troops in Saigon, they would come out of the field, get drunk, and start fighting. To control this, the sergeants would start playing guitars and singing during the initial stages of drinking. Soon the troops would put their arms around one another and join in on the sing-along. In a short while they would pass out, and violence would be avoided.

We went for breakfast in the officers' mess where I introduced him to Lieutenant Colonel Hefner and the other MSC officers. We then went to the helipad and jumped into Lieutenant Colonel Hefner's copter with Major Martinet and the other officers.

At the third fire support base we were being briefed by the company commander when we heard the explosions of mortar shells being "walked in" to our area. The VC would land a shell to the right and then to the left as they zeroed in on their target. We all hit the dirt and lay there as the explosions continued. Major Downey remained standing throughout the attack and continued to talk in a calm voice: "War is interesting, isn't it? Sort of exciting, really." We all looked up at him in amazement from our prone positions on the ground. It was obvious that Major Downey wasn't going to experience any anxiety during his tour of the division.

We went on to the headquarters base camp in Lai Khe, where we met with our techs, inspected the clearing station, and then had lunch in their mess hall. We stopped in our most remote base camp in Dau Tieng to meet the Bravo Company techs and look at their clearing station. Then we returned to our own base camp to have dinner and go to the club for a few drinks. Michael stayed over and then took off in the morning but returned a few weeks later. He called me from headquarters in Vung Tau. I told him we were having a "party" with the pilots and that there would be plenty of steaks and beer if he could make it. He said he would be delighted and showed up that evening. As we were sitting around with the pilots after our cookout, one of them asked me if I had flown in a Bronco yet. The pilots were always giving the docs rides in their aircraft, and almost all of us had flown in most of the various helicopters and planes used in country. The Bronco was a split-tailed airplane that dove straight down to mark a target for the jets, then pulled out and went straight up to avoid enemy fire. When I replied that I hadn't flown in one, Michael broke in.

"You MUST fly in a Bronco—haven't got a hair on your derriere if you don't fly in a Bronco."

I looked at him in surprise. "Lieutenant Colonel Hefner flew in one the other day and he threw up."

"Oh yes, you DO upchuck," he answered without blinking. Everyone laughed.

"Why the hell do you want me to go up in a Bronco and puke?" I asked incredulously.

"It's part of the experience, old chap."

THERE IS A SITUATION IN THE ARMY that I think of as pseudo-counterphobic behavior. It superficially resembles counterphobic behavior, but there is really no fear on the part of the perpetrator. Doctors were a special category in the military. We were somewhat like loose cannons because we had rank but usually were not planning on staying in the army. Because we didn't care what went into our own personnel folders, it was always possible that we could do something that would inadvertently mess up a Regular Army officer's career path. The result was that as long as we did our jobs, the army gave us quite a bit of slack. For example, several of the doctors were at the support command officers' club one night playing liar's dice with the Regular Army officers around the crowded bar. The dice had made it around the bar twice when the commanding general approached the table and said that he wanted in. Guarino responded that he would have to wait until this game was over. The Regular Army colonels, lieutenant colonels, and majors were shocked that anyone would speak back to the general, much less refuse his request. One the majors yelled at Guarino to give the general the dice: "He's the general, for Christ's sake."

"No, those are the rules!" Guarino yelled back. The general looked down at the table.

"Who said that!"

"I did, sir," said Guarino.

"A medical officer—I thought so." The general turned to face the Regular Army officers at the bar and said, "None of you have the balls to speak up."

The general waited his turn and stuck by the rules as Captain Guarino had insisted. From my limited military experience, the big brass will usually stick up for what is right. One of the enlisted men at the base camp gate refused to admit a general who didn't have the password of the day. The general chewed him out initially, but when the private persisted in following his orders, the general complimented him and the next day ordered him promoted.

I SAW NO LRRPs as psychiatric patients during my year in Vietnam. One LRRP brought in a soldier who had "frozen" during his first firefight and remained in a catatonic state. The Ranger was a tall, lean, tired-looking veteran with a Fu Manchu mustache. He wore tiger-striped fatigues and carried captured weapons.

"Hey, doc, this is my third year in country."

"What?"

"Yeah, I extended—I've been here three years."

"What are you doing extending in Vietnam?"

"Well, I believe in what we are doing here—stopping the spread of communism and helping protect the democracy of South Vietnam."

"Bull!"

"Well, actually I'm here because I know that they need experienced men in Vietnam. Look at this kid I brought in today. They need guys like me who have been here awhile and know what's going on."

"I think that's also bull!"

"Okay, to tell you the truth doc, I like killing people."

"That I believe."

The LRRPs were elite troops who had completed the rigorous Ranger training program. The acronym for the LRRP qualities was TESTICLES: teamwork, enthusiasm, stamina, tenacity, initiative, courage, loyalty, excellence, and a sense of humor. They were highly motivated and disciplined and looked forward to combat. They also seemed to experience less stress than most of the soldiers we saw.

These kinds of individuals are aggressive but are able to channel their aggression in socially acceptable ways. These are also the men who often become heroes on the battlefield; for example, Joe Hooper, who was the most decorated soldier in Vietnam and a Medal of Honor recipient, said that he looked forward to being in combat and had thoughts of becoming a prisoner of war so he could escape and assassinate the enemy leaders.

Shortly after I arrived in Vietnam, the medical officers had a party with the pilots of the 1st Aviation Battalion, which was located near us in the base camp. After steaks and beer the pilots told several of us that there was a fellow they wanted us to meet. Some of us accompanied them to a hootch in their area of the base camp. Inside was a tall, fit, neatly groomed man in his thirties wearing starched fatigues with no insignias or rank. He welcomed us in. He handed each of us each a balloon-shaped wine glass and filled the glasses with red wine. Nuts and cheeses were available on the crate that served as a coffee table. He then opened up a violin case, took out the violin, and began playing classical music. I remember thinking that this was pretty civilized—drinking great wine and listening to classical music while in a war zone in Vietnam. After several renditions and refills, we excused ourselves, thanked the man for his hospitality, and complimented him on his virtuosity.

After we left the hootch, I asked the pilots who he was. They said that he was the number-one man on the VC wanted list. He was an assassin who went into villages at night and killed Viet Cong, leaving his personal calling card in the teeth of his victims. The pilots said that he had a successful business in California and that there was no record of his being in Vietnam. They didn't know for sure but speculated that he was associated with the Phoenix program in Vietnam, which was responsible for the execution of about twenty thousand Viet Cong suspects. The program was sometimes referred to as "Pacification by Assassination."

Recent findings in psychiatry suggest that individuals with a genetic predisposition for fearlessness who are raised in a loving, stable family tend to go into socially acceptable but risky occupations such as test pilot, race car driver, law enforcement, or military service. Others with the same genetic predisposition but who are raised in abusive homes tend to become antisocial and to hurt others as adults. Professional government personnel who are engaged in "wet work" (assassination) are in between these two groups.

MEN TEND TO UTILIZE COUNTERPHOBIC PIMPING to flood one another with the worst possible fears to help the new person deny the danger and to let go of attachments at home. I would speculate that women would probably cope with the stress of war differently. Women are more verbal and tend to share their feelings with one another. The female war correspondents in Vietnam who described their experiences in the book *War Torn* seemed to rely less on drugs and alcohol and more on sex to relieve their tension while there. Sex would be more available to female soldiers. My guess would be that women would also show some of the counterphobic pimping that men engage in and also the REMF phenomenon, but more subtly and indirectly than their male counterparts. For example, veteran men greeted newcomers in Vietnam by telling them, with liberal use of the "f" word, that they were going to be killed and by telling graphic war stories. The newcomers responded by forgetting about "the world" back home, deciding that they weren't any more likely to be killed than the veterans, and denying the danger.

A female soldier in Vietnam might have greeted a new soldier by welcoming her to the country, reassuring her that things are probably not as bad as she had imagined, and letting her know that there are plenty of men to choose from—one good thing in the military. If the new soldier expresses anxiety about the danger, she might be told that there had been rocket attacks and a scary night when the enemy came into the perimeter, but for the most part it had been fine. She might be frightened at first but it's not so bad when she gets used to it. She could be lucky and get assigned to Saigon or Long Binh. The veteran soldier would again reassure her and say she would be available if the new soldier needed anything.

WE NEEDED SOME COUNTERPHOBIA to overcome our initial anxiety and to be able to function in Vietnam. Homophobia, a fear of homosexuality and one's own latent homosexual feelings, is an uncomfortable topic within the military.

It is not surprising that the military is uncomfortable with homosexuality. You have a large group of men eating, sleeping, showering, and going to the john together. The majority are adolescent males who generally tend to be homophobic. They often work in areas for extended periods of time in locales where there are few or no women. You can also add to this that the military provides for the individual's dependency needs. You are told when to get up, provided with food, assigned specific functions, and told when to go to bed. Everything is provided, including most of your thinking. The basic soldier image is one of aggressive manliness. You get to carry weapons, travel the world, meet interesting people, and sometimes shoot at them. The idea of a passive homosexual male soldier threatens that image. I don't want to get too psychological about this, but for many reasons homosexuality seems to cause discomfort and a negative reaction among many soldiers in the military.

Homophobia can result in the irrational punishment of homosexual individuals. While I was at Fort Knox, we had a situation in which a sergeant had killed his unfaithful wife and her lover after discussing the matter with another sergeant at the NCO club. Although the killings were clearly premeditated, he was sentenced to minimal prison time for what was considered an understandable crime of passion. At the same time on the same post, a lieutenant was arrested for paying a paperboy to perform fellatio. It was proven that the paperboy had been making a good deal of money by performing sexual acts on a number of male customers on the post. The commanding general was furious that one of his officers would commit a homosexual act. He stated that he would like to see the lieutenant executed, but since this wasn't likely, he wanted him sent to a federal prison for life. We were able to admit the lieutenant to the psychiatric unit and medically discharge him from the service.

One morning I was seated at my desk in the psychiatric hootch with my feet up, smoking my pipe and looking through some of the data we had collected. A tough-looking soldier from a field unit came in and asked Pattburg if he could speak with the division psychiatrist. His boots and fatigues were covered with red dust. He had a steel pot and was carrying his M16. Pattburg looked up at me, and I nodded and motioned for him to come back. He stood in front of my desk and saluted. I returned his salute.

"I'm gay, doc—I just wanted you to know that I'm gay and I've been in a combat unit all year."

I mumbled something like, "Thanks for telling me" or "Okay." He turned around and left the office. I never saw him again.

I have often thought about this young man and the fact that he made a special effort to seek me out just to let me know he was gay. At that time, homosexuality was still considered a psychiatric illness to be treated. Earlier, Freud had written that homosexuality was nothing to be ashamed of; it wasn't a vice or an illness but a variation of sexual expression. The first gay rights march in the United States took place in 1970 in Greenwich Village. In 1973 the American Psychiatric Association eliminated homosexuality as a diagnosis. It was then thought of as an alternative lifestyle rather than an illness. The rationale was that the orientation toward homosexuality in an individual was not a choice, although the expression was.

It may have been that the gay soldier wanted to show the division psychiatrist that the official position about homosexuality espoused by organized psychiatry in 1969 was wrong. Also, at that time, homosexuals were excluded from the military. In fact, many men who were trying to avoid serving in Vietnam claimed to be homosexual for that reason. The Fort Knox Mental Hygiene Clinic had so many of these men that they assigned a specialist to interview men claiming to be gay. This fellow had effeminate mannerisms himself. He would sit straight up and look wide-eyed at his client, stressing the advantages for gay people in the military. He would also ask in a matter-of-fact manner graphic questions about the client's sexual habits. The combination of the specialist's effeminate speech and mannerisms, the detailed questioning, and his obvious curiosity about the soldier being interviewed often caused those feigning homosexuality to bolt from the room. Individuals who persisted in claiming they were gay were investigated by the Criminal Investigation Division, a process that included interviewing all their sexual contacts and documenting detailed questions about their sexual habits. This, of course, was embarrassing to the individuals as well as to their sexual contacts. They were discharged from the army if it was established that they were gay.

IN THE MILITARY you can't express your anger directly to individuals above you without severe consequences. Therefore, the anger is often expressed indirectly.

"Passive-aggressive" is a term that was first used by American military psychiatrists in World War II. It refers to situations in which an individual's assertiveness has been curtailed so that a direct expression of negative feelings is not possible. In such situations, the person can deal with anger only passively and indirectly. The aggression may be expressed in the form of obstructionism, pouting, procrastination, intentional inefficiency, or stubbornness. Sometimes, passive aggression is the only means through which justice can be served within an authoritarian organization.

When Major Martinet bullied the enlisted men, they could not express their anger directly to him. He was particularly hard on the soldier who drove his jeep. While Major Martinet was attending meetings indoors, he would insist that his driver remain seated in the jeep and bake in the 120-degree sun.

One day the major volunteered to pick up a visiting general who was coming to inspect the medical battalion. He had his driver take him to the airport to pick up the general. Major Martinet met the general, ready to ingratiate himself, and escorted him to the jeep. The general was seated in the right front seat of the jeep, which, according to military protocol, is where the highest-ranking officer sits. The major sat in the back, then whacked his driver with his swagger stick. "Make it snappy, son—the general doesn't want to be kept waiting." "Yes, sir!" his driver responded and took a hard left, whereupon the general and his seat flew out of the jeep and into the ditch. Major Martinet found himself in the ditch trying to help the general up. He was sweating bullets trying to apologize and explain the situation to the very angry general. Major Martinet never figured out that his driver had loosened the bolts holding the general's seat to the jeep prior to the trip.

People tried to find projects in Vietnam to keep themselves busy to help the time pass more quickly. Lieutenant Colonel Koberle's project was to install a large sign for the medical battalion. He then had the Vietnamese sign painter put at the top: "1st Medical Battalion, Lt. Col. Eberhardt Koberle Commanding Officer." Beneath this self-effacing title was the 1st Medical Battalion emblem and the emblems of all the other units in the division. While admiring the sign, which the lieutenant colonel hoped would become a lasting monument to his tour in Vietnam, he began to worry that the heavy rains during the monsoon season might cause the sign to fade over time. He then hired a Vietnamese carpenter to construct a roof over the sign to protect it from the elements. After the roof was finished, Lieutenant Colonel Koberle saw that the unfinished wood and shingles didn't match the sign. He called in the first sergeant and told him to have the roof painted white to match the sign. The sergeant grabbed the first private he saw and said, "The lieutenant colonel wants his sign painted." The private, who wasn't paid to think, painted the entire sign, which obliterated Lieutenant Colonel Koberle's pet project. He was furious but couldn't do anything to the private, who had merely followed his orders.

A similar incident occurred in another support command unit. The commander of the 1st Engineering Battalion coped with his tour in Vietnam by growing banana plants next to his hootch. He watered them daily during the dry season and carefully nurtured them throughout his tour of duty. Prior to the visit of a senior officer to the unit, he ordered the first sergeant to have the men "trim the grass" in the company area. This was a jungle base camp that was attacked fairly frequently by rockets and mortars. The first sergeant had a platoon fall in and repeated the lieutenant colonel's orders. The enlisted men calmly cut down every plant, vine, shrub, weed, and banana plant in the area. The lieutenant colonel ranted, raved, and cursed them for their stupidity, but they were merely carrying out orders.

As shown, passive aggression can be downright funny. We had a skinny black dentist from Cleveland named Maurice (pseudonym) who reminded us of Klinger on *M*A*S*H*. He had finished dental school and borrowed the money he needed to set up a private dental practice. He joined the army reserves hoping that this would keep him from being drafted. Instead, his reserve unit was activated and sent to Vietnam. Maurice had to sell his equipment at a loss, had to pay to get out of his office lease, and was stuck with the bank loans taken out to start his practice. When he arrived in country, he was assigned to a combat infantry unit. At that point, he stopped wearing army uniforms. Instead, he wore tropical sport shirts, flip-flops, and boxer shorts—anything but an army uniform. No one got close enough to Maurice during the year to really know what he thought. My guess is that he was thinking that the army took him from his practice, put him in debt, and sent him to a combat division in Vietnam—there was nothing more they could do to him.

The dental hootch was located next to the psychiatric hootch. It had a bunker made out of old shell containers. A cage with a live monkey was located outside, and a sign was posted: "No extraction too difficult, no cavity too great, anesthesia first," which was a parody of the 1st Infantry Division motto, "No mission too difficult, no sacrifice too great, duty first."

A visiting general and his party were inspecting the medical company one day. This was a big deal. We had officers stationed at the clearing station, the psychiatry headquarters, and the optometry hootch, as well as at the dental hootch, to show the general through these facilities and answer his questions. Lieutenant Colonel

Hefner, Major Martinet, Captain Guarino, and Captain Hamilton accompanied the general and his party throughout the tour. As our brass were pointing out highlights of the company area, the general spotted Maurice dancing on top of the elevated barrel that was used as an outdoor shower. The dentist was wearing a bright red Hawaiian sports shirt covered with large green parrots, green boxer shorts, and flip-flops. He was slowly bopping and gyrating around to some internal beat that only he was hearing. "What is that supposed to be?" growled the general. "A dentist, sir," answered Captain Guarino. "He wants to go home." "Does he drill teeth?" asked the general. "Yes, sir," answered Guarino. "Humph," responded the general who continued on with his inspection. He didn't care what Maurice did as long as he drilled teeth.

Maurice kept to himself. When he came to the officers' club, he would have a drink, dance around by himself, and then leave to hole up in his "house" on "the Ghetto." Galen, Zappia, Guarino, and I lived on "Broadway," which was our name for the gravel path between our hootches. Maurice, Pabst, and Hamilton lived the next "street" over, which they called "the Ghetto." He was elusive. When I looked over my hundreds of pictures taken during my year in Vietnam, Maurice is the only one of the medical and medical service officers who is missing from the photos.

One day I heard screaming and loud laughter coming from the area of the dental hootch. I turned the corner of our building in time to see an infantry soldier run screaming out of the back door of the dental facility. The dental corpsmen were doubled over, rolling on the ground with laughter. They were finally able to tell me that an infantryman who was apprehensive about seeing a dentist had been sent by his unit because of a toothache. He was nervously sitting in the dental chair when Maurice entered the hootch wearing his "uniform" and looked in the tense soldier's mouth. Maurice asked the corpsman what he thought was wrong with him. The corpsman replied that Maurice was supposed to be the doctor.

Maurice looked into the even more frightened soldier's mouth again, commenting that he never should have left the motor pool. The soldier's eyes widened at the thought that a black mechanic in bizarre attire from the motor pool was going to work on his mouth. Maurice announced that he was going to have to "blast." He pulled out a foot of dental floss, stuck it between two of the soldier's back teeth, lit the end of it, and went over to the corner of the hootch where he crouched down with his eyes squinted and his fingers in his ears. The terrified soldier looked down at the "fuse" burning closer and closer to his mouth. He jerked out the dental floss and ran screaming from the building. I asked the corpsmen how Maurice had reacted to all of this. They said that he didn't show any emotion at all. He just got up slowly, went outside, and started dancing. We all had our ways of coping with Vietnam. Maurice danced his way through the year.

I WASN'T ABOVE USING a little PA manipulation myself. When I first arrived in the division, John got me a jeep and had the Vietnamese painter paint "Division Psychiatrist" on the front. We could always get a helicopter ride to anywhere in the division, but the jeep was an important piece of equipment because it allowed us to go to places such as Saigon, Long Binh, Lai Khe, and Bien Hoa. After the jeep had been totaled on the trip to Saigon, I put in a request, with John's assistance, for a new jeep but heard nothing for a couple of weeks. John told me that Lieutenant Colonel Koberle had to approve the request and it was sitting on his desk.

I then wrote a memorandum to the division surgeon at headquarters company in Lai Khe through the commander of 1st Medical Battalion (Lieutenant Colonel Koberle) indicating that all psychiatric unit consultations in the division would be curtailed until such time as we acquired suitable transportation. A few days later, Lieutenant Colonel Koberle stormed into my office, red faced and furious, waving the memorandum in his hand.

"Vhat the heck do you tink you are doing, Vizard?"

"We need a jeep if we are going to get out to the units and consult with them."

"Are you trying to make me look bad, Vizard?"

"No, sir, that wasn't my intent."

"Den vhy are you sending dis memo on to da division surgeon?"

"Sir, you are the division surgeon."

"Huh? Ya? I guess that's right. Okay, you can have your jeep—but I better not catch you out of line in any vay."

"Yes, sir."

Soon we had a brand-new jeep, and the Vietnamese painter once again spiffed it up with "Division Psychiatrist" on the front. John told me to keep a low profile because the lieutenant colonel would love to nail me before he left country.

Lieutenant Colonel Koberle did hold a ceremony for me and pinned on the oak leaves that signified my promotion to major. Being a field-grade officer instead of company grade was of some help during unit consultations because it caused some lifers to mistake me for one of their own. I went from "Bac-si Dai Uy" (doctor captain) which rhymed, to "Bac-si Thieu Ta," which did not rhyme and which I could never remember.

DENIAL, COUNTERPHOBIA, HARD WORK, the breaks in and out of the country, the MEDCAPS, the "parties," and self-medication got us through the year. We were becoming two-digit midgets, short timers, and finally were actually preparing to leave country. We started thinking of home and had the opportunity to welcome a planeload of FNGs who came in on our freedom bird. We went our separate ways and were surprised to find that Vietnam had largely been ignored and forgotten by the civilians at home. We were ignored or greeted with hostility by most of the civilians we met. Despite the lack of welcome, we put our medals and uniforms away and took up our lives as civilians. We tried to put our memories away as well but found this to be more difficult. The people at home were able to forget Vietnam, but we could not.

CHAPTER 16

Short and Leaving Vietnam

Most medical officers were not Regular Army and were not planning on staying in the military beyond their obligatory two years. Some guys were getting out of the military as soon as they got home, whereas others had a few months to a year to serve before they were discharged. The doctors who were assigned to military posts when they returned caught some ribbing from those of us who were getting out. We told them how fortunate they were to be able to buy cheap shaving lotion and toilet paper at the post commissary.

Sometimes guys got into trouble as they were getting short. Even the straitlaced First Sergeant Ivanoff found himself in trouble near the end of his tour, and John and I had to bail him out of jail. In an unusual act of socialization, the first sergeant had accompanied some other NCOs to a villa owned by civilian engineers in the middle of the jungle. Gambling, drugs, women, and booze were available at these parties for the military personnel. By chance, an MP bird colonel was flying over that area and spotted the large collection of military vehicles parked around the remote villa. He called his troops and had them surround the villa and arrest the military personnel inside. The MPs contacted the units, asking them to pick up their personnel. Lieutenant Colonel Hefner sent John and me to do the honors. When we arrived at the lockup, we had to sign for Sergeant Ivanoff. Two guards brought out the downcast sergeant, who couldn't look us in the eye. His bootlaces had been removed to prevent him from committing suicide in the jail. He did not say a word as he laced his boots. We drove him in silence to the base camp, where the entire Alpha Medical Company stood waiting on each side of the road, snickering and cheering at his embarrassment.

When we got ready to return home, the medical battalion went as a unit. This was unusual in 1970. Typically, people went through the process of emotionally detaching from their units and left one at a time when their year was up. We didn't get to pimp each other because we all packed up and flew out together. The 1st Infantry Division was withdrawn so that the Army of the Republic of Vietnam (ARVN) could take over our mission. Of course, that was a joke and we all knew it. The ARVN, according to the word in our division, couldn't fight their way out of a wet paper bag. Preparing the South Vietnamese to assume the full responsibility of the war effort was one of General Abrams's top priorities. He was ordered to withdraw U.S. troops before he could achieve this goal.

We expected that it would take a couple of days to get on the plane and leave country, so we all wore our comfortable fatigues. We shipped off our hold baggage, gave away or threw away a lot of stuff, and packed our bags for the flight home. We headed down to Bien Hoa to the 90th Replacement Station where we had stayed when we first arrived in country. I remembered it as being a mosquito-infested, hot, crowded, smelly place when we came into country. Again, perception is influenced by attitude. We were euphoric about leaving country, and the milieu in the camp now seemed to be a pleasant one for all of us as we prepared to return to "the world" on our freedom bird. We played cards, started the days with Bloody Marys, told jokes, and fantasized about what home would be like and what we would do when we got there.

Major Martinet wore his starched khakis and the chest full of medals he had awarded himself. He thought he had some pull and would be leaving country as soon as he arrived in Bien Hoa. What he did not know was that his driver and some of the other enlisted men had called their friends at USARV headquarters and had them lose his orders.

When he found that he couldn't leave the first day, he got on the phone and started chewing out people at USARV headquarters. The second day his uniform looked more wrinkled and sweat soaked, and the major looked more dejected. As we prepared to board our plane at Tan Son Nhut Airport the third day, we waved good-bye to a confused, disheveled Major Martinet, who remained at the replacement station. He was the only one there who didn't know why he was still in country. We speculated about how and when he might get to go home. We all agreed that there was justice in the world—even in the army in Vietnam.

This time we formed the double line waiting to board the plane and greeted the FNGs who arrived looking young, confused, sad, and scared in their sweaty fatigues as they walked between us. Now we were the welcoming group who gleefully told them they were going to die, that they should kill themselves now, and that they would be going home in a body bag. We laughed and slapped each other on the back as we boarded our plane. The pilot announced, "You are the shortest guys in Vietnam," which produced a huge cheer from the passengers. The trip back was easier and seemed faster than the trip over had been. I remember that the flight attendants on the way home seemed more attractive than the ones on the way to Vietnam (but Ruby Begonia was beginning to look sort of cute after a year in Vietnam as well). When our plane touched down on the U.S. soil of the runway at Travis Air Force Base, we let out another loud cheer.

In Vietnam we had been preoccupied with the war and what was going on around us there. We read the *Stars and Stripes,* which primarily focused on what the military was doing in Vietnam, with secondary news from the States and around the world. To adapt to Vietnam, we focused on our lives and routine there. We spoke very little about "the world," and it seemed that "the world" had done the same with Vietnam. If the subject came up, people at home said, "Oh, is that still going on?" Those of us who were there in Vietnam still had vivid memories of the experiences we wished we could forget, whereas those who weren't there had forgotten the war.

After landing at Travis, we took cabs to San Francisco International for commercial flights home. In San Francisco, people looked away from us or through us. Some who did make eye contact were hostile and seemed to feel we were baby killers or somehow responsible for the atrocities and the war itself. From my arrival in

California until I reached home, the only kind word I heard was from a cab driver in Chicago, who said, "Welcome home." I don't know if he was a veteran himself or why he said it, but I got a lump in my throat and nearly wept when he did.

When I returned from Vietnam, I was permitted to process out. At first I was scheduled to go to Fort Sam and teach for a few weeks until my time was up, but this was changed and I was permitted to process out at Fort Sheridan in Chicago. When I arrived home, my office partner had fifteen patients in the hospital. He was eager to go on vacation; so the day I returned, he took off and left me with the practice. I was extremely busy trying to get oriented to the new setting but managed to set aside a day to go up to Fort Sheridan. I came in early, made rounds in the hospital, and took off for Chicago. I spoke to the civil servant, who gave me a pile of papers and said that she would schedule me with the various doctors and laboratory tests that I needed for my discharge physical. When I asked how long it would take, she responded that it could usually be completed in a week. "A week!" I exclaimed, "I've got patients in the hospital." She assured me that it would take at least that long. I then found a WAC and explained the situation to her—I told her I wasn't going to make any claims against the government—I just wanted out. She took my paperwork and found the doctors having lunch and told them what was going on. They dry-labbed my paperwork over lunch—filling out all of the required lab results, the EKG, X-rays, physical exams, and eye tests. The WAC had the papers back to me in an hour. I took them to the surprised government employee, who said she had never had anyone go through the process this quickly. Since having the blanks filled was her main concern, she began processing the papers. She look at me and, based on my age, said, "I'm sure that this discharge is at the convenience of the government." I said that I was pretty sure it was also. She finished the paperwork, and I was officially out of the army. By making the discharge at the government's convenience, I was not obligated to attend reserve meetings or have any more association with the military.

Once home, I used my main coping device, hard work, to adjust to civilian private practice. I did have a couple of out-of-control drinking parties at home during which I screamed and carried on as we had in Vietnam, causing some of the onlookers to think that the experience had driven me over the edge. This toned down with time, and the drinking diminished. Although I occasionally have a martini now, I observe the "breast principle" (one isn't enough and three are too many). In Vietnam it was one martini, two martini, three martini, FLOOR!

I have had little contact with my colleagues from Vietnam. I joined the Veterans of Foreign Wars but never attended a meeting. The only time I have been inside a VFW facility was to take a course on hunting with my son. I support the VFW, however, and may become more active within the organization in the future. The VFW has been supportive of Vietnam veterans and an advocate for them when the rest of the nation turned their backs. The VFW recently sponsored a series of documentary videotapes in conjunction with ABC titled *Service with Honor,* which documents the heroic actions of soldiers in Vietnam. It makes me feel good to watch them and even better that the VFW backed this project.

I saw Bob Anzinger and his new wife once and spoke to Ross Guarino on the phone. He's retired from cardiovascular surgery and doing well. I saw Gasper Falzone's name associated with counseling veterans in New York, and I have been corresponding by e-mail with Walt Smith. Mike Weissman called me at my office last year. John Hamilton and I finally got in touch this past year. We exchanged pictures and caught up on the past thirty-four years. My Australian buddy Michael Downey and I have visited each other and explored the outback together. He and I still keep in touch with Christmas cards and an occasional phone call. Al Breeland stopped by with his son. He had just retired from the CIA and was on his way to take a position at a psychiatric hospital out West. That has been the extent of my contacts with my old buddies over the past thirty-five years.

I later had the good fortune of recruiting an excellent head nurse for my office, Eric Traub, RN, MSN. Eric had seen considerable action in Vietnam as a combat medic with the 82nd Airborne Division. On rare occasions, we would talk about our Vietnam experiences after a few beers. Most Vietnam veterans I've met did not mention that they had been in Vietnam unless they knew I had served there. Even then, it would be an acknowledgment that they had done a tour and that would end the conversation. A couple of years ago, I sat next to a Mexican American businessman on a flight to Cancun, Mexico. For some reason, he turned to me and asked if I had been in Vietnam. When I said I had and he was convinced that I had, he began telling me of his service in a special unit. He said he found that everyone in the unit looked like him—short and dark skinned. He described some of his extensive combat experiences in Vietnam and Cambodia. He concluded by saying, "I haven't mentioned this stuff in years." Heroism in Vietnam seemed to consist more of survival than self-sacrifice for higher values. Vietnam veterans feel that they were misled by the government and rejected by their civilian peers. Following our experience in Vietnam, we have a tendency to hold everyone in equal distrust.

From all the stories of drinking, throwing optometrists through doors, and such, the reader may conclude that I have been flawed by my experience in Vietnam and that perhaps I'm one of the many supposed victims of PTSD. I attribute my crude behavior to my getting away from religion, my childhood patterns of behavior, compulsive work, and self-medication with alcohol. I was operating under the delusion that I was in control of my life. I was that way before I went to Vietnam. I should add that I've maintained my busy practice since my discharge in 1970. I was board-certified in Psychiatry by the American Board of Neurology and Psychiatry (ABNP), and later with qualifications in Geriatric Psychiatry; was a board examiner for the ABNP for a number of years and received a certificate in appreciation for this service; and was president of the McLean County Medical Society and secretary of that organization for nine years. I was also president of the McLean County Board of Health and the BroMenn Medical Center hospital medical staff and chairman of the Illinois Medical Society's Council on Mental Health and Addiction. I published more than fifteen papers in psychiatry and presented a number of these at the annual American Psychiatric Association meetings. I was elected to fellowship status in the American Psychiatric Association based on my contributions to psychiatry and recently became a Distinguished Life Fellow.

The combination of near-death experiences from heart attacks and open-heart surgery; marriage to my wonderful wife, Debbie; the adoption of Sarah and Matt; and the informal adoption of Alvis have resulted in a change to a more balanced lifestyle and a lessening of my compulsive ways. I no longer have time pressure.

It isn't unusual for my patients to be busier than I am these days. I love my life and feel very blessed. I'm happy I had the opportunity to serve my country.

We weren't greeted warmly when we returned, but I have no regrets and am proud that I served. I support my son's wish to enlist. I feel it is important to support our military and our government in these troubled times. I make a special effort to welcome and praise our returning veterans.

> The willingness with which our young people are likely to serve in any war, no matter how justified, shall be directly proportional as to how they perceive veterans of earlier wars and how they were treated and appreciated by this country.
>
> —George Washington

CHAPTER 17

And I Say to Myself

We came home and got on with our lives. We put away or threw away our medals, stopped talking about Vietnam, and focused on our civilian lives, careers, and families. For the most part we used less drugs and alcohol back in "the world." We typically didn't talk about Vietnam unless the other person had been there as well. We didn't attempt to contact the buddies we served with overseas.

Despite this seeming return to normality, I think most of us have been affected by the experience. The "Where were you when I was in Vietnam?" and "I'm not taking anything off anybody" chips on the shoulder cause problems with authority and with relationships. There is a feeling that "No one gave a damn about me when I was there or when I came home, so why should I give a damn about them?" This applies to the government and to individuals in the community and leads to a calloused, self-centered, "me-first" style of thinking. Vietnam veterans share a mistrust of the government and politicians in general. Initially, there was a reluctance to permit our sons and daughters to serve in the military. Veterans tended to feel that others did not and really could not understand them because others could not understand what they experienced in Vietnam. This produced distance and isolation from others at home. Of course, I had many of these feelings long before Vietnam. 'Nam only made them stronger.

We think we recognize the extreme forms of these symptoms in a few individuals: the Rambo-isolationist, armed to the teeth, living in the woods; the veteran who is unable to maintain a job; the veteran who can't maintain a relationship; the chemically dependent veteran; the veteran who demonstrates explosive violence. The authors of *Stolen Valor* investigated many of these individuals, who still dress as if they were living in the sixties and just got out of Vietnam, and found that many were never in Vietnam or, if they were, served in support areas and sustained little or no exposure to actual combat. Unfortunately, these few "wannabes" portray the image of Vietnam veterans as long-haired, drug-using, fatigue-wearing, half-crazed losers. Of course, I don't feel that individuals who didn't serve in Vietnam should represent those who did, nor should they receive compensation under false pretenses. On the other hand, I don't think we do enough for our veterans, especially those who served in Vietnam. Those who have psychological problems (including the showboats in Rambo garb)—whether directly caused by Vietnam or not—should have access to treatment.

When I arrived in Vietnam, I read a good deal of the military psychiatry literature. My predecessor left me the two volumes of *Neuropsychiatry in World War II,* edited by Lt. Gen. Leonard D. Heaton, which I read cover to cover. I found it exciting to read that the division psychiatrist in the 1st Infantry Division in World War II was reporting many of the same observations that I was making in Vietnam. He noted that Big Red One (1st Infantry Division) soldiers complained that they were doing the fighting for other divisions and there were rumors that the division was going to be withdrawn. I found that our division soldiers in Vietnam were saying the same things. I initially looked for cases of combat exhaustion and found very few. I attributed this finding to our improved psychiatric techniques. I later learned that combat exhaustion, hysterical reactions, and psychosomatic complaints frequently seen by World War II psychiatrists were relatively minor problems in Vietnam. Instead, personality disorders, chemical dependency, and racial conflict were more prevalent. We medically evacuated a few patients out of the division and out of the country for psychiatric reasons. Far more soldiers were administratively discharged because of behavioral problems.

My impression was that soldiers in World War II had the feeling they were morally in the right and were supported by the folks back home. Men who avoided service were shunned. Soldiers did not know how long they would be in service. They were in for the duration. They trained together and were shipped out with their combat units and returned with what was left of their units. We did not have air superiority in World War II, and our troops were exposed to strafing and bombing. Combat was more intense and much more sustained in that war. Lieutenant Colonel Hefner told us that his tank unit took on replacements every two weeks and was re-formed because of the heavy losses they sustained. For the most part World War II was fought with large troop movements. Men were sometimes patched up and sent back into battle because there was no way to evacuate them. A local physician told me that when he was in the Pacific, they were operating on men in tents. The operating lights were so inadequate that they were unable to see what they were doing. They cabled the surgeon general in Washington requesting brighter lights and received the response, "Make bigger incisions." It took longer to get the wounded to surgical treatment facilities in World War II, and those facilities were primitive compared to those of Vietnam. As a result, severely wounded men were more likely to die in the field.

Psychiatry in World War II, under the leadership of Gen. William Menninger, was psychoanalytically oriented. Initially there was an effort to screen out "neurotics" in the induction centers by having psychiatrists read to each recruit a lengthy list of questions designed by Harry Stack Sullivan. Soon so many applicants were being screened out that Washington put a stop to the practice. Later, a follow-up study showed that the group previously identified as "neurotic" seemed to actually function better in combat, and it was hypothesized that these men functioned better when the source of their fear was external to themselves. Psychiatric casualties were a great concern initially in World War II. The principles of "immediacy, proximity, and expectancy" that had been developed in World War I were rediscovered, and psychiatrists were assigned to combat divisions. Psychotropic medicines were limited to a few barbiturates, paraldehyde, and chloral hydrate. Sodium amytal interviews were successful in relieving symptoms, but psychiatrists were unable to return these patients to the field. The diagnosis of "combat exhaustion" replaced "shell shock" of World War I and "nostalgia" of the Civil War. It was felt during World War II that anyone given enough stress for a long enough period of time would have a breaking point. This went along with the psychoanalytic concept that individuals would find themselves on a continuum between normality and psychosis depending on their ability to cope with anxiety.

At the time of my military service, psychiatry was on the cusp between psychoanalysis and biological psychiatry. The introduction of lithium in 1970 swung the pendulum toward biology because it was difficult to claim that a salt that controlled a major mental illness (manic depression/bipolar disorder) was a "chemical straitjacket" or an "upper," as the analysts had labeled the major tranquilizers and antidepressants. In Vietnam, we used Thorazine and Mellaril as major tranquilizers, Valium and Librium as minor tranquilizers, and Tofranil and Elavil as antidepressants. I did a few sodium amytal interviews, mainly for the benefit of the technicians who had not seen this technique used. We attempted to carry out preventive psychiatry programs in the division by identifying and protecting high-risk individuals, identifying and lessening high-stress periods in units, and monitoring stress in the units throughout the division and intervening when they appeared to be elevated. There were a few classic combat-induced stress reactions, but the big problems in Vietnam appeared to be those of drugs and alcohol; racial conflict; personality disorders; and rebellion against the establishment, which had been imported from the United States. Elite units like the LRRPs, Special Forces, and Delta had low psychiatric casualty rates in Vietnam, presumably because they were well trained and highly motivated.

I have seen a number of Vietnam veterans as patients over the years. Some cases were clearly related to traumatic experiences in combat, but most were for problems other than PTSD. I've recently seen returning soldiers from Afghanistan and Iraq who were suffering from PTSD, chemical dependency, and family problems related to their readjustment to civilian life.

Despite the public perception of Vietnam veterans as disturbed and psychologically damaged, I have seen only a few Vietnam-related matters in a busy practice that has extended over thirty years. For example, I saw a young patient in civilian practice after getting home from Vietnam who was initially felt to be chronically depressed. He had failed to respond to conventional treatment and was referred to me by another psychiatrist. He showed cognitive problems, his EEG showed slow waves, and his liver and kidney function studies were abnormal. We were able to determine that he had been in a field unit in Vietnam and had used C-4 as a cooking fuel. Unfortunately, the brain damage he sustained was irreversible. We were able to explain his symptoms and lack of response to treatment to his family, who arranged for him to have his long-term care with the Veterans Administration.

Also in civilian practice I was asked to see a young female refugee from Vietnam. She was staying with a family in town. The host was a veterinarian. He noted that the young woman was taking Mellaril on a regular basis, and he contacted me to refill her medicine for her. I insisted on seeing her before prescribing. She was apprehensive about seeing an American doctor, so I arranged to meet her accompanied by her family and her host sponsors at the hospital. I listened to my Vietnamese language tapes and read a Vietnamese-language book in preparation for the consultation. I tried to greet them in Vietnamese. They looked at me with blank expressions as though I were from another planet—so much for trying to speak a tonal language (I had experienced the same difficulty while in Vietnam). I brought the framed picture of Dr. Hiep and me at the Bien Hoa hospital to show the patient that I had been in Vietnam. She smiled and became more animated as she explained that Dr. Hiep had been her doctor in Vietnam and she was so happy that I knew her doctor. As a postscript, this patient had facial grimacing and difficulties with balance and coordination. A brain scan revealed a large acoustic neuroma (a benign tumor of the acoustic nerve) that required neurosurgery.

A few years ago a local faculty member called to ask if I would be willing to advise a Russian doctor he was sponsoring. I said yes, and a few days later, he escorted a female Russian ophthalmologist to my office. Her English was good, and she appeared to be an intelligent, energetic young woman. She wanted to go into neuropsychiatry and wanted to know the best training programs for this specialty. I suggested a few and gave her the names of some psychiatrists and neurologists I knew who were associated with programs that might fit her requirements. As we talked, she looked around my office and spotted a plaque from Vietnam. She asked if I had been in Vietnam and when I said I had, she said that her husband had also served there. He had been a Russian military advisor to the NVA and had been stationed in Hanoi. I thought how much had changed since I had served in Vietnam. Here I was giving friendly advice to the wife of one of our former enemies.

I thought our efforts to prevent psychiatric casualties and to intervene at the organizational level in Vietnam were primarily of historical interest today. The world and war have changed since Vietnam. We are not importing problems of racial strife, drug use, and anti-authoritarian rebellion from the United States to Iraq as we did in Vietnam. We initially had well-trained, highly motivated, volunteer soldiers in Iraq. There is no draft. Men frequently have the support of going to the combat theater with their units and returning from the battle area with their units. The initial combat was intense with relatively few casualties by our military and was over in a short period of time. The military is racially integrated at all levels. Commanders have more training with regard to racial problems and the ability to recognize signs of mental illness in their troops. The majority of citizens at home continue to support the president and the military troops in combat.

However, as the occupation of Iraq continues, we are beginning to see more similarities with the situation in Vietnam and an increasing number of psychiatric casualties. The suicide rate is up among soldiers in Iraq. Prozac is becoming one of the most commonly prescribed medicines for our troops there. Boredom, loneliness, homesickness, difficulty telling friend from foe, women and children as the enemy, close-quarters fighting in which you see the people you kill, periodic danger from a hostile environment, oppressive heat, uncertainty about military goals, forced retention (men who have served their time are now being retained and sent back)—all resemble the stresses soldiers endured in Vietnam. Antiwar talk at home is increasing, as is the criticism of our political leaders. In addition, explosive injuries produce horrendous wounds that have a negative effect on troop morale. Many replacements are reservists who are not as motivated and as well trained nor as experienced as the elite troops who initiated the battle there.

The soldiers in Iraq don't have illegal drugs available to them—only bootleg liquor. Is this a plus or minus in terms of stress reduction? We "self-medicated" in Vietnam. The troops in Iraq have instant contact with home through e-mail and satellite phones. In Vietnam we wrote letters that took several days each way, tapes that we mailed, and an occasional patched-through phone call using several volunteer civilian HAM radio operators. When "calling" by this method, each person had to say "over" at the end of a statement so the other person could start talking. There wasn't much intimacy with these calls. One officer in the medical unit was having difficulty understanding his wife and kept saying, "Can't understand—say again, over." Finally, the voice of one of the HAM operators broke in and said, "Your wife said she missed her period and she thinks she's pregnant, sir." I don't know if the instant communication available to soldiers in Iraq is good or bad for their morale. We coped with Vietnam by forgetting "the world" and focusing on our day-to-day tasks. When we started thinking of home as a reality, we had "the short-timer's syndrome" and became anxious for our safety. I wonder if the ability to communicate in Iraq might not maintain a closer tie with home for the soldiers there and, at the same time, increase their concern for their own safety.

I am a little worried about our efforts to try to appear as though we are "good guys" who are playing soccer with the kids and helping rebuild Iraq in an attempt to lessen the anger of other Middle Eastern nations. I remember a senior officer in Vietnam telling me that our troops had taught some Vietnamese kids to play baseball and that this supported his conviction that we were "winning the hearts and minds of the people." It was wrong for a few of our soldiers to abuse Iraqi prisoners, but the situation was sensationalized by the videotapes and, in my opinion, blown out of proportion. It was rumored that Vietnamese prisoners were often vigorously interrogated and thrown out of helicopters in some cases. This was wrong, and a greater offense, but did not receive the sort of publicity and public outcry that the recent videotapes from Iraq engendered. We can kill the terrorists or not kill the terrorists. They hate us either way. As the occupation drags on and more body bags return home, we can also expect to see more unrest and more antiwar demonstrations in the United States. I believe that the terrorists think they learned a lesson from Vietnam. Draw out the war and keep killing American soldiers, and eventually the antiwar forces at home will pressure the government to withdraw. I hope that our country also learned from Vietnam and that we will continue to support our government and our troops for as long as it takes to complete the mission.

After my return home from 'Nam, I tried to forget the whole experience. I didn't wear anything green for several years. I carried my own load of guilt going into Vietnam. In addition, I felt a vague sense of guilt in response to the criticism by the antiwar groups—particularly those from my colleagues in psychiatry. When I first got back, I had a few episodes in which I would drink too much, become very angry, and vent some primal screams. In college and medical school I had a tendency to get into fights when drinking. After Vietnam it was more of a generalized rage, but it was enough to cause some concern and anxiety in those around me at the time. Initially, I had recurrent dreams of opening a body bag and seeing my brother's face. I didn't want to look in the dream but felt forced to do so. For years I continued to be a type-A, driven, compulsive psychiatrist who worked from 5:30 A.M. to 10 or 11 P.M. weekdays, did daily hospital rounds, kept Saturday office hours, and took calls throughout the night. My kids turned out well despite my being a workaholic.

My oldest daughter, Cathy, married Dan Ward; and her younger sister, Barby, married Bill White. I now have five beautiful grandchildren. The girls could not have picked better husbands. They are both former jocks who have bizarre senses of humor. I wonder why my daughters happened to pick guys with those characteristics.

When the girls left home for college, married, and began their own careers, it was obvious that there was little going on between my ex and me, and our marriage ended. My situation was different from that of most of my divorced Vietnam buddies in that they were in love when they got married, whereas we married for very irrational reasons. Prior to 'Nam I felt I didn't deserve much. Survivor guilt after my brother's suicide and guilt about not having an affective illness were factors in my feeling that I didn't deserve happiness or success in life. I wanted to please my parents and, although I rebelled in small ways, never did anything that was blatantly against their will. I was competitive and a workaholic but often acted in a way to undermine my success.

My tour in Vietnam served as an emotional atonement for some of my perceived past sins. I also began to recognize that some of my adult knee-jerk reactions were the products of my earlier emotional trauma. In any event, I allowed myself to think a little more of my own happiness after Vietnam. Periodically throughout our marriage my ex would tell me to get out, and I would respond by trying to correct whatever she was mad about at the time. When she once more asked me to leave, I surprised her by calmly agreeing. I moved out a few days later, and we divorced not long after that. This was upsetting to the entire family, who shared my ex's view that I was having a midlife crisis and behaving irrationally.

I had a good friend, Debbie, over the years who was an excellent nurse. She was chief of the chemical-dependency unit and later the surgical floor. She had trained at Barnes Hospital in St. Louis. I found myself hanging around her nursing station in order to talk with her. She was younger than I, and I didn't consciously think of her as a romantic partner. On an impulse I asked her out and then tried to talk her out of going because I anticipated rejection. To my surprise she accepted. We fell in love, and both feel that our getting together had to be the result of divine intervention. We were married by the minister who married my two oldest daughters. I adopted Debbie's two children, Sarah and Matt, and later we informally adopted Alvis. By the grace of God I found Debbie, my "intended," who taught me the meaning of love and how to have fun dancing. She was a former cheerleader who continues to encourage and cheer the family and our patients on. She is now my office nurse. Having a spouse in the office can sometimes result in problems for the office and for the relationship. In our case it hasn't. We maintain a professional relationship at work, and we enjoy being around one another each day.

Two years after we were married I went to see a therapist while Debbie and the kids were in Chicago shopping. I was feeling "burned out," and Debbie suggested I talk with a therapist about my being the family "hero" and the difficulties I had balancing my life. I remember the therapist asking me, "How do you want your life to be?" I didn't have a clue because I thought in terms of what everyone else wanted or needed. I didn't think I had a choice in the matter. I awoke the next morning with chest pain and shortness of breath. I drove myself to the hospital, where my heart stopped. I had two heart attacks, a balloon procedure, and a single-vessel bypass. This near-death experience, along with my marriage to Debbie, helped me realign my priorities in life. God, family, friends, and doing something nice for others seemed to be the order of business. I had a triple bypass a few years later, followed by a couple of balloon procedures and a stent. I recycled through cardiac rehab so many times that I think I broke the hospital record for time clocked on a treadmill. I slowed down and eliminated the stressful aspects of my practice. I found out what it meant to have a loving relationship. Debbie did some couch time after her divorce from her abusive first husband and was very open in talking about herself. We are coauthoring a book, *Loving an Adult Child of an Alcoholic.* Her love and introspection helped me look at my own patterns and understand how some of them might be having a negative effect on my adult relationships and my own happiness. Debbie loosened me up and got me dancing, writing, and learning how to enjoy life. Like Jack Nicholson in *As Good As It Gets,* my compulsiveness was cured by love. I really didn't think much about Vietnam, but apparently I had suppressed many of my feelings.

When Robert McNamara admitted in the early 1990s that, from the beginning, he did not think we would win in Vietnam, I became very angry. When Donna Shalala said that the best and the brightest (including her boss Bill Clinton) did not go to Vietnam, I felt more anger than I knew I had about the war. I was involved in a Bible class when I experienced the resurgence of anger about Vietnam. When I opened the Bible for the week's lesson, I read a passage about supporting the government. I thought that if the Christians could support the Roman government at a time when they were being crucified and fed to lions, I should be able to support a government who merely sent us to Vietnam and didn't tell us the whole story. As they say in AA, "The wise man has many cuts; the happy man doesn't count the scars." My experiences in Vietnam, religion, maturation, near-death experiences, and a loving family have all been major factors producing change in my life in recent years.

These are some things I think I've learned from Vietnam and life. I've learned that the most important thing in life is God, and God is love. Looking back on my year in the division in 'Nam, I can see that the thing that kept us going was our affection for one another and for our soldier-patients. You can get through just about anything in life if you love and know you are loved. When you are without love, life is hell.

I learned from John that a black man and a white man looking at the same set of circumstances will likely see them differently. Neither is wrong, but to understand one another, each needs to try to experience events from the other's perspective. John was an intelligent professional soldier and an outstanding athlete who was forced to ignore racial slurs and prejudice exhibited by white men who were his inferiors in every way. Despite this, John took the time to try to teach me and to help me keep myself out of trouble in Vietnam. I feel that because of John's friendship in 'Nam, I have a better understanding of some of the pressures a black man has to tolerate in our society and more admiration and respect for black men in general. I hope he benefited from our relationship as well. John and I have had many of the same experiences in life and now are "brothers in Christ."

The one brief visit with the gay infantryman made a lasting impression on me. It helped me understand how difficult it must have been for a gay man to function in a heterosexual military organization. I think of that tough combat soldier whenever gay political issues are discussed. I doubt if this soldier realized what an impact his brief visit had on me. As I look back, it seems that my life and character haven't been shaped so much by major events as by small day-to-day interactions with others.

My experiences in Vietnam changed some of my social views. Since Vietnam, I have felt that women should be able to serve in combat. I'm sure that if a woman had served in a combat division, as I did, she would not take any guff off any man afterward—especially a man who hadn't been there. From what I've read, women in Israel who have served in the military are very strong and self-confident as a result of their service experience. I don't have any doubt that women are as courageous as men in combat.

Vietnam caused me to be hypersensitive to administrative baloney. Doctors in our hospital were assigned to hospital committees. The administration would present some ridiculous proposal, and the private practitioners on the committee would say it was nonsense. The minutes of the meeting, when distributed to the board and to the medical staff, would state, "The doctors on the committee enthusiastically endorsed the administration's proposal." This reminded me of the descriptions of military morale in Vietnam by *Stars and Stripes.* I wrote an order for the hospital social service department to obtain a social history on nearly every patient I admitted to the hospital. It rarely happened. The hospital presented a study to the board indicating that 100 percent of the social histories requested by staff physicians had been completed by the social work department. When I said I knew from my own experience that this wasn't true, the social service department explained that if the patient refused to permit them to take a social history, or if the social workers were unable to reach a family member to obtain a social history, these requests for social histories were excluded from the survey. This reminded me of the body counts in Vietnam, which gave the higher-ups the numbers they wanted to see.

Two of the legacies of Vietnam that are prominent in the media are PTSD and Agent Orange. Even though I saw some bad things in Vietnam, I do not see myself as a victim of PTSD due to Vietnam. (I *could* make a case for my having had PTSD prior to Vietnam as a result of my childhood trauma.) Dr. Jonathan Shay (author of *Achilles in Vietnam* and *Odysseus in America*) describes his work with Vietnam veterans in the VA. Dr. Shay notes that isolation of feelings, compulsive work, and the tendency to snatch defeat from the jaws of victory are common traits among his patients with PTSD. I had those traits long before I arrived in 'Nam.

Recent studies report that as many as one-third of the Vietnam veterans show psychiatric symptoms. This has not been my personal observation over the years. I am usually surprised to learn that a new patient of mine has been in Vietnam.

There are many dedicated VA counselors and therapists, in addition to Dr. Shay, who work with Vietnam veterans who have symptoms of PTSD. Of course, the diagnosis itself was pushed by the antiwar activists on the basis of unscientific accounts made by a biased population of veterans and wannabes. Whether you believe that many Vietnam veterans are still suffering from the trauma of Vietnam or not—veterans who are seeking help for psychological problems deserve assistance. There are some recent PET-scan findings that appear to demonstrate the neurochemical basis for reactions to severe stress. It appears that the limbic system, particularly the amygdala, is responsible for the stress-related symptoms; and the "flashbulb memory" it retains explains the patient's reexperience of the trauma in civilian life—for example, the veteran who reacts to a car backfiring as if he were in Vietnam being fired upon by the enemy. *Mind Wide Open* by Steven Johnson provides an excellent update on the current literature in this regard. We treated acute gross stress reactions with Thorazine in the combat areas. In *dauerschlaft,* or sleep therapy, we utilized the sedative effect of the major tranquilizer together with rest, rehydration, a warm meal, supportive counseling, and contact with unit members.

Today's soldiers in Iraq should receive better psychiatric treatment. Instead of using major tranquilizers to sedate them, we would now give them a selective serotonin reuptake inhibitor (SSRI), such as Zoloft or Paxil, which is more effective in treating PTSD and does not carry the potential for severe side effects associated with the early major tranquilizers, such as Thorazine and Mellaril. In cases where antipsychotic medicines would be indicated, today we would use the newer atypical antipsychotics (Geodone, Zyprexa, Risperdal, Abilify, or Seroquel). There are several other SSRIs on the market, but only Zoloft and Paxil have been approved by the FDA for the treatment of PTSD, and from my reading and experience, they would be the drugs of choice. In Vietnam we used the old tricyclic antidepressants (Tofranil and Elavil) to treat depression and anxiety disorders. Today we would use the SSRIs; and the newer dual-acting antidepressants, which have fewer side effects, may be more effective in some instances and work more quickly. Indicators of unit stress could be monitored more quickly and accurately today. We relied on monthly statistical reports to monitor stress indices within the division's units. Today, this data could be available on computer as soon as it was entered by each unit. We had difficulty communicating with doctors and commanding officers within various units because the phone calls were patched through and were frequently interrupted or terminated due to technical problems. Satellite phones would ensure clear, uninterrupted communication with the units. The Internet would provide rapid availability of resource material and contact with consultants anywhere in the world.

I would continue to advocate unit evaluation and consultation by the combat psychiatrists to try to help commanders and battalion surgeons reduce the stress of their units and help them recognize and protect high-risk individuals within the units. I think it is helpful for the treatment team's morale to do research in addition to providing direct service and unit consultation. Many questions come to my mind when I think of our troops in Iraq. For example, does self-medication with alcohol and/or illegal drugs increase or decrease troop stress? Which medicines are most useful and in what doses? Does constant contact with home through e-mail and satellite phones aid or impair a soldier's adjustment to the combat area? What programs could be instituted to keep troops busy and occupied in the combat area? How can the support within the units themselves be fostered? How can the military goals be clarified for the troops on the ground? Support at home for our leaders and for our troops is an important factor in maintaining unit morale. Do the news media have a responsibility to try to help foster this support? Are there ways that old combat psychiatrists like me could contribute?

Agent Orange could be a cause of some of my current problems. Herbicides were used in Vietnam beginning in 1962. During 1967, the peak year, 4.8 million gallons of herbicide defoliated 1.2 million acres. Cheaper agents such as Agent Orange were used later in the war. The last military herbicides were destroyed in 1977. In 1984 the manufacturers of herbicides paid a settlement to veterans' groups that provided approximately one thousand dollars per veteran. Since that time there have been scientific studies that demonstrate a higher incidence of some illnesses among Vietnam veterans who were exposed to Agent Orange and a higher incidence of some birth defects among their children.

My heart disease, type II diabetes, and peripheral neuropathy might be examples of the increased incidence of these physical problems among those of us who were exposed to Agent Orange. My diabetes II and my having been in Vietnam have automatically qualified me to obtain my medications from the Veterans Administration. I've been impressed by the kindness and professionalism of the VA staff. John Hamilton informed me that he has also had open-heart surgery and now has been diagnosed with type II diabetes.

My mental health team and I tried to do our best to help our soldier-patients thirty-five years ago in Vietnam, and I believe that we did help many and did reduce the stress in some of the units we worked with in the division. Later, when I examined my own navel in therapy and read books like *Mad House* by Clea Simon, I was able to see how some of my childhood paradigms were repeated in my own behavior in Vietnam. The trauma of seeing dead young men brought up my feelings about my brother. My rebellion against being set up to get a Silver Star was my reflex reaction to any situation in which I was being expected to play the role of the "good son." I had turned my back on my religious upbringing at that stage in my life because I felt that God didn't save my brother and that I'd have to do the saving myself. My choice of psychiatry was in itself a little rebellious but more acceptable to the family after my brother became a victim of mental illness.

I COPED WITH MY OWN TOUR in Vietnam by focusing on my work, forgetting about home, isolating my negative feelings, becoming an observer, chronicling events, and occasionally self-medicating with alcohol. I served with a great group of guys in Vietnam. We helped each other, and we tried to help our soldier-patients. These loving relationships sustained us in Vietnam. Loving activities, my defense mechanisms, the R&Rs, the surprise trip home at Christmas, and my in-country trips all helped me get through the year. When I got home, I published my findings in several journals; put my rough book and medals on the shelf; and turned into a neurotic, compulsive, driven, private practitioner of psychiatry. Before Vietnam I didn't feel I deserved much in life. Vietnam had the positive effect of making me feel that maybe I was entitled to some happiness. I had always felt alienated and guilt ridden. My self-criticism and estrangement were accentuated by the public's negative attitude (including that of a number of my psychiatric peers) toward Vietnam and Vietnam veterans. I was sad and a little guilty about 'Nam after the Communists took over in 1975. For the most part I tried not to think about Vietnam. I focused on my work and on the day-to-day events at home and went on with my life.

　　　　　　　　　　　　　　　　　　CHAPTER 17

I SOMETIMES BECOME SAD thinking of the future. Life is so good now that I hate to give it up. I don't fear death, but I hate to think of leaving Deb, the family, friends, and my patients. *Shadow Lands* portrayed the life of C. S. Lewis (played by Anthony Hopkins), who lost his mother at an early age and protected himself from further pain and loss by distancing himself from others, focusing on intellectual pursuits, and controlling his emotions. He falls in love with a passionate woman who jars him out of his compulsive lifestyle. She is then diagnosed with cancer and dies. He is overwhelmed with grief but tells her son that it is better to experience the pain of loss than to protect oneself and miss having a loving relationship. As a Christian I know that I will be with God and that God is love. Perhaps I have become too attached to this brief existence, but I love Deb, my family, my good friends, my work as a psychiatrist, and my recent efforts to become a writer. I feel as though my grandparents, parents, uncle, cousin, and brother, who have passed on before me, are still with me in spirit. If it is possible, I will be with my loved ones as well after I leave this world. But enough of this morbid rumination; I want to pass on a few things that I think I have learned over the years.

The following things I *think* I've learned are probably more the result of other life events and my introspection than from the Vietnam experience. I think they are still worth passing on.

I've learned that it is better to say what you really think and feel rather than what you anticipate others want to hear. You lose some people by doing this, but you end up with friends who think and feel as you do. When you say what you think others want to hear, it distances you from them because they really don't know you.

I've learned that when you do for others, hoping they will like you, it usually doesn't work out that way. On the other hand, doing for others without expecting anything back makes you feel good. There is an ancient hospital in Europe that has a sign over the entrance that reads "Enter, do good works and leave." Not a bad rule to follow in work and in life.

I've learned that when I've done things to show off or try to make myself look important, it usually turns out badly.

I've learned that prayer is a good thing. Since my near-death experiences, I awaken being thankful that I'm still around. I count my blessings each morning, and it's downhill all day after that. I thank God each evening for my many blessings and ask him to help me live my life in a way that will bring honor and glory to his name. I ask him to help me be a better son, husband, father, brother, grandfather, uncle, cousin, friend, and physician.

I learned in golf that it's better to get excited about the good shots and forget the bad ones. This works in life as well. My dad always focused on the positive. His favorite song was *What a Wonderful World,* written by George Weiss and Bob Thiele, and made popular by Louis Armstrong. The lyrics bring me to the end I want.

I hear babies cryin', I watch them grow
They'll learn much more than I'll ever know
And I think to myself, what a wonderful world
Oh, yeah.

Index

ISBN-13: 978-1-58544-482-3
ISBN-10: 1-58544-482-0

9 781585 444823   54400